Existentialism and Romantic Love

Existentialism and Romantic Love

Skye Cleary
Columbia University, New York, USA

palgrave
macmillan

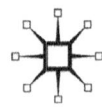

© Skye Cleary 2015

All rights reserved. No reproduction, copy or transmission of this publication may be made without written permission.

No portion of this publication may be reproduced, copied or transmitted save with written permission or in accordance with the provisions of the Copyright, Designs and Patents Act 1988, or under the terms of any licence permitting limited copying issued by the Copyright Licensing Agency, Saffron House, 6–10 Kirby Street, London EC1N 8TS.

Any person who does any unauthorized act in relation to this publication may be liable to criminal prosecution and civil claims for damages.

The author has asserted her right to be identified as the author of this work in accordance with the Copyright, Designs and Patents Act 1988.

First published 2015 by
PALGRAVE MACMILLAN

Palgrave Macmillan in the UK is an imprint of Macmillan Publishers Limited, registered in England, company number 785998, of Houndmills, Basingstoke, Hampshire RG21 6XS.

Palgrave Macmillan in the US is a division of St Martin's Press LLC, 175 Fifth Avenue, New York, NY 10010.

Palgrave Macmillan is the global academic imprint of the above companies and has companies and representatives throughout the world.

Palgrave® and Macmillan® are registered trademarks in the United States, the United Kingdom, Europe and other countries.

ISBN: 978–1–137–45579–6

This book is printed on paper suitable for recycling and made from fully managed and sustained forest sources. Logging, pulping and manufacturing processes are expected to conform to the environmental regulations of the country of origin.

A catalogue record for this book is available from the British Library.

Library of Congress Cataloging-in-Publication Data

Cleary, Skye, 1975–
   Existentialism and romantic love / Skye Cleary, Columbia University, New York, USA.
     pages cm
    ISBN 978–1–137–45579–6 (hardback)
   1. Love. 2. Existentialism. I. Title.
BD436.C49 2015
128'.46—dc23   2015002149

To Nick and Dylan

Contents

Acknowledgments		viii
1	Introduction	1
2	Max Stirner and Loving Egoistically	21
3	Søren Kierkegaard and Loving Aesthetically	45
4	Friedrich Nietzsche and Loving Powerfully	71
5	Jean-Paul Sartre and Loving Sadomasochistically	99
6	Simone de Beauvoir and Loving Authentically	125
7	Conclusion	160
Notes		178
References		196
Index		204

Acknowledgments

Many thanks to Professor Robert Spillane and Dr Steven Segal for their guidance and inspiration during my doctoral research at Macquarie Graduate School of Management. I am very grateful to my editor Brendan George of Palgrave Macmillan for his support of this project. Special thanks to Sam Smith for the cover design of this book and her star friendship. For their relentless encouragement and love, my deepest appreciation to Nick and Dylan. To all my friends, colleagues at MGSM and Columbia University, and my mum, thank you for your enthusiasm, support, and feedback.

Grateful acknowledgments are made to Dover Publications for permission to quote from the copyrighted text of Max Stirner's *The Ego and His Own*.

1
Introduction

The attempt to understand romantic loving has become big business. The popularity of matchmaking industries, internet dating, romance novels, relationship self-help books, and celebrity relationship counselors are just a few examples of how the dynamics of loving relationships remain of perennial interest. Expectations about romantic loving are grand, but there seems to be an issue with the way we understand it because reality often falls short of the ideal. Romantic loving suggests images of perfect happiness, harmony, understanding, and intimacy that make the lovers feel as if they are made for each other. The ideal is alluring but flawed, because romantic loving often involves conflicts and disappointments.

This book is an existential study of romantic loving. Its central argument is that existential philosophies reveal to us the notion that once lovers free themselves from preconceived ideals about how romantic lovers *ought* to behave, and free themselves from being slaves to their passions, they will be free to create relationships that complement and enhance their personal, authentic endeavors. Love is a passion to be chosen and mastered, not sacrificed to. One argument is that although romantic lovers lose certain freedoms, the love they acquire compensates.[1] However, I argue that one of the key contributions of the existential approach to romantic loving is its criticism of such an assumption. After all, it is by no means given that the benefits of romantic love necessarily outweigh the costs.

Existential philosophies provide a meaningful framework through which the dominant ideas about romantic loving can be critically examined because they explore the space between the ideals of romantic loving and the compromises lovers make in order to try to achieve those ideals. Five existential philosophers have been selected for study because their narratives provide the means by which the roots of dissatisfactions and frustrations within our everyday ideas about romantic loving can be examined.

While every existential philosopher interprets being in the world differently, there is a common emphasis on concrete personal experience, freedom, authenticity, responsibility, individuality, awareness of death, and personal determination of values. It is unsurprising, therefore, that such philosophers would consider the question of romantic loving. This includes Max Stirner (1806–1856), Søren Kierkegaard (1813–1855), Friedrich Nietzsche (1844–1900), Jean-Paul Sartre (1905–1980), and Simone de Beauvoir (1908–1986), who contribute significantly to the idea of romantic loving. The five existential philosophers do not provide a single solution, but rather a five-pronged critique that helps us to understand both how romantic loving can go awry and how it can be reinvigorated. An analysis of such existential notions as freedom, power, choice, authenticity, and anxiety challenges our assumptions regarding the nature and meaning of romantic loving.

The existential perspective lends itself well to such an analysis, since relationships are an important part of existential discourse. Existential philosophers acknowledge that we are born into webs of relationships, and they explore how relations with others infuse our world with meaning and modify our possibilities. Existential thinking brings to light complexities, knowledge, and expressions of romantic loving because it provides a language to understand and reflect on our being in the world and being with others, and it expands our knowledge about possibilities and dynamics of relationships. Existential philosophies remain relevant because they deal with everyday human problems.[2]

What is romantic loving?

In 1300 BC the ancient Egyptians wrote love poems. Around 350 BC Plato classified love into different forms. The Roman poet Ovid wrote erotic poetry in 19 BC. Heloise and Abelard famously exchanged letters about their love for each other in the twelfth century. In the late 1500s Shakespeare wrote plays about love. While the literature of romantic loving dates as far back as the ancient Egyptians, only more recently has it been referred to as "romantic" and become a mass phenomenon, particularly in the Western world. This section addresses a few key historical developments that have influenced our understanding of romantic loving in the twenty-first century Western world and some of the dominant current definitions of romantic loving.

Historically, associations between men and women were marriages based on economic alliances that aimed at either maintaining power and wealth or providing extra labor for domestic production. Coupling was arranged as a matter of economic convenience, and so passionate love usually occurred outside marriage and was based on the natural functions of sex and lust. The love story generally ended in sexual union – until the Middle Ages when the phenomenon of courtly love became popular.

Sometimes courtly love manifested as a knight's secretive admiration for a socially superior and unattainable female. Because the relationship was unconsummated, the love was idealized. This is why the pinnacle of love in great romance stories ends with lovers seeking unity in death: *Liebestod* (a metaphorical orgasm).[3] William Shakespeare's *Romeo and Juliet* and Richard Wagner's *Tristan and Isolde* are two pertinent examples. However, Robert Solomon and Kathleen Higgins argue that although courtly love was often consummated within the higher classes of society, it was a slow process, and the focus was on courting because it was based on the lovers' worth, charms, whims, and desires instead of economics.[4]

The use of the term "romantic" proliferated in the Middle Ages when things were likened to the Roman Empire, in which everything seemed magnificent, heroic, adventurous, and passionate. In the late eighteenth century, art, music, literature, and philosophy that emphasized emotions, imagination, creativity, nature, freedom, individualism, and the concrete over abstract reasoning, logic, rationality, and convention became known as "Romantic".[5]

Narratives of love as romantic bloomed during the nineteenth century, at the same time that romance literature proliferated and when romance came to be equated with courting. With the growth of capitalism and industrialization, the requirement for economic-based marriages became obsolete because domestic production declined and corporations, not families, controlled wealth. Capitalism and the growth of individual liberties in Western society meant that courtship and coupling became a matter of personal choice rather than parental arrangement.

In the second half of the twentieth century, such developments as legal and technological advances in contraception, abortion, divorce, equal opportunity legislation, changes in traditional roles and growth of women's participation in the workforce, created greater possibilities and variations in forms of relationships. Feminism awakened women's psychosocial freedom to pursue economic independence and shifted the power dynamics in relationships. Elisabeth Badinter highlights that birth control has endowed Western women with a new kind of power, springing from two sources in particular. First, economic independence means that women are able to survive financially and socially without men, giving them the "atomic bomb that is separation or divorce".[6] Second, a father need not be consulted in procreation-related decisions. Women are no longer required to marry, stay married, and have children in order to gain social approval and be perceived as successful in life.

The effect has been that in the Western world, the traditional nuclear family has broken down and more people are living alone. Robert Solomon proposes that with the weakening of familial and community bonds, romantic love has grown in importance since it contributes to an individual's sense of belonging, if only temporarily. Moreover, it has been possible only since women have been able to choose their partners and have been treated as objects of love rather than as property.[7]

Romantic loving, while incorporating elements of both passionate and courtly love, raised the sexual to the sublime and encompassed the life trajectories and futures of individuals as they wrote their own narratives. This shift in ideas about love meant not only that was it socially acceptable to marry a lover, but also that the ideal of romantic love culminated in marriage, as we see in Shakespeare's plays. Thus, romantic love united passionate loving and marriage, sexual matters became more important, and the social and economic barriers around romantic liaisons shattered.

Definitions and understandings of romantic loving are wide, varied, and changeable. Some of our modern ideas about love retain key themes of Romanticism, and yet other theories are also popular. There are six major ways of conceptualizing romantic loving in the Western world today, outlined below. Since romantic loving is not a purely philosophical discussion, psychological, anthropological, and biological perspectives are also incorporated.[8]

Merging

First, the conception of romantic loving that most clearly echoes ideas that evolved during the Romantic period is that of merging, which is an idea derived from the ancient Greeks. For example, Plato described love in terms of merging in *Symposium*. Plato's character Aristophanes explains that people used to be round creatures with four arms, four legs, and two faces. They attacked the gods and as punishment, Zeus cut them all in two. Since then, people have been searching for their other half so that they can reunite into their original whole. This myth encouraged the idea of romantic loving as a union of two people, who in compensating for each other's deficiencies together make a single entity. That there is only one other person capable of doing this fostered the idea that finding one's other half would result in perfect happiness, making it a monogamous and eternal bond, as well as one that allows for complete disclosure to, and understanding of, one another.

Many modern definitions of romantic love incorporate aspects of Aristophanes' myth. For example, Martin Dillon proposes that romantic love is "to consummate a union with the beautiful object that betokens sheer pleasure", but the inherent contradiction is that while lovers crave perfection, reality cannot live up to the ideal.[9] Robert Nozick describes romantic love as longing for a "we", resulting in a new entity or unit that "pools" well-being, autonomy, and decisions.[10] Aaron Ben-Ze'ev and Ruhama Goussinsky describe romantic loving as uncompromising, unconditional, comprehensive, and encompassing the beliefs that "The beloved is everything to the lover and hence love is all you need; true love lasts forever and can conquer all; true lovers are united – they are one and the same person; love is irreplaceable and exclusive; and love is pure and can do no evil".[11] Just as Christians embrace the ideal of merging with God to become a total unity, Irving Singer argues that the Romantics' ideal of "organic unity" explains the ideal of merging in love: culminating in marriage, the bond of romantic love promises eternal oneness, and provides value and meaning in life.[12] However, Singer proposes that the problem with the merging ideal is that it assumes submission and dependence. Instead, he proposes a "bestowal" model of love based on interdependence, which balances the benefits lovers derive from each other with concern for each others' welfare.[13]

However, romantic love is also conceived as opposition, tension, or a dialectic between lovers' desire to merge their souls and their need to assert their individuality, freedom, and autonomy, which all together is the foundation for romantic love. Robert Solomon is a key exponent of this view. He suggests that there are at least four key components of romantic love. One, it must involve sexual desire (although sexual consummation is not necessary). Two, it must include a desire for reciprocity (but actual reciprocity is irrelevant). Three, it must be personal, that is, love of a particular individual. And four, it aims to create a shared identity. This shared identity is based on something much deeper than companionship, pleasure, and usefulness: it is a process of developing a new shared self together – in and through each other. A central feature of romantic love is that it involves the desire or hope that it will endure. This is why, Solomon proposes, the legendary libertine Don Juan does not love: he is involved with too many women, does not allow time for a dialectic to develop, and knows that the relationship will not last more than a few days at most.[14]

Similar stories

A second approach views loving in terms of a personally constructed narrative. According to Robert Sternberg, people fall in love because they have similar stories and complementary roles, and greater differences in lovers' stories mean that there is greater risk of discontentment with their relationship.[15] Examples include when lovers refer to having things in common, mutual interests, or shared histories. Linnell Secomb adopts a similar approach. She describes paradoxes and complexities of love stories by comparing Mary Shelley's *Frankenstein* to Friedrich Nietzsche's speculations on love and Simone de Beauvoir's philosophy of love to the narratives of the television series *Desperate Housewives*.[16]

Passion or companionship

A third approach defines romantic loving as either passionate love or companionate love – or a combination of both. One theory is that romantic love is like an emotional rollercoaster ride. It starts out intense and exciting, but over time passion slows, and if lovers are lucky, their relationship develops into companionate love, characterized primarily by affection and sharing their lives. However, Susan Hendrick and Clyde Hendrick propose that passion and friendship are not mutually exclusive and both are necessary in romantic relationships.[17]

Passion and intimacy

A fourth approach defines romantic love as a combination of passion and intimacy. For example, Robert Sternberg described different types of love in terms of three components: passion, intimacy, and decision/commitment.[18] Passion includes such elements as sexual attraction and aspiring for unity. Intimacy is about being caring, supportive, and highly regarding and feeling close to one another. Lovers *decide* to be in a relationship but make a *commitment* to maintain it. According to this classification, a relationship based on intimacy alone is "liking". A relationship based on passion only is "infatuated love". Decision and commitment in the absence of passion and intimacy is "empty love". "Fatuitous love" involves passion, decision, and commitment. "Companionate love" involves intimacy and commitment. One example of companionate love is marriage after sexual passion has atrophied. "Romantic love" is a combination of intimacy and passion. "Consummate love" involves all three components of intimacy, passion, and decision/commitment, and, according to Sternberg, romantic lovers aim for this.

Self-expansion

A fifth approach considers romantic loving to be a means of expanding one's boundaries or reaching beyond oneself. For example, Arthur Aron and Elaine Aron proposed that loving is a means of self-expansion, through knowledge, experiences, social connections, and resources.[19] Peter Koestenbaum described romantic loving as a way that people grow and transcend by reaching beyond their given situations.[20] Charles Lindholm reasons that romantic love is not only a justification for sex, but rather is a desire to exceed our boundaries; however, the ideal of salvation that lovers crave is a mirage.[21]

Evolution

A sixth approach focuses on the biological aspects of loving. Evolutionary theory proposes that romantic love's greatest function is reproductive survival, and it is defined in terms of passion for procreative purposes and intimacy for relationship stamina and survival of offspring.[22] Arthur Schopenhauer is one philosopher who takes such a view. He proposed that love is determined by sexual impulse which appears as a "voluptuous illusion" that directs individuals toward those who seem to promise happiness and pleasure. The human species benefits because generations reproduce, but individuals are much less satisfied.[23]

Based on these definitions, the ideas of romantic loving – against which existential themes are compared and contrasted in this book – include the following:

1. Romantic loving is passionate, meaning that it is not just about sex, but often includes sex or, at least, sexual desirability.
2. Romantic loving is personal, meaning that it is love of a particular individual and appreciation of that person's unique qualities.
3. Romantic loving involves a yearning for some kind of union. This is described in a myriad of forms, such as a desire to merge, to create a shared identity, to share selves, to become interdependent, to entwine lives such that the lovers' boundaries are blurred or overcome, or to expand oneself. This can also be understood as lovers' shifting their focus from "I" to "we", whereby many decisions are made taking into account the interests of both parties.
4. The ideal of love during the Romantic period was to establish permanent unions, especially through marriage, and those relationships

would transform lovers' lives to such an extent that everything would take on a new meaning and even become the meaning of life itself. However, more recent ideas about romantic love do not always include the requirement that the relationship last forever. Lovers do expect it to last beyond the initial moments of passion and hope that it will last, but passion can cool over time and the relationship either ceases or evolves into companionate love. Thus, commitment is not a central feature of romantic love, unlike marital love.

5. While passion is a necessary feature of romantic loving, some also insist on companionship and intimacy since these latter elements balance the potential selfishness of an overt focus on passionate loving by including such considerations as concern for the beloved's welfare.[24]

While not all the existential philosophers in this study refer to the type of love they speak of as "romantic", they all describe love in one or more of these themes outlined above. Gary Cox proposes that the existentialists' view of love is not romantic, because they do not believe in love as an abstract force or amorous sunset walks along the beach. However, Cox also said, "If your idea of romance is somewhat more gothic and stormy, full of heartache, yearning and the thwarted desire to possess; breaking up, making up and breaking up again, tears before bedtime and tears in the rain, then maybe it is romantic".[25]

I argue that existential philosophers offer a critique of preconceived ideas about the nature of, and behavior associated with, romantic loving and argue for reconceptions of it, in order to emphasize possibilities for creating authentically meaningful relationships. Stirner's alternative is egoistic loving and Kierkegaard's alternative is initially ethical love (marriage) and ultimately religious love.

Although Nietzsche's musings on love refer mostly to "the love story", eros, or sexual love, he refers to elements of romantic love discussed above. For example, he says that love is a desire to bridge two separate "I"s,[26] and he criticizes the idea of love as merging when it is understood as mutual renunciation.[27] He warns about the dangerous persuasiveness of love at first sight and being misled by "blue eyes or heaving bosoms".[28] Ultimately, Nietzsche suggests that marriage and friendship are stronger bases for interpersonal relationships than romance.

Sartre does not specifically refer to love as romantic, but his language indicates that he was exploring and criticizing the merging model of romantic loving. For example, he describes the ideal of love as uniting with, assimilating, or absorbing the beloved. He uses *Tristan and Isolde* as an example of passion in love and refers to such romantic platitudes as being "made for each other" and "soul mates", wanting to be the world for one another and each other's *raison d'être*, and being willing to do anything for each other as proof of love.[29] Although Sartre does not provide a comprehensive reconstruction of romantic loving in his *magnum opus*, *Being and Nothingness*, he does hint toward alternative understandings elsewhere.

Beauvoir also discusses romantic loving in terms of romantic attractions, desires, musings, and daydreams in *The Second Sex* and explores examples of romantic loving in her fictional works. Her chapter in *The Second Sex* entitled "The Woman in Love" is a critique of women's romantic loving behavior and the ideal of merging. She proposes authentic love as an alternative.

The next section outlines some of the key features of existential thinking before proceeding to identify the questions that it raises with respect to romantic loving as outlined above.

What is existentialism?

Defining existentialism is not a simple task, because none of the writers associated with it was writing for an "existential school". Moreover, the very idea of being "an existentialist" or "achieving authenticity" is contrary to existential thinking because it implies an endpoint rather than a continuous process and suggests that there is a role or external criteria to which one ought to subscribe. Furthermore, the term "existential" was not used as a philosophical category until the mid-twentieth century, which means that some philosophers, notably Stirner, Kierkegaard, and Nietzsche, were only retrospectively described as existentialists.

Nevertheless, a few central themes characterize existential thinking, which have been called "overlapping traits" or "family resemblance[s]".[30] The existential philosophers were concerned with finding meaning in life. Like the Romantics, they reacted vigorously to the Enlightenment, which emphasized objectivity and detachment at the expense of the individual subjective experience and passion. Although the existential philosophers agreed with the Romantics on a number of such issues as subjectivity, uniqueness, and irrationality of human existence, according to Robert Spillane, existentialism was Romanticism's "rebellious adolescent" because it discarded spirituality.[31] Instead, existential philosophers emphasized concrete living over abstract pondering, and these elements contradicted G.W.F. Hegel's (1770–1831) system building, idealism, and belief in the power of reasoning.[32] Hegel's system sought to uncover the underlying order to the universe with its emphasis on the whole (the absolute ideal) rather than the individual. Existential philosophers disagreed because they saw that such a system fails to establish personal principles that are worth living for. Yet, Hegel was important to several existential philosophers because of his analysis of self-consciousness and exposition of the master-slave dialectic. Edmund Husserl's (1859–1938) phenomenology was also particularly influential in the development of existential thinking, most importantly with regard to methodology and intentionality: actions are directed toward objects, and meaning is derived through our awareness of them.[33] Moreover, talking with his friend Raymond Aron about phenomenology introduced Sartre to the notion that we can philosophize about apricot cocktails; that is, philosophy does not have to be only an intellectual exercise but can be used to understand everyday living.[34]

By the 1940s existentialism had become popular due to the influence of Karl Jaspers, Gabriel Marcel, Martin Heidegger, Maurice Merleau-Ponty, Jean-Paul Sartre, Simone de Beauvoir, and Albert Camus. They provided a philosophy that was particularly conducive to dealing with the extreme situations and great human suffering that occurred during the Second World War because it accounted for the absurdity of existence and stressed the importance of individual freedom. Every day, people faced significant choices and life-or-death consequences. For example, if tortured, will I betray my friends and colleagues, thereby condemning them to certain death?

Six of the key themes that characterize existential thinking are as follows.

Choice and freedom

Existential thinking starts with the fact that we are cast into the world: having not chosen to be born, we arrive without a guidebook and without having had any say in how the world around us was built.[35] Yet, once we are conscious, we must choose. Because every action is a choice, we always have choices, and so there is no escaping or, as Sartre put it, "no exit" from our freedom: we are "condemned to be free".[36] In terms of loving, freedom means that individuals are free to choose the meaning and importance they attribute to love. However, there are two aspects to freedom: freedom *to* implies that one has the power to do something, and freedom *from* is what we mean by liberty. According to the existential philosophers of the twentieth century, both types of freedom were at the forefront of thought: freedom *from* oppression and freedom _to_ choose one's actions.[37] Robert Solomon described romantic love as "freedom _from_ determination by our families, from arranged marriages and fixed community roles" and freedom _to_ create relationships and break up, which was not the case for most people before the rise of romantic loving.[38]

Responsibility

With freedom comes responsibility for one's choices. This is a consequence of Sartre's maxim that "existence precedes essence": individuals exist first, start with nothing, and are free to create themselves through their choices and actions. Individuals are free to choose their relationships, and those relationships are a reflection of the people they choose to be. Responsibility is, according to Peter Koestenbaum, realizing and acting in accordance with the fact that individuals design, build, and construct their own lives.[39] Loving distorts our understanding of such freedom because lovers want to define or be defined by the beloved. However, existentially, it is up to individuals to take responsibility for defining themselves and creating their own values.

Anxiety

Awareness of freedom and responsibility creates anxiety, which is also referred to as anguish or angst. Aspects of romantic attachments can relieve anxieties. For example, Mario Mikulincer et al. argue that loving relationships can act as a "a death-anxiety buffering mechanism", since the sense of security, protection, comfort, self-esteem, and social validation that close relationships provide may serve as defensive devices with respect to existential anxiety about the threat of mortality.[40] However, the weight of responsibility that comes with choosing our lives also tends to weigh heavily upon individuals, and this is why they are tempted to deny their freedom and thus enter into what Sartre refers to as "bad faith" _(mauvaise foi)_. One is in bad faith when one allows one's role or situation to rule one's choices and actions. Further to this, existential philosophies reject essential human nature, personality traits, or psychological determinism, which is the view that one is the victim of one's environment, culture, society, childhood, upbringing, genetics, or passions.[41] When Sartre wrote that even in chains one is free, he meant that even if one is not free from oppression, one is still free to think as one chooses.[42] Similarly, since actions are voluntary, individuals choose to act passionately. What is important is what one does to transcend one's facticity, that is, to overcome one's given situation.

Authenticity

While not all existential philosophers refer specifically to authenticity, they all have their own version of the term. Authenticity is deliberately to choose in accordance with what one thinks is genuine and right for oneself, actively to decide whether to accept external pressures and to take responsibility for making choices and associated consequences insofar as they can be foreseen.[43] It is taking charge of one's life or, in other words, being one's own person. An authentic individual is sovereign, unique, self-governing, and self-defining, and one creates oneself through transcending and striving toward goals. According to John Macquarrie, existential authenticity relies on a form of self-mastery in order not to allow oneself to be manipulated by such externalities as moral codes, ideals, duties, roles, or expectations of others.[44]

Being-with

Although existential philosophers have been accused of focusing overtly on the individual at the expense of community, this book shows that for the existential philosophers, human existence can be understood only in and through our relationships.[45] Although "being-with" is primarily a Heideggerian concept, David Cooper argues that the underlying concept that holds for other existentialists is that other people are a fact of life.[46] William Sadler also argues that "being-with" is the human condition, and he defines authentic freedom as being engaged in situations that open possibilities beyond solitary existence. Sadler credits romantic love, when it is not "smothered in the fog of sentimentalism", as "a very significant existential possibility" because it unveils new worlds, new realities, new structures of existence, new modes of being, and new meanings.[47]

Peter Koestenbaum also elaborated on the importance of others, particularly romantic lovers, in the existential context. Love is the choice to create and reflect each other mutually, verifying and illuminating each other's uniqueness because this is how we learn that we exist and who we are. A key theme of authentic love is resistance between, but welcoming of, two independent consciousnesses acting like positive and negative magnets within a single magnetic field.[48]

Leaping

Existential philosophers acknowledged that narratives were insufficient to describe and understand human existence. Some of them faced the abyss of a world where they saw God as dead, invalid, or estranged and where no values could replace the Christian system that was undermined by the empirical rationality of the Enlightenment. Stirner announced that man killed God; Nietzsche declared that God is dead; Kierkegaard suggested that God had been estranged by organized religion; and Beauvoir and Sartre were radical atheists. As Steven Segal argued, disruptions and uncertainties in previously taken-for-granted conventions of our lives provoke existential anxiety.[49] This vacuum left a nihilistic desert for twentieth-century individuals to negotiate.

Yet, this is only the beginning of the story. In an effort to overcome nihilism and anxiety, existential philosophers consider individuals to be responsible for creating their own meaning. Values must be personally and passionately chosen and created through engagement and concrete action.[50] However, each philosopher's approach is different. It shall be seen that Stirner laughs at the abyss and, refusing to leap across it, leaps into it; to overcome the anxiety of the abyss, Kierkegaard leaps into duty and faith; Nietzsche attempts to construct a new morality and embraces the aristocratic ideal of the *Übermensch*; pessimistic about the conflictual nature of relationships, Sartre clambers out of the abyss into Marxism; and Beauvoir leaps into a form of humanism, seeking harmonious relationships based on friendship.

"The leap" is an existential term that originated with Kierkegaard as a leap to faith.[51] The leap is the recognition that there is uncertainty and lack of rationale to choose with confidence about the potential outcomes. It is a commitment to oneself: a bold and risky metamorphosis of choosing the life one wants to lead, or for purposes of this book, the loving relationship that one wants. It is beyond the realms of feelings and reasoning. That is, it is not based only on satisfying sexual impulses, nor is it based on whether the relationship is efficient, beneficial, or socially acceptable; rather, it is based on willing.[52] The existential leap to a faith of love is the decisive declaration that "I choose you", even if others do not approve and even if the relationship is not physically consummated. A leap is not, however, a commitment to the beloved. It is rather a commitment to the life one chooses to create for oneself.

Approach

The five philosophers considered in this study emphasized different aspects of the above themes of both romantic loving and existential concepts. This book considers their views about romantic loving and aims to shed light on the following: the common themes of romantic loving from an existential perspective; the problems that existential philosophies pose for the traditional understanding of romantic loving; and the solutions that existential philosophies offer to overcome those problems.

There are five key points for discussion that will allow us to unpack the central themes of, problems with, and possible solutions to romantic loving from an existential perspective. First, romantic loving involves the idea of creating a union and becoming a "we" instead of two "I"s. Yet, the idea of lovers blurring the boundaries between them brings into question the independent nature of individuals. Moreover, if merging is problematic, then how well can lovers know each other, and how much can they know about themselves through each other? Not all mirrors provide accurate reflections.

Second, many people expect that romantic loving relationships will relieve anxieties because they seem to create meaning in lovers' lives, or at least provide a foundation on which everything else takes on new meaning. Since, existentially, meaning must be created in life, it would seem to make sense that in the absence of anything else, lovers become each other's *raison d'être*. However, founding meaning in one's life on an evanescent relationship makes it inherently precarious. The existential question is: can romantic loving validly relieve anxiety by creating meaning in life, and if so, to what extent?

Third, to what extent does choice play a role in romantic loving? Lovers choose with whom to develop a relationship and how much time and effort they invest in it. However, some elements are uncontrollable, in particular finding the "right person" at the "right time" who chooses to reciprocate. If, existentially, we are condemned to choose, how can we reconcile this with the passionate elements of loving? Moreover, is it unromantic to suggest that romantic loving can be chosen since that means everyone is a potential lover?

Fourth, we have seen that loving relationships support lovers' freedom by opening up possibilities that did not exist without the other. For example, loving relationships offer individuals different perspectives, encouragement, confidence, support, and advice. However, lovers are not free to do whatever they like without repercussion. Lovers expect to be taken into account or consulted when the other makes decisions. The key issues are whether it is possible to love without restricting freedom and whether it is existentially valid to choose to restrict one's freedom.

Fifth, to what extent can individuals be authentic within a romantic loving relationship? Since we create our essence, identity is not fixed and is constructed in light of loving relationships. The desire to be with the other, to avoid disappointment, and to support each other's well-being and happiness means that concessions, sacrifices, and negotiations are commonplace. For example, lovers modify goals, shift priorities, and forego possibilities for the sake of each other. However, if lovers must consider each other when making decisions, it would appear that the ability to make authentic choices is contradicted. Denying or evading one's freedom – in this case by appeal to another person – is bad faith.

An exploration of these issues through the works of five existential philosophers will assist in exploring and understanding the ways in which our ideas about romantic loving shape our understanding of our freedom or power to act by calling into question lovers' desire for independence, the choices they make, how they act authentically, and how they find meaning through romantic loving.

This book proceeds chronologically and phenomenologically by linking what we know about each philosopher's experience with the philosophy that each develops. Thus, the concepts are contextually embedded, which is important because existential philosophies are concerned with everyday living. However, although existentialism is a lived philosophy, it cannot be assumed that all the philosophers always lived by the principles they wrote about. For example, Sartre wrote that he was neither nauseous nor authentic, but he considered himself to be a guide giving directions to others.[53]

In light of this, a secondary theme that is pursued is: to what extent are their philosophies consistent with their lived experiences, as the philosophers themselves describe and reflect on them? Such a pursuit could be criticized as presenting an *ad hominem* argument. However, according to Béla Szabados, it can be dangerous to ignore philosophers' personalities because philosophizing is a personal interpretation of truth.[54] Similarly, Ray Monk argues that biography is important for understanding a person's thinking because it considers connections and differences between what people say and do, allows us to see different facets of the words, and – to use Wittgenstein's words – avoids "aspect blindness".[55] Kierkegaard would also have approved since, as shall be seen, he emphasizes the importance of the subjective experience of the existing individual.

Further to these views, since existential philosophers emphasize passionate engagement and concrete living, the way they experience romantic loving is central to their philosophies. Moreover, some of the philosophers invite us to consider the personal. Simone de Beauvoir and Jean-Paul Sartre wrote autobiographies, and many of Beauvoir's, Sartre's, and Kierkegaard's personal journals and letters were published. In these writings, they each reflect on both their lives and their philosophies.

Nietzsche goes so far as to suggest that all philosophy is personal and autobiographical.[56] Thus, I consider romantic loving not only as the philosophers conceptualized it but also as they concretely lived, described, and reflected on it through their writing. This approach provides a means for practical reflection on the experience of romantic loving rather than abstract philosophical discourse.

Structure

Chapter 2 reviews the philosophy of Max Stirner, who sets the existential stage in his defense of individuals as creative and self-governing. For Stirner, life is to be squandered and lovers are to be enjoyed, and the only constraint is one's power. One loves oneself being in love and lovers ignite the experience. Stirner specifically criticized romantic relationships for being suffocated by dependency, duty, and obligation. His preferred view of loving is a union formed not only for passionate enjoyment, but also in order to extend one's power in the world. Such unions do not, however, involve any illusions or metaphors about blurring the boundaries between two lovers as Plato described in *Symposium*. Stirner was a strong advocate for conceiving of loving as a choice and provided an account of maintaining self-ownership within a loving relationship.

Chapter 3 discusses the ideas of Søren Kierkegaard, a Christian philosopher who saw romantic loving as part of an immature and anxiety-ridden "aesthetic" lifestyle. In *Either/Or* Kierkegaard criticized romantic love for being weak since it depends on beauty and sensuality, and thus it is immediate and lacks reflection. Instead, Kierkegaard suggested that by embracing a duty to one's lover through marriage, and ultimately a duty to God to love our neighbors, individuals could live more fully and meaningfully. To this end, he compared such aesthetes as Mozart's *Don Giovanni* and "Johannes the Seducer" – men interested in passionate love and with no concern for enduring relationships – with Judge William, an ethicist, who advocates marriage based on commitment in the face of perishing passion. I explore the conditions under which romantic loving can be conceived of as an existential stance, and although the duty to love supports the nature of loving as a choice, it raises the question: is there anything meaningful left of romantic loving in the ethical and religious modes?

Chapter 4 investigates the ideas of Friedrich Nietzsche, who saw romantic loving as a frivolous power game that distracts attention from pursuit of the ideal of the *Übermensch*. However, Nietzsche appreciated that worthwhile relationships open up possibilities for individuals by pushing them to achieve more than they could have alone, and such relations as friendship and marriage are more suitable than romantic love for doing so. Nevertheless, by drawing on his understanding of friendship, it is possible to reconcile his ideals of aristocratic anarchism and romantic loving.

Chapter 5 explores Jean-Paul Sartre's view that romantic loving relationships are inherently frustrating because they are sadomasochistic encounters, aimed at becoming complete, that ultimately end in bad faith. While his dominant view was that loving is a choice, it was not his final word. He emphasized the limiting aspects of relationships because love is an attempt to capture the lover's freedom. Sartre leaves us with an instrumental view of romantic loving that is an unreliable strategy for becoming complete, and his attempts to provide an alternative conception are inconclusive.

Chapter 6 considers the work of Simone de Beauvoir. She differs from her predecessors in her emphasis on situations, which limit freedom. In particular, Beauvoir explored the difficulties in reconciling loving and authenticity because lovers tend to have differing priorities. Moreover, she highlighted that existential anxiety cannot be relieved through positing a lover as one's *raison d'être*. However, Beauvoir was ambiguous as to the viability of maintaining a romantic loving relationship and authenticity unless lovers' priorities coincide with each other.

Chapter 7 summarizes existential problems of romantic loving and associated solutions, highlighting common themes and differences, while addressing the questions raised in this introductory chapter.

Selection of five existential philosophers

While questions may be raised as to whether all of the five philosophers I have selected can be officially classified as "existentialists", I have included them because they contributed significantly to the development of existential ideas. This is why I discuss loving existential*ly* (rather than the philosophy of existential*ists*) and why I used the following two selection criteria for inclusion in this book: (1) they develop existential themes, and (2) they address romantic loving. Consistent with David Cooper, I am conducting this study on the basis that "The important thing is not the card-carrying credentials of this or that writer, but his [or her] contribution to the development of that structure".[57]

Many other philosophers are often associated with the existential school, but they are not included in this study because they have not considered romantic loving in sufficient detail. For example, while Martin Heidegger addressed the notion of care, he did not address romantic loving in any depth. Albert Camus did not explicitly address romantic loving and claimed he was neither an existentialist nor a philosopher.[58] Karl Jaspers also rejected the label of existentialist.[59] While Maurice Merleau-Ponty's work does cover existential themes, he is more often considered a phenomenologist.[60]

Such religious existential philosophers as Gabriel Marcel, Emmanuel Levinas, and Martin Buber have been excluded because this book is concerned with the atheistic development of existential thinking. Søren Kierkegaard is the exception because of his pivotal role: he is often referred to as the first existential philosopher.[61]

Nietzsche is a potentially contentious inclusion as an existential philosopher because his vitalistic idea of the will to power as a determining motivational force conflicts with the existential notion of existence preceding essence. Notwithstanding this caveat, it is difficult to ignore similarities between Nietzsche's ideas and such existential ideas as authenticity. Many scholars reference him as a pioneer of existentialism,[62] and like Kierkegaard, Nietzsche is an existential philosopher, if not an existentialist.

Kierkegaard and Nietzsche are a more usual introduction to existentialism but Max Stirner provides an alternative and much-neglected route since he anticipated many existential ideas, especially with respect to individuals as creative nothingnesses. John Carroll pointed out that Stirner raised existential questions regarding the nature of being and existence preceding essence long before Nietzsche, Heidegger, and Sartre.[63]

Although Sartre reluctantly accepted the "existential" label, as David Cooper says, if he is not an existentialist, "then no one is".[64] However, only Sartre's early works can be considered existential. Like Sartre, Beauvoir was not only initially reluctant to accept the existential label but also rejected the suggestion that she was a philosopher at all.[65] Nevertheless, she wrote about existential themes in her fictional and philosophical works, and today she is considered to be not only a novelist but also a significant contributor to existential thinking.[66]

While more philosophers could have been included in a broader examination, these five philosophers are the most significant for this investigation. By drawing on this particular group of five philosophers, possibilities open up for understanding how our common conceptions about romantic loving shape lovers' awareness about what they are free *from* and free *to* do. Such a discussion creates new opportunities to clarify and understand possible sources of conflict and frustration with romantic loving.

Scope

This book is about romantic loving between adult women and adult men. Focusing on romantic loving means that, first, this book is not about companionate or conjugal loving or love that develops in arranged marriages. While marriage is mentioned on occasion, it is only when it is useful to, or contrasts with, the discussion of romantic loving. Although marriage today is sometimes considered the culmination of romantic loving relationships in Western culture, marriage is just one legal association in which romantic loving can play a role. Second, this book is about relationships between grown-ups. It is not about love between parents and children, gods and mortals, humans and their furry or feathered companions, or humans and such inanimate objects as teddy bears or the Eiffel Tower. Third, this book is about heterosexual loving relationships. Fourth, this book focuses on loving as opposed to love: it shall be seen that the existential view is that love becomes meaningful through actions directed toward another, and not as an abstract entity or mystical force that exists independently of individuals. Fifth, this book is about loving relationships in the Western world because romantic love is predominantly a Western cultural phenomenon.[67] Although further exploration would likely uncover interesting similarities, differences, and other insights between other forms and contexts of relationships mentioned above, the scope of this book is limited to human, adult, heterosexual loving relations in Western society.

One final point to note before proceeding is that an important caveat is to what extent the views the philosophers express in nonfiction works and via pseudonyms are their own. Kierkegaard often used indirect methods of communication to encourage his readers to question themselves. This means that we need to be careful to note what was written by Kierkegaard's pseudonyms as compared to the views he held personally and openly acknowledged. Nietzsche's writing contains many potential contradictions that have created much speculation as to whether he intended to be systematic. Added to this, Nietzsche rarely argued, but rather aimed to provide methods and insights, likening his aphorisms to mountain peaks, implying that he was writing for those who did not need valleys of explanations.[68] Much of Beauvoir's and

Sartre's philosophies was expressed through novels and plays, and thus references to those works are given careful consideration with respect to their stated philosophy.

Both philosophical texts and fictional works have been analyzed because, congruent with the existential emphasis on action, we see painted through the philosophers' fictional works concrete examples of philosophical issues. The criticism may be raised that fictional characters are unreliable philosophical representatives. To this I propose that often the affinity between philosophy and literature is obvious and direct. At times, they articulate their philosophy even better through fiction because it provides personal and intimate case studies, allows analysis of concrete actions, and reinforces and exemplifies theories. Fiction allows engagement with philosophical ideas from different angles, helps with understanding and exploring philosophical ideas from a more personal perspective, and provides authors with the flexibility to construct contexts and situations that illustrate examples of their arguments.

Kierkegaard, for example, thought indirect communication was a better way of relating his ideas. Felicity Joseph et al. argue that the existential philosophers' use of literature and indirect communication is strategic since they resist methodologies and systems. Instead, literature and indirect communication show concrete living, thereby appealing to and engaging "a fuller range of human faculties (emotion, imagination, empathy, etc.) than abstract intellectual theory".[69]

Colin Davis argues that for the existential writers, literature pushes the boundaries of philosophical thinking because it opens up new opportunities for illuminating challenges and tensions between theory and practice.[70] However, it must be kept in mind that their literary works cannot always be taken at face value because they are a ground for exploration of their ideas. Thus, they sometimes illustrate contradictory themes and do not always present a definitive conclusion.

2
Max Stirner and Loving Egoistically

Max Stirner was a radical philosopher of personal power and extreme individualism. *Der Einzige und sein Eigentum*, published in English as *The Ego and His Own* ("*Der Einzige*"), dedicated "To my sweetheart Marie Dähnhardt", his second wife, begins and ends with a quote from Goethe: "All things are nothing to me".[1] Stirner's philosophy unfolds from this central theme, which places individuals at the center of their world. Individuals wield their power to gain control of their predicaments through acquiring property. They sever ties with everyone and everything, including authorities, religion, morals, values, truth, emotions, and intellect, which he dismissed as abstractions or "spooks".[2] Individuals hold nothing sacred and are masters of their own metaphysical universe. Having broken ties with everything, an individual is solitary, or in Stirner's words, a "unique one". Stirner's emphasis on enjoyment, frivolity, and personal interest encourages us to ask: why would one engage in a romantic relationship that lacks these essential ingredients?

Der Einzige burst onto the Berlin philosophical scene and sparked such outrage that the censors initially banned it. A week later, they lifted the ban, asserting that no one would take it seriously. Karl Marx and Friedrich Engels took it seriously enough to warrant a direct retaliation in *The German Ideology* that was longer than *Der Einzige* itself. Undoubtedly, Stirner was fully aware of the controversy that his philosophy would spark. But he cared neither about what anyone thought nor about whether his book upset anyone. In fact, he speculated that it would only bring his readers trouble and grief. Stirner announces that his relationship to his readers is one of utility since he is a writer, and it interests him to have a paying audience.[3]

Contrary to his declarations, it is possible that *Der Einzige* and Stirner's response to his critics is a form of conversation. Considering the difference between content and process, Stirner's work describes others as instruments, which is the content of his work, and publishing his book initiates a form of dialogue. He perpetuated this dialogue through a response to criticisms of *Der Einzige*, called *Kleinere Schriften und seine Entgegnungen auf die Kritik seines Werkes "Der Einzige und sein Eigenthum"* (*"Kleinere Schriften"*). Perpetuating this dialogue is the process of his work, and this is why his work can be treated as philosophy rather than a personal tract.

Stirner's philosophy has often been neglected and dismissed as undiplomatic or unorthodox.[4] Manners and moral judgments aside, he provides some relevant insights into an existential critique of romantic loving. Stirner provides an alternate route to loving existentially, compared to Kierkegaard and Nietzsche, because of his idea that the individual is a creative nothingness. Existential thinkers have largely neglected Stirner, even though he anticipated many of the issues that they faced.[5] While there are significant differences between Stirner and other existential thinkers, particularly with respect to the nature of commitment and anxiety, the commonalities and relevance to romantic loving are significant enough to warrant a careful and serious examination.[6]

Before proceeding to romantic loving, let us first place Stirner briefly in context. *Der Einzige* was released in 1845, during the rise of liberal economic theory under the influence of Adam Smith and when the utilitarian ideas of Jeremy Bentham and John Stuart Mill were taking hold and emphasizing individualism and *laissez-faire* capitalism. In a similar vein, Stirner was rebelling against authorities, institutions, and organized religion, and he called for individual liberation and for individuals to seize and act upon their personal power. Such ideals as humanism or communism, Stirner argued, are artificial structures that humans create and voluntarily subordinate themselves to. Liberating oneself from such spooks is of utmost importance for establishing Stirner's unique one as the ultimate authority and for returning power to the individual.

Stirner's methodology, terminology, and themes have been likened to Hegel's, but it was against Hegel that Stirner was rebelling.[7] Both Hegel and Stirner dismissed abstract notions of freedom and argued for freedom manifested tangibly in property. However, Stirner takes it further than did Hegel. Hegel advocated integration with society and state, while Stirner took an individual-centric approach. Stirner clearly rejected Hegel's concept of freedom as an ethical step that requires membership of social institutions overseen by the state. For Hegel, Stirner's unrestrained libertarian conception of freedom would have been barbaric.

As subtly as a sledgehammer, Stirner begins by decimating the idea that we are supposed to devote ourselves to higher causes, including God, nations, humankind, or any other general cause. While Sultans and God would claim unselfishly to serve their people, Stirner proposed that so-called higher beings are ultimately concerned with themselves, since anyone who stands against them incurs their wrath or is supposed to be sent to hell. Stirner finds no justification to adopt another's cause, and so he chooses his own. Following Feuerbach, Stirner took humans to be supreme, and *Der Einzige* aimed better to understand what this means. This chapter aims to understand the implications of this in the context of romantic relationships.

Problems of romantic loving

Stirner's problem with romantic love was twofold: that it should be unselfish and that it evokes a duty to others. First, Stirner was contemptuous of anything that creates a liability, including relationships. His reasoning is as follows. Romantic relationships induce an obligation to love each other forever and an expectation to feel a certain way. Duty calls for acquiescence and self-sacrifice, and it operates for the sake of others rather than in accordance with one's own judgment or interest. Obeying a duty to love is tantamount to self-renunciation because it overrides the choice to love, it and enslaves lovers to the ideal of love because what lovers *should* do dominates the relationship. Lovers are obliged to give each other love like paying a toll, and thus they do not own their love, and this dynamic makes loving relationships manic. According to Stirner, the other is not sacred, love is not sacred, and promises are not sacred. One should not turn love into a spook and subordinate oneself to it. Religious, mystical, marital, and familial loving also generate obligations. The only difference is the object to which one is obligated. Infatuation and sensual love are similarly problematic: infatuation is driven by a *must*, and sensual love is driven by dependence on the beloved.[8]

Responsibility, accountability, obligation, and commitment are annihilated in Stirner's moral vacuum. Certainly, he would take little issue with accepting responsibility for his actions in saying, "yes, I did it". However, he did not accept *accountability* to others. He wrote: "Let us therefore not aspire to community, but to *one-sidedness*. Let us not seek the most comprehensive commune, 'human society', but let us seek in others only means and organs which we may use as our property!"[9] The sanctity of the promise is also obliterated. Keeping promises, for the sake of the promise, is an illegitimate constraint because it is another attempt to bind the individual. Stirner equates being free from obligations to owning himself: "A leap from this bridge makes me free!"[10]

The unique one must embrace the heroism of the lie and be willing to break one's word so that one establishes oneself as self-determining instead of bound by morality and ethics.[11] There is no acknowledgment of good and evil to guide one's choices, and objective moral values are illegitimate since the individual is the measure of right and wrong: "If it is right for me, it is right".[12] For Stirner, the only important truth is that which is lived: the freely chosen personal subjective truth. Stirner would dismiss the realist objection that there is a physical aspect to reality that is independent of our knowledge of it. His emphasis on subjective truth links him to existential thinking.

In *Kleinere Schriften*, Stirner scoffed at the idea that loving necessarily involves self-sacrifice and unselfishness. If we want sacrificial relationships without enjoyment, he recommends looking in a lunatic asylum.[13] Nevertheless, he did not rule out the possibility of such values as community and cooperation.[14] He proposed that one engages with the community and others for one's own profit, not for anyone's sake, even though others may derive advantages from it. The unique one embraces life and all enjoyable experiences that come with it. Stirner even takes it to the extreme of a love of mankind, thereby allowing what is commonly perceived as altruism and charity to become acceptable because one loves loving.[15] If one derives a sense of enjoyment and happiness from communing with others, then so be it. Stirner's objection would be turning community into a spook.

The implication of such an attitude is that there is no possibility of connecting or establishing a solid basis of mutual understanding with another, because individuals exist in opposition. From the moment we are thrust into the world, Stirner says that we find ourselves in combat with others – that is, asserting, defending, and trying to grasp ourselves.

There is no possibility for "intersubjectivity" or merging, because "opposition vanishes in complete – *severance* or singleness".[16] Every individual is therefore doomed to solitude. Taking a binary view of subject and object, Stirner is consistent in his view that truth is subjective. As he can know only his subjective experience with any certainty, anyone else's subjectivity is foreign and incomprehensible to him. Stirner digs a chasm across which it is difficult to imagine any bridge that could carry a sustainable human relationship, let alone a romantic one. However, instead of unselfishly loving others, Stirner argued for the importance of loving oneself.

Stirner's solution

The alternative to romantic love, Stirner proposed, is self-love, and it shall be seen that relationships based on egoistic unions support this. For Stirner, loving oneself means to appreciate oneself as a "unique one". Stirner called an individual "unique" because humans are different in terms of their bodies, desires, actions, and experiences.[17] Never again will this exact human form exist. Moreover, being "unique" is a form of self-government in which individuals refuse to be subordinated to anyone or anything. Stirner declares, "Nothing is more to me than myself!"[18]

This does not imply that Stirner is solipsistic. Although the unique one is the center of his or her own world, one does not hold the view that nothing else exists besides oneself. One recognizes the existence of property and other people (as property), even if one's attitude is to treat everything as objects. Becoming unique involves owning oneself, accepting oneself as one is, and taking a selfish interest in oneself, as outlined below.

Owning oneself

The first integral feature of loving oneself is "owning" oneself. There are three facets to self-ownership: recognizing one's chains, embracing one's power, and creating oneself.

Recognizing one's chains

Stirner referred to *Eigenheit*, which in the English translation appears as "ownness" or self-ownership. "Ownness" – as Stirner refers to it – is ownership of one's ideas, body, and objects that one finds interesting. It is about being self-determining and self-creating, ensuring one chooses for one's own sake and on one's own terms, and not because one thinks one should or is coerced into it. It involves shaking free from the cobwebs that entrap and the pressures that push and pull one in different directions. It could also be argued that Stirner's *Eigenheit* is an embryonic understanding of existential authenticity, since the German word for authenticity is *Eigentlich*, and *eigen* means one's own.

Stirner saw life as a constant battle for self-possession by raising our consciousness to recognize the fetters that bind us. Consciousness-raising is very important to Stirner because "Unconsciously and involuntarily we all strive towards ownness...But what I do unconsciously I half-do."[19] This indicates that Stirner distinguished between the quality and strength of one's actions, which is not far removed from what some of the later existential thinkers described as immanent living versus transcendental living. Immanent living blindly accepts the chains, while transcending involves striving to break the chains. Seeing the chains is the first battle. Then, it becomes a matter of breaking free and seizing our power to act in accordance with our choices.

Embracing one's power

Albert Camus pointed out that for Stirner to live is to transgress and to be in a constant state of rebellion against society and the environment.[20] The unique one refuses to subordinate oneself to not only constraints such as the law and societal norms but also so-called virtues and vices such as love and avarice. Self-mastery has external and internal dimensions, requiring that one neither subordinates oneself to others nor is ruled by appetites or emotions such as sensuality.[21]

Certainly, Stirner's total apathy to any higher authority even justifies crime. Other people's claims on property are not respected. Possession is property, and possession is defined by power.[22] Indeed, if crime is necessary to overcome a constraint on the individual, then Stirner does so without remorse. Such a philosophy could be construed as highly dangerous and hurtful for anyone who encounters such a person. While Stirner's philosophy does allow for the legitimacy of criminal action, even murder, he approaches it in a very specific way. He provides an example of a man who greedily pursues materialism for his selfish pleasure alone. Stirner rejects this kind of egoism as trivial because an avaricious person has become a slave to one ruling passion: the spook of material gratification.[23] Similarly, an infatuated person is a slave to love, possessed by desire.

However, Stirner's philosophy is no excuse for petty crime, reckless greed, or obsessive infatuation. The crime is justified only if it is an assertion of one's autonomy, free from any pressure, conditioning, or emotion, for increasing the property in which one takes an interest. One can pursue the possessions of the material world, provided one remains the master and not the slave.

It is only when one is free from such spooks as obligations and expectations that one is able to truly own oneself. However, for Stirner, freedom is also a spook. Being free is not something to seek or win but rather to recognize and assume. Many people who think that they are idealists are, in fact, egoists, and pretending otherwise is absurd and a form of "self-denial".[24] Being free is Stirner's starting point: once one recognizes one is free, shaking off all ties, what then? What matters then is how one makes the world one's own.

Stirner was more interested in "freedom *to*", that is, what one has the power to do rather than what one is "free *from*". Stirner discounts this latter aspect of freedom and the libertarian claim that often accompanies it. While Jean-Paul Sartre later said that we are never so free as when we are in chains, Stirner proposes that being "inwardly free" is true but useless.[25] Freedom is a pyrrhic victory if one does not have the power to act freely. One's power determines what one can be free *from*. Instead of pursuing "freedom", Stirner acted from and for his own power.

Stirner admits that while we can free ourselves from most things, we tend not to be free from everything.[26] He did not deny facticity; that is, certain situations and restrictions are imposed upon individuals beyond their control. For example, he was all too aware that his own and his mother's illnesses were hindrances to his higher education and career. Power is more important to Stirner than freedom because he understood that there were limits beyond his control to how he could exert his power and preserve his own life in order to squander it. Keenly aware of the power of others, he used his own power where he could. He was not interested in fighting battles for the sake of more property. Martyrdom is not for the unique one, because there is nothing – no person, cause, belief, or principle – that is more important than oneself. Stirner recognized that some people do exert more power than he. So, he stressed the importance of how one uses things within one's grasp.

Possession is of utmost importance to Stirner because the unique one maximizes pleasure through exercising one's power to appropriate what one is interested in. The unique one defines oneself through property:

My power is *my* property.
My power *gives* me property.
My power *am* I myself, and through it am I my property.[27]

In Machiavellian terms, one desires something only for its use or as a means to a pleasing end. This includes other people. Stirner views the object of the game of human relations to be possession of the other, and it has to be that way if one is to own oneself.

One uses the power one has to enjoy life, but should one's power not be enough for something one wants, there is no reason to upset oneself about it. With hints of stoicism and pragmatism, he is willing to fight for his property, but if he fails, he is ready to give it up and walk away smiling because all things are nothing to him.[28]

Creating oneself

Owning oneself involves realizing that one creates oneself and one's world. In a passage that echoes what Friedrich Nietzsche later came to refer to as overcoming, Stirner said: "You are yourself a higher being than you are, and surpass yourself".[29] The individual is never static but rather continuously in a process, always transcending, always creating a new self and constantly choosing identities and transforming oneself. For Stirner, the self is a "nothingness", or more specifically, a "creative nothing".[30] One is one's own creator. He did not literally mean that he creates everything in a God-like sense but rather that one creates one's own metaphysical identity. There are no pre-determined roles in society that the unique one must adhere to, nor are there any set vocations that the person must live up to because that would be an attempt to be something that the unique one *is* not and chooses not to become.

The implication that this has for conceptions of the human condition is that no one is born with a personality. No one is born introverted or extroverted, nor can people inherit their behavior. One is a transitory entity that continually develops and creates its own existence, extending as far as one's power enables. Since one is not pre-determined, one exists first in the world and is free to create oneself through actions and projects. One is what one makes of the world.[31] One uses one's creativity to surpass conditioning and assert oneself as a sovereign individual. This is the root of Stirner's objection to romantic love: if lovers conform to pre-established expectations about how they should feel and behave, then they do not own themselves. To own themselves, lovers would create themselves as unique lovers.

The existential thinkers will also adopt this principle of the individual in the process of becoming and overcoming oneself. Thus, Stirner was the first to articulate the existential idea that "existence precedes essence", which is a key reason he can be placed as a progenitor of atheistic existentialism.

Also like the later existential thinkers, Stirner's attitude to life stems from the fact that he finds nothing given on which to found the meaning of his life. Stirner articulated a phrase that Nietzsche later echoed: "Man has killed God".[32] However, for Stirner, God ought never to have been taken seriously. Like many of the existential thinkers, Stirner attempted to answer the question: how does one live in a world without inherent meaning and ready-made reasons for existence? Logical thinking leads Stirner to the abyss of a nihilistic world: the same predicament the later existential thinkers confronted.

However, what differentiates Stirner from the other existential philosophers is his solution to the nihilistic world. Nihilism was not a problem for Stirner. It was his facticity, and he was not anxious about it. For Stirner, anxiety and frustration are not fundamental aspects of life, unless one so chooses. Stirner did not rule out the possibility of negative emotions, but as a nominalist, he did not reify them. Rather, we emote negatively or positively. He did not seem to view emoting negatively as personally useful or beneficial since it would be inconsistent with enjoying and squandering his life. Stirner chose not to act anxiously. He refused to act in ways that compromised him.

Albert Camus, who also attempted to embrace the nihilistic truth of the world, said of Stirner that he laughs at the abyss, adventures into the absurd, and takes nihilism to its logical conclusion. By shedding ties with all things that threaten to hinder the individual, one sweeps oneself clear of outside clutter.[33] The unique one, as a creative nothing, awakens, annihilates everything, and is liberated in this self-created desert. Nevertheless, Stirner did not end with nihilism, because he proposed, as other existential philosophers came to advise, that individuals are creative nothingnesses with the power to craft meaning where they will. Stirner ignores the immanence of death and embraces life. Without God or any higher being, entity, or ideal to serve, the only thing left for Stirner is himself: the isolated individual. Without an anchor, the unique one seeks not to discover one's true self but to discover one's frivolity.

Accepting oneself

A second element of loving oneself, for Stirner, is accepting oneself completely. Notwithstanding Stirner's discussion about surpassing oneself, Stirner said we should be happy just the way we are. "We are perfect altogether!" he said, "For we are, every moment, all that we can be; and we never need be more".[34] Stirner's point is that just because one is constantly in flux and instantly able to change, this does not mean that one should change. There is no ideal self toward which we ought to strive. Certainly, one is constantly becoming, but only in a sense of always being fluid, never tied to anyone or anything. One does not become toward anything in particular.

One might be compelled to point out, however, if the aim is to squander and dissolve oneself, then surely there are moments when one is not perfect, that is, when one ignores or foregoes possibilities for squandering. Elsewhere, Stirner urges us to recognize that if we are honest with ourselves, we will realize that we are actually egoists.[35] This is further evidence that Stirner does advocate striving toward consciousness-raising and self-awareness. Stirner might respond that his aim is to avoid the situation whereby one wishes one had squeezed more out of a situation. Nevertheless, there ought to be no problem with recognizing in hindsight that one had other possibilities and learning how to take advantage of other possibilities in the future.

Stirner's description of the unique one can be vague and opens Stirner up to the criticism that the unique one is a spook.[36] In *Kleinere Schriften*, he identified that the difficulty in meaningfully describing the unique one is that by its very nature as a creative nothing, it is always changing. A better understanding of the unique one can only be obtained through recognizing it as isolated, solitary, and a creative nothingness, as Stirner himself. Yet, exactly these qualities prohibit it from being fully described. In being unique at every moment, it cannot exist a second time.[37]

Stirner's description of the unique one is also comparable to an analogy used by Jean-Paul Sartre, who claimed it is not possible truly to understand another because as one grasps for another's essence, it escapes, and one is left with an empty coat in one's hands.[38] Similarly, the unique one's essence can never be fully grasped because it is intangible and always becoming. Thus, a description is meaningless at any point in time because, by the time it is articulated, the unique one has changed. A person is never static and can never be defined absolutely and attempting to do so is a matter of reconciling the irreconcilable. Yet, surely there is nothing more concrete to individuals than their own existence.[39] The unique one is a concrete being, not an ideal to strive toward. Embracing the fact that individuals are egoists is raising one's consciousness to reality, not striving toward an ideal. It is not sacred, because it is up to individuals to decide how to live, squander, and dissolve themselves.

Taking a selfish interest in oneself

A third necessary condition of loving oneself involves taking an egoistic and selfish interest in satisfying oneself.[40] This means that one does things in which one is interested and that one enjoys rather than things one is expected to do or accepts a duty to do. In this sense, the world takes on value through the meaning one chooses and imposes on it. Stirner reiterates the importance of following one's own interests in *Kleinere Schriften*. Unless it is a *selfish* interest, it is superficial because anything else is a general or abstract interest. Something becomes interesting and valuable only if *you* appreciate it, despite its value to others.[41] For example, a beloved is not intrinsically or objectively lovable. As soon as the unique one loses interest, the beloved loses the value that was bestowed upon them. Stirner says this kind of person is not worse than anyone else; but rather, according to Stirner, such a person is more "definite" and "practical".[42] Thus, disinterested concern is not a feature of Stirnerian relationships.

Stirner also referred to other people as potentially useful or interesting objects, to be consumed like food. Lovers are interesting because they nourish passions and increase enjoyment and pleasure in life. He said, "I can love, love with a full heart, and let the most consuming glow of passion burn in my heart, without taking the beloved one for anything else than the *nourishment* of my passion, on which it ever refreshes itself anew".[43]

The implication of loving oneself above all else is not self-preservation but almost the opposite. Instead of the Delphic maxim to know oneself, Stirner advocates getting value out of oneself.[44] A fulfilling life is not one in which one discovers one's true self. Rather, it is one in which the individual "burns the candle at both ends". It is a matter of squeezing as much enjoyment out of existence as possible, and that involves consuming, squandering, and even risking life.[45] He would have advocated the mantra *carpe diem* and leaping head first into adventures.

For Stirner, what is meaningful is what one has the power or "might" to do. Stirner reduced everything to possession, which poses the question: what can I use my might to attain that is of interest to me? And what can I do to transcend the influences that threaten me? In loving relationships, Stirner emphasized the importance of being free from preconceived expectations about how lovers should feel and obligations always to feel lovingly toward that individual. Once one frees oneself from such ties, then one is free to choose relationships and endeavors that interest one. The next section addresses the question of romantic loving relationships for an individual who distinguishes oneself as "unique".

Loving others

Superficially, it would appear that Stirner's approach to others is caustic. Stirner would seem to desecrate any opportunity for positive human relations when he talks about other people being mere objects to be devoured and exploited. One can live a cloistered existence, but it is not a necessary consequence of Stirner's philosophy.

Stirner maintained that a great way to get value out of oneself is through relationships with others. Stirner warns that one would really be missing out on immense joy and pleasure if one did not concern oneself with others, and he says that one who loves another is richer than one who does not.[46]

Stirner loves because it makes him happy and feels natural.[47] But at the same time, love is a conscious choice, and he is not simply succumbing to internal desires. One loves the feeling of being in love, and the other's admirable qualities spark loving feelings and enjoyment. In this context, the unique one loves another just as he or she would love oysters or wine, which taste and smell good or provide an interesting, enjoyable experience.[48] Just as the unique one is indifferent to the bottle in which the wine is presented, one is indifferent to other qualities that the lover displays. One can still claim to "love" the wine, even if one does not love the bottle, which is nevertheless an essential component of the wine. If the wine turns sour, then one no longer loves the wine. Similarly, if the beloved stops demonstrating enjoyable qualities, then the unique one's love dissolves into indifference. The implication of such an attitude is that loving is entirely conditional because if it is not right for the unique one, then there is no obligation to continue the relationship, since "I fix the purchase price of my love quite at my pleasure".[49] There is no need or desire to understand or acknowledge the other's subjectivity, because one treats others as objects. As the beloved's subjectivity is not recognized and one defines oneself in terms of property, love becomes a power relationship.

Nonetheless, Stirner insists that his approach is open to love, devotion, sacrifices, and sincerity.[50] Moreover, Stirner explicitly established the possibility of romantic loving when he said:

> I can with joy sacrifice to him numberless enjoyments, I can deny myself numberless things for the enhancement of *his* pleasure, and I can hazard for him what without him was the dearest to me, my life, my welfare, my freedom. Why, it constitutes my pleasure and my happiness to refresh myself with his happiness and his pleasure.[51]

This suggests that a unique one can still do all those things traditionally associated with romantic loving that are not, on the surface, of direct or immediate benefit or enjoyment, such as giving, sharing, compromising, sacrificing, being caring and compassionate, and concerning oneself with the beloved's welfare and happiness: "If I see the loved one suffer, I suffer with him, and I know no rest till I have tried everything to comfort and cheer him; if I see him glad, I too become glad over his joy".[52]

However, these actions are always considered in relation to the unique one's benefit: "But, because I cannot bear the troubled crease on the beloved forehead, for that reason, and therefore for my sake, I kiss it away. If I did not love this person, he might go right on making creases, they would not trouble me; I am only driving away *my* trouble".[53] Even if the unique one is deeply concerned for the beloved, the beloved is still considered property. The unique one treats the beloved as one would one's eyes: they have a use, and one enjoys and cares for them but ultimately owes them nothing.[54] Stirner is not raising Cartesian dualistic issues here, because for him, there is no essence behind appearances and no mind behind a body. One is one's body and one can choose to do what one wills with it. One is what one does. One is an embodied consciousness in the sense that there is no "self" that can be definitively described.

A unique one is not concerned for the beloved as an end in itself. One's actions are driven by the desire to receive something in exchange, even if it is simply the warm feeling of doing something nice for the beloved. The unique one trades one passion for another.[55] One gives as a means to an end. The happiness of the beloved is preferred to the sacrifice. While Stirner can be read to be cynical, selfish, and self-centered, he does concern himself for the beloved's welfare and this allows for romantic possibilities.

Despite Stirner's apparent willingness to sacrifice his life, welfare, freedom, and most other things for the beloved, he insisted that he does not sacrifice himself.[56] He is willing to sacrifice everything except his "owness" – that is, those self-chosen principles by which he defines himself: "Yes, I *utilize* the world and men! With this I can keep myself open to every impression without being torn away from myself by one of them".[57] He is keeping himself open to all kinds of potentially enjoyable and interesting experiences. Stirner realized that others open up possibilities that he would not have had alone and being with others can be highly rewarding.

One can engage with others as long as one chooses the ties, actively chooses the relationship, and does not lose self-ownership in the process. A unique one ensures this by choosing obligations and the extent to which one attaches oneself to them.[58] Despite Stirner's distancing the unique one from others, the isolated individual needs other people for the enjoyable experience of loving.

The attitude outlined above can be manipulative, exploitative, and thus self-defeating because if the beloved does not appreciate being used and treated as an object, then the relationship collapses. Then, a unique one not only is closed off to other possibilities that a more sustainable and continuing relationship could provide, but also risks loneliness and seclusion. Stirner's second wife, Marie Dähnhardt, suggested that for Stirner, this was the result of his approach to life. Stirner's two marriages were brief. His first wife, Agnes Clara Kunigunde Butz, was the daughter of his proprietor. She was young and poorly educated, and Stirner married her probably for her housekeeping skills. Accidentally seeing her naked once, he never touched her again. She died while giving birth to a stillborn child less than a year after the marriage. In stark contrast to Butz, Marie Dähnhardt left behind Christianity and her family to live more freely in Berlin where she met Stirner at the *Young Hegelians* philosophy discussion group. She smoked cigars, drank beer, played billiards, and even went with the men when they visited brothels. Stirner and his witnesses were playing cards at Stirner's apartment when the pastor arrived for the wedding ceremony. Dähnhardt arrived late and without a wedding dress. Having forgotten to buy wedding rings, they improvised with two copper rings that came from a witness's bag and were married without a bible.[59]

In little more than two years after his second wedding, Stirner had squandered Dähnhardt's inheritance on a failed milk shop cooperative, and they separated – with little love lost on her side. Stirner's biographer, John Henry Mackay, contacted her after Stirner's death. She had converted to Catholicism, retired in a religious institution, refused to see Mackay in person, and sent him surly responses to his queries. Dähnhardt said that she had neither respected nor loved Stirner; he was "too selfish to have true friends", and she described him as "very sly".[60] Why she married Stirner remains a mystery, and Mackay concludes that she undoubtedly never understood her husband's philosophy. However, she may have understood the man. Stirner ended up bankrupt, with few friends, and he died alone from what was probably an infection from a wasp sting.[61]

Superficially, it could be argued that the fact Stirner was married meant that he did not live his philosophy, which condemns obligations to others. Yet, there is no indication that Stirner took his marriage commitments seriously or that he accepted any kind of obligation to his wives. Moreover, his frequent moves to avoid debt collectors and two stints in debtor's jail suggest he also rejected any obligation to those from whom he borrowed money. Indeed, Marie Dähnhardt's comments to John Henry Mackay would seem to support the argument that Stirner did indeed live his philosophy, and there is no indication that Stirner regretted or was unhappy with his life choices.

The risk in Stirner's anarchism taken to its logical conclusion is that if one does away with morality, then one also does away with society.

Undoubtedly, society also does away with the unique one, which would explain why Stirner had so few friends. In Albert Camus' analysis of Stirner in *L'Homme Revolte*, he anticipates that if Stirner's philosophy were adopted *en masse*, then rampant nihilists drunk on destruction would raze the world into ruins. Survivors would awaken in this desert and have to figure out for themselves what to do next.[62] Stirner suggested that we form egoistic unions, as follows.

Loving unions

It is clear from the above discussion that loving relationships with others are possible for Stirner, even though they are based on exploitation. The question arises as to whether loving is possible between unique ones and whether it would be in Stirner's best interest not to enlighten lovers about his attitude.[63] One might expect that a "self-denying" lover would be reluctant to become involved with Stirner if they knew his philosophy. Moreover, it is possible that Stirner would better be able to gain possession of those things he is interested in by manipulating others and appealing to their generosity and kindness. While such an attitude is possible within Stirner's philosophy, there are two reasons that Stirner resists the conclusion that others ought to be ignorant of his intentions.

First, Stirner suggests that he would actually prefer to engage with selfish – instead of kind – people. Kindness is given in response to one who begs for help, and thus one is dependent on a chance encounter with another who shows mercy or pity and must be accepted. On the other hand, selfishness "demands *reciprocity* (as thou to me, so I to thee), does nothing 'gratis', and may be won and–*bought*".[64] Nevertheless, Stirner did not accept obligations to others, so acts of kindness are irrelevant to him since he would have no intention of reciprocating unless it pleased him to do so.

Second, Stirner specifically considered the possibility of relationships between unique ones. Stirner was not utopian, not interested in providing a framework for future society, and not advocating that everyone ought to adopt his philosophy. Politically, Stirner's egoist is a radical anarchist, and so he rejects the state and the law. Indeed, Stirner did not support any economic or political system, because he viewed them as oppressive exploiters of the individual: socialism subordinates the individual to the state and capitalism to the firm.[65] However, Stirner recognized that society is a fact of our existence and chose to live in it so that he could exploit it. To such an end, he outlined a form of relationships that he imagined could increase his power. Thus, being anti-social is not a necessary feature of Stirner's philosophy.

Stirner proposed that a means of establishing viable relationships is a free and voluntary association without hierarchy or domination, where everyone pursues his or her individual goals, which happen to be mutually beneficial. He called it a "Union of Egoists".[66] The purpose of such a relationship is to amplify individual power by together achieving more than could be managed alone.[67] To this end, people come to agreements and understandings. Stirner avoids turning the union into a spook and being subordinated to it by insisting on two key criteria: the union is formed for one's own benefit, and one does not let oneself be possessed by it. He wrote, "a union is only your instrument, or the sword with which you sharpen and increase your natural force; the union exists for you and through you".[68] Moreover, the union is self-creating; it does not restrict itself by turning into something fixed and weighed down by rules and expectations.[69] Despite Stirner's apparent distaste for commitments, he did allow ties to be made, as long as one remains ready to break them. "As *own* you are *really rid of everything*, and what clings to you *you have accepted*; it is your choice and your pleasure".[70]

Like Hegel, Stirner refers to loving in terms of a union. Hegel thought that a true loving union exists only between equals who annul opposition and overcome objectivity. While in a corporeal sense the lovers are still individuals, they strive to overcome their otherness and unite into "living whole".[71] Not sharing property damages the relationship because it means it is not a complete union.

For Stirner, it is irrelevant whether the two are alike in power, and opposition, objectivity, and separation are facts of life. For Stirner, there can be no possibility of a true union as Hegel envisaged, because every relationship is in opposition and based on exploitation. However, in Stirner's opinion, this is not pejorative. On the contrary, Stirner thought it is to be cherished because obligations to others suffocate individuals. Others are not to be part of one's self-definition, because as Stirner said, "If you are connected, you cannot leave each other; if a 'tie' clasps you, you are something only *with another*".[72] The unique one preserves and defines one's uniqueness through distance from other people. Thus, despite the unique one's solitude and attempts to detach oneself from others, one still needs others to define oneself. Stirner's liberating approach suggests that although there is a world full of people, it is up to individuals to choose how much they allow others to influence and define them.

Stirner's union is based on a voluntary exchange. Respect and reciprocity exist insofar as the other is significant, or in other words, the relationship brings something of value. It is not a matter of breaking promises or commitments for the sake of breaking them, but rather only if they compromise one's self-assertion and self-determination. Thus, breaking promises is possible and acceptable but not automatic. Nevertheless, such relationships are rendered unreliable and tenuous to say the least.

Key considerations

There are three key questions arising from Stirner's philosophy with respect to romantic loving that are considered below: whether it is tautological, narcissistic, or actually romantic.

First, one of the key risks of Stirner's framework is that it is conceived as narcissistic because of its overt self-centeredness. However, it is not entirely closed off from others, because it supports unions. It does not necessarily come at the expense of others and result in reclusiveness. Moreover, whereas narcissists love the idea of themselves, Stirner and other Romantics are not afraid to annihilate and create themselves anew at every turn.[73]

Second, Stirner asserted that everyone is an egoist even if some deny it because they prefer to create the illusion of altruism. First of all, stating that everyone is an egoist even if they deny it is unfalsifiable. Furthermore, if everyone is an egoist, then Stirner's argument amounts to the tautology that one cannot act against one's will.[74] Moreover, by asserting that one loves because one feels pleasure, Stirner is simply restating his general argument that the egoist has no motives or purposes that are not its own. While Stirner acknowledged that such an argument is clearly tautological, he advises that it is ethically significant.

Stirner might have argued that it is a mistake to assume that there is a motivating force behind the action. It is true but redundant that one cannot act against one's will because the act is the will. It is a tautology if one separates action from the will, which Stirner would not do. The unique one does not do what one wants; rather, one is what one does and therefore cannot be anything other than what one wants. Often, one does not know one's motivation at the time of one's actions, but the meaning is revealed through doing, as is one's knowledge as to whether the action is interesting or enjoyable. Furthermore, since for Stirner truth is subjective, he chooses to accept that he exists in the world, consciously acts, seems to be able to override many of the influences around him, and does not see himself as part of anything greater. If it is true for him, it is true. Moreover, Stirner did not say that there are no reasons to act, just that reasons are not enough. One does not need a reason to do things, and here we see latent underpinnings of the existential point that rationality and desires do not explain all behavior.

Although there are elements of Stirner's philosophy that are synonymous with psychological egoism (such as self-interest as the motivation for behavior), he does not fit perfectly into this category, because his focus is not on immediate gratification of current and impulsive desires. He did not say that all actions are always egoistic, nor that everyone is motivated by self-interest.[75] In fact, he said that most people do not act egoistically.

Stirner acts in accordance with what he finds interesting and enjoyable in life. It is not a tautology if it is understood in existential terms: he acts, he learns, he becomes. He does not know what interests him until he throws himself into it. The opposite of self-interest is supposedly altruism, doing things for the good of others. Yet, Stirner said that this is hypocritical because if it interests one to pursue altruistic or humanitarian activities, then one does it. His point is that by freely choosing to engage oneself in activities, one owns oneself. We are individuals and free to pursue things that interest us.

A third issue is whether Stirner's reformulation of love – with its emphasis on oneself, treating others as objects, and relationships based on exchange – can be considered romantic. Reconsidering the definition of romantic loving outlined in the introduction, there are latent romantic elements that not only support the union, but also open up a window for rich and rewarding romantic relationships.

Anticipating the criticism that he is talking about something other than the sweet experience that the rest of us call "love", Stirner argues that it is the most appropriate expression that exists.[76] Even so, *Der Einzige* created so much controversy on publication that Stirner published a response to his critics addressing (among other things) the issue whether his construction of loving in *Der Einzige* is really love as we know it. In *Kleinere Schriften*, Stirner asked one of his critics if he has ever had a lover where both found enjoyment and neither felt short-changed. He also asked what this person would do if he met a couple of friends on the street who invited him to go for a drink: does he go out of a duty to the friendship or because he thinks it would be fun? Stirner proposed that in both cases, an egoistic union has been formed for a short time with the goal of enjoyment.[77]

The passionate elements of romantic loving are entirely consistent with Stirner's philosophy. Pursuing a relationship with another who sparks one's interests and nourishes one's passions is highly enriching for a unique one. Indulging in the sensual aspects of romantic loving is also unproblematic for Stirner, as long as one stays in control of one's urges and as long as one does not become dependent on the beloved. Stirner did not advocate unrestrained hedonism whereby one maximizes pleasure and minimizes pain, because there are instances where he will accept pain and suffering. Moreover, he is principled in that, although he endorsed frivolity, he did not accept blindly pursuing one's desires, because that would imply one is controlled by one's passions.

Furthermore, the unique one does not greedily exploit another person for only the sake of more property. To do so runs the risk of avarice because it involves subordinating oneself to one's desire for more possessions. Stirner is not tied to his property, just as he is not tied to anything or anyone, and this stops his philosophy from being construed as materialistic or greedy. One uses property to assert oneself as unique, just as one uses objects to enjoy. The unique one is defined through one's possessions because they have a use. Like Hegel, Stirner sees his freedom concretely manifested in the property he accumulates. Thus, he uses property as a currency or measure or evidence of his power within his particular context.

Stirner's understanding of romantic loving also supports the idea that it is love of a particular person who is appreciated for his or her unique qualities. However, it is not unconditional love of the individual, because that would turn the beloved into something sacred. Rather, love of the individual is based on the enjoyment one derives from loving the other. Consider this in Irving Singer's terms of appraisal and bestowal: on one hand, it is an appraisive attitude since one's love is fueled by the other's charming qualities; on the other hand, it is a bestowal because there need not be any particular reasons for loving a particular person, other than being the particular object that one chooses to love.

Stirner's main critique of romantic love is aimed at the expectation that the relationship ought to last forever and the obligations that romantic love assumes in order to attempt to secure the love eternally. This is clearly a critique of love that grew out of the Romantic period. However, more modern understandings of romantic love suppose that, although romantic lovers hope that the relationship will last forever, there is no obligation as such for it to do so. Certainly, lovers often *want* to promise everlasting love and, although the hope that it will last forever is a central feature of romantic loving, making and keeping such a promise is not. If Stirner's view denies that romantic loving includes the desire or hope for lasting relationships, then it must be deemed unromantic. However, this is not a necessary conclusion of Stirner's view.

For example, although little is known about Stirner's love life, the short-term nature of his own relationships and his ex-wife's comments do bring into question the viability of long-term relationships. If relationships are built on enjoyment, then in tough times, when there is no enjoyment, the risk of the relationship breaking down is significant. Traditional loving relationships are built on the commitment to stick together through thick and thin, in sickness and in health. In theory, working through problems together strengthens the bond and deepens the respect and understanding for one another, in anticipation of a more enjoyable and better life in the long run. This is not so different from Stirner's idea of loving relationships: he will kiss away the worry lines and help the other, in order to restore a more enjoyable future – albeit for himself and not the worrier. If a person exhibits strongly admirable qualities, then small challenges along the way are tackled to achieve the longer-term enjoyment of them. A small sacrifice here is the means to a greater end in the future. Stirner did allow for adjustments and compromises, albeit on his terms.

Stirner's own experience of loving indicates that he chose shorter-term egoistic unions, demonstrated by his short marriage to Marie Dähnhardt, his lack of enduring friends, and his frequent moves to avoid repayment of his debts. However, others adopting the same egoistic principles could end up in long-term relationships in which both continue to interest one another and both appreciate qualities in the other which change over time. Even if youth and beauty were the initial interests, as those qualities evaporate the interest could be replaced with others, such as intellectual stimulation or entertaining companionship.

Egoistic loving relationships encompass the spectrum of possibilities from Don Giovanni's thousands of fleeting affairs to a happy marriage lasting a lifetime. Without externally imposed rules, the onus is on individuals to choose. How long the lovers' interests, enjoyment, and loving feelings are aligned defines how sustainable the relationship is. However, duration will be sacrificed in favor of self-ownership.

Where a loving relationship, as Stirner constructs it, can break down is where one party values honesty and is deceived, expects to be loved independent of the other's benefit, or misunderstands the basis of the relationship and is surprised by the consequences. Indeed, lying and breaking promises is perfectly acceptable to Stirner. On the other hand, it is also perfectly consistent in Stirner's philosophy not to lie if it so pleases the unique one. There is much to be said for two lovers understanding each other's philosophies.

Acknowledging that either lover is free to leave at any time and will not stay out of duty can strengthen the bond, for example, by acknowledging that the relationship is based on such factors as benefits from and enjoyment of each other's company, anticipated benefits and enjoyment, and battling the world together more powerfully than each could alone. However, for Stirner, egoistic loving is the mutual recognition of two unique ones, two powers, who enjoy each other's company as long as they both benefit from it. Reciprocity is not a necessary requirement, since Stirner loves himself and loves the feelings of love that the other inspires, and this need not include loving actions from the beloved. However, Stirner realizes there is much to be enjoyed in reciprocal relationships, and insofar as he wants to engage in a loving relationship, there is latent reciprocity because the relationship will not exist if the beloved is not benefiting from it. Further to this, Stirner's passion will go hungry if the object of his love is not cooperative.

Stirner clearly did not accept the idea that love is a harmonious merging with another being to create a blissful "we". Nevertheless, unions for the purposes of enjoyment or increasing one's property and possessions, and extending oneself in the world, are not only acceptable but also desirable. Stirner opens up the possibility of a romantic relationship as a union based on mutual enjoyment or in which lovers come together and intertwine lives for the purposes of extending themselves and their boundaries in the world. Thus, the lovers achieve more together than they could alone.

If romantic loving is about accepting the beloved's welfare as one's own, while in a loving relationship, then Stirner's philosophy of loving is romantic. However, it must come with the qualification that he does so only insofar as it does not conflict with his own interests, which mean more to him than loving. Thus, he is not sacrificing anything important to him. For Stirner, sacrifices do not prove the depth of one's love. Stirner's philosophy can be understood as a critique of romantic loving that is based on "agapaic" sacrificing of oneself.

Stirner acknowledged that he did not enter a relationship for the sake of the ideal of love, for the sake of another, or for the sake of maintaining a relationship based on a prior commitment that compromises his ownness. Rather, Stirner took into account his life as a project and one that is constantly being created. He was strategic and realized that the time comes when some passions will be traded for others and sacrifices will be made, albeit on his terms. He was interested in effective use of power to expend his life, and to this end, he was interested in the consequences of his actions. Even the ultimate sacrifice – death – is within Stirner's realm of possibilities, and it is in this sense that he draws close to the existential question: under what conditions does one want to live? If the choice were either to sacrifice one's life or to betray one's ownness, such as subordinating oneself to the will of others, then losing one's life is a valid option. However, self-preservation was not Stirner's goal. He was interested in squandering his life.

The unique one exploits the other in the pursuit of interesting and enjoyable experiences. For his own happiness, Stirner would hazard anything and everything, including his life, for his beloved. The unique one is a risk-taker and preserves his life only in order to squander it. Yet, the enjoyable loving experience might well be worth the risk. For example, the most interesting and exciting experience of loving could be with another unique one. Certainly, there is a great risk the beloved will exploit and exert power over the unique one. However, it is consistent for the unique one to choose to get value out of oneself by engaging in a highly risky loving relationship. Moreover, if the unique one does lose property or even life to the beloved, then Stirner would say that he would smile when he is beaten and acknowledge that all things are nothing to him.

Romantic loving is consistent with Stirner's philosophy when it is understood as two individuals doing what they enjoy most and coincidentally finding interest in and being attracted to each other. Stirner loves himself and loves another for himself, and sometimes that aligns with another who takes an interest in him too. In a negative sense, we can paint the unique one as a vampire, prowling around in the world, looking for fresh quarry, in order to feed. With a loving interest, the unique one and the beloved work strategically together, increasing their property more effectively than either individual working alone. They stalk prey, consume others, and enjoy life and each other. Not all lovers will be unique ones, and those who are not will be consumed. This is the predatory possibility in Stirner's work. Nevertheless, this is not the necessary outcome, because although Stirner did not allow for compromise politically, he did in loving relationships, and those exceptions are up to the unique one to negotiate.

All relationships, including loving ones, are power relationships, according to Stirner. The unique one appropriates a lover just as any other treasured possession from which he derives pleasure. Stirner's formulation of a loving relationship is based on appreciation of enjoyable, charming, and unique qualities in another human. Love as a duty or moral obligation is indifferent to those qualities and thus devalues the individual; it is also a recipe for a miserable loving relationship. Stirner rightly raises the issue as to why anyone would want an unenjoyable and uninteresting loving relationship, characterized by sacrifices and obligations without any benefit to the individuals.

Stirner's unique one is set against the world with battles at every turn. His philosophy is certainly not for those who want a quiet and peaceful life. Moreover, Stirner's mantra that "all things are nothing to me" can be difficult to adopt into everyday psychology. For example, Marx and Engels criticize "Saint Max" or "Sancho" (Stirner) for creating an ideal individual that most people are not strong enough to live up to.[78] Stirner's philosophy emphasizes individual power and loving others, but not subservience. One associates with another only as long as one is in control of the association.

For Stirner, one ought to own oneself rather than be owned by a set of rules or norms. One can compromise on anything except what one deems to be right and important for oneself – that is, one's self-chosen principles. Thus, according to Stirner, the only commitment one can make without compromising authenticity (ownness) is to oneself. In leaping to oneself, one does not subordinate oneself to any higher entity or external source of values. Thus, one takes up residence within the abyss of a world without given meaning. The commitments one makes are only to upholding oneself as a free and creative nothingness, directed toward one's chosen ends. However, Stirner's approach is beyond affirming one's freedom because he assumed his freedom to begin with and did not treat it as a value to be adopted or something to strive toward. More important than freedom is what one has the power to do. Thus, for Stirner, freedom would not take the existential philosopher far enough.

Stirner clearly foreshadowed many existential ideas, and in his insistence on the contingency and primacy of becoming and in his rejection of anything other than individual choice as the singular voice of authority, he can properly be described as proto-existentialist. He pinpoints some of the most fundamental principles of living and loving existentially – for example, "existence precedes essence", the understanding of an individual as a creative nothingness, transcendental living as preferred to acting immanently or half-consciously – and although Stirner was more interested in power, his self-owning unique one has much in common with the existential understanding of freedom as the starting point of the authentic individual. He outlines an ultra-authentic stance in his focus on owning oneself and in the weight he places on choosing how to live and love free from the constraints of anything other than what one finds interesting and enjoyable.

The strength of Stirner's philosophy is his emphasis on uncompromising self-ownership and the risk that it can come at the expense of obligations to others, rendering loving relationships anything but stable and secure. Such an attitude need not necessarily cause anxiety if one owns one's passions. It also reflects loving as a choice because it is based on strengthening and nourishing oneself through the other. Committing to oneself while rejecting obligations to others means that existing is defined by power rather than freedom. Relations with others are power-based and, through egoistic unions, are instrumental in their contribution to enriching oneself. Owning oneself enables one to be free to pursue enjoyable and interesting relationships. The extent to which one can own oneself depends on only one's power to relate to people that one loves.

3
Søren Kierkegaard and Loving Aesthetically

For Søren Kierkegaard, passion and pleasure are at the heart of romantic loving, which he categorizes as part of an aesthetic lifestyle. For one of Kierkegaard's aesthetic protagonists, Johannes the Seducer, romantic loving is beautiful because it is intoxicating and extraordinarily interesting and transforms one's life so much that it feels as if it is of mythological proportions.[1] One of Kierkegaard's pseudonyms asks, "What, after all, is a human being without love?"[2] and another says that loving relationships give one "the courage to attempt and risk everything".[3] Elsewhere, Kierkegaard wrote that "to love human beings is still the only thing worth living for; without this love you do not really live".[4] However, Kierkegaard also viewed aesthetic loving relationships as inadequate because they are fleeting and immature, reflecting a lack of self-development and destined to end in despair. To overcome this despair and become a fulfilled individual, Kierkegaard recommended a leap into marriage and faith.

This chapter discusses Kierkegaard's view of aesthetic loving relationships, through two of his aesthetic characters: Don Giovanni and Johannes the Seducer. I want to show that they do not fit neatly into Kierkegaard's aesthetic spheres, and also note that there is little of romantic love left in Kierkegaard's preferred spheres. First, it will be worthwhile noting some of Kierkegaard's influences and key ideas underlying his philosophy, particularly the importance of the subjective perspective and his pseudonymous approach to writing.

Hegel was the most famous modern philosopher of Kierkegaard's time. Johannes Climacus, Kierkegaard's pseudonymous author of *Concluding Unscientific Postscript*, disputed Hegel's system for two main reasons. First, he attacked it as useless and abstract because it does not help address the problems of everyday life.[5] Second, Hegel argued that people could feel a part of something bigger than themselves by being involved in a community, such as joining a church group. But Climacus worried that this produced unreflective masses who blindly accept what the clergy tell them, rather than working it out for themselves. Climacus was disappointed that people simply took it for granted that they were Christians merely because at that time in Denmark it was the expected and proper thing to do.[6] Although these views are expressed by a pseudonym, entries in Kierkegaard's journals suggest that he concurred on a personal level.[7]

Kierkegaard's emphasis on the individual and the personal passionate subjective human experience earned him recognition as the first existential philosopher. His exploration of subjective experience, personal decisions free from external influences, self-determination, and responsibility for one's choices was radical for his time. Jean-Paul Sartre described Kierkegaard as an "anti-philosopher" because he rejected philosophy that had come before him and started afresh.[8] Emmanuel Levinas accused Kierkegaard of tainting all philosophy with "an exhibitionistic, immodest subjectivity".[9] These kinds of statements give an indication of Kierkegaard's radical ideas and how they differed from those post-Cartesian philosophers who revered disinterested objectivity and the scientific method.

Kierkegaard wanted simply "That Single Individual" to be written on his tombstone.[10] The clergy, who found his writings to be outrageous, thwarted his wish. At Kierkegaard's funeral, the Archdeacon tried to undermine Kierkegaard's work by advising the huge crowd not to misunderstand or accept what he had written because even Kierkegaard did not realize that he had "gone too far".[11] But this did not dissuade the many generations of people who have since given his work serious consideration.

Although Kierkegaard and Stirner lived at the same time, it is unlikely that they knew of each other. Like Stirner, Kierkegaard emphasized personally lived experiences and relationality. Unlike Stirner, Kierkegaard was a Christian and suggested that Christianity was a good choice of belief system because it promises eternal happiness. Yet, eternal happiness is not to be found in a church that preaches so-called objective truths about the meaning of life. Rather, it can be found only with a passionate personal interest in one's existence and in creating a personal relationship with God.[12] It also appears to be why Kierkegaard addressed the "single individual". In *The Crowd is Untruth* he criticized groups (the crowd) for being abstract and impersonal, discouraging individual thinking, rendering individuals anonymous and irresponsible, and being a place in which to hide like a coward.[13]

Climacus protests that objective truths are deceptive because they do not account for the existing subject and the situation of that subject. (He neglects to consider logically necessary truths.) Objective truth is inhumane and abstract because in trying to be objective, one must give up one's passionate personal interest. He complains that people in his age and society have indeed lost their passion for living. Without passion, there is a "negativity that pervades existence", and it is as if "in our age we do not exist at all".[14] Furthermore, overemphasizing objective results neglects individual decisiveness. Kierkegaard sought something that he could be passionate about – "to find *the idea for which I am willing to live and die*".[15]

One implication of truth as subjectivity is that it cannot be communicated directly, that is, with objective certainty. Kierkegaard published many works under pseudonyms. He used indirect communication as a means of distancing himself from the words. Although he accepted legal and literary responsibility for his writing, his aim was to remove any preconceived notions that the reader may have about him or his work, that is, to release the reader from dragging "the weight of my personal reality".[16] The effect is that Kierkegaard suggests rather than dictates. Kierkegaard wanted to challenge his readers to dispute his ideas, to take responsibility for interpreting the text's meaning, and to create their subjective truth. In order to do this, he composed deliberately inflammatory statements and used irony to challenge the reader to question the true meaning of the text. As such, the reader can never be certain when Kierkegaard is being ironic, and this forces the reader to make judgments. Accordingly, there is ambiguity as to how much Kierkegaard's pseudonymous works reflect his own views. Kierkegaard said that to attribute all quotes to him is to confuse and exploit his writing, to portray him as mad, and to make one a "charlatan or a literary toper".[17] This is why I attribute quotes to the relevant pseudonym, rather than Kierkegaard, and also draw upon his journals, letters, and non-pseudonymous works to complement the analysis.

Kierkegaard's method of using indirect communication, pseudonyms, fragmentary pieces, and postscripts was a rebellion against systematic philosophy. However, he did suggest a type of system by describing the path of self-fulfillment in terms of three lifestyles: aesthetic, ethical, and religious. These three modes of existence are not necessarily rigid steps that one must take, but rather they are the phases that one can expect to experience on the existential journey of finding meaning in life. *Either/Or* was one of Kierkegaard's first works outlining the individual experience of life and love.

Victor Eremita, the editor of *Either/Or* (another of Kierkegaard's pseudonyms), explains that he fell in love with and bought a second-hand desk. Frustrated with a jammed door, he kicked the desk and a secret drawer popped out. Inside it were letters and essays. Victor hypothesizes that two different people wrote them: an aesthete and an ethicist, whom he refers to as "A" and "B" (or Judge William), respectively. *Either/Or* introduces the reader to the seminal choices one faces: either the aesthetic or the ethical. However, flaws are identified in both lifestyles, and the book ends with a sermon that hints at another (higher) alternative: the religious.

Problems of romantic loving

The aesthetic sphere is the first phase of life and, like a child, is bursting with possibilities. The aesthete drifts through a pleasure-seeking life, guided by sensualism and immediate gratification, free from commitment to anyone or anything, free from social and moral responsibility, and devoted to hedonism. This phase is represented in part one of *Either/Or*, portrayed as fun, exciting, dramatic, poetic, and curiously mesmerizing. It starts by alerting the reader to the dangers of the aesthetic life, which include depression about its inherent emptiness and meaninglessness, and then turns to the floating elation of falling in love and the exhilaration of seduction. Aside from the depressing beginning, his description is so enchanting that at times it seems to advocate pursuing a richer aesthetic life.

The author of the aesthetic writings in *Either/Or*, "A", outlines three levels within the aesthetic sphere: dreaming, seeking, and desiring. Dreaming, the first stage, is a vague craving for something unknown. Desire is aroused, and in the second stage one seeks to satisfy the craving. Papageno in Mozart's *Magic Flute* is a prime example. Papageno accompanies a handsome prince on a quest to rescue a beautiful woman with whom the prince has fallen in love. Papageno has no specific object of desire but is excited about the adventure and possibility of discovery. The third stage is fully fledged desire. Mozart's *Don Giovanni*, arguably one of opera's most unscrupulous seducers, is the ultimate representative of this sphere according to "A". Unlike Papageno, who enjoys the adventure of discovery, Don Giovanni is on a specific mission.[18] Johannes, the protagonist and author of the legendary *Seducer's Diary* (the "*Diary*") in *Either/Or*, also inhabits this third stage. While Don Giovanni is constantly and impulsively in pursuit of satisfying his erotic desires, Johannes is more developed because he reflects and recognizes the meaninglessness and emptiness of his life. To overcome his boredom, he entertains himself by manipulating love interests.

Johannes and Don Giovanni are the focus of the analysis that follows. While there are other characters representing possibilities within the aesthetic lifestyle outlined in Kierkegaard's later work *Stages on Life's Way* (1845), they are not addressed, because they are at a similar stage of existence as Johannes. Also important to note is that "Don Juan" refers to the name of the legend and "Don Giovanni" is the title of and character in Mozart's opera. While the pseudonymous author is referred to as "A" so that Kierkegaard will not turn in his grave to call me a charlatan, there is evidence to suggest that the essay on Mozart's *Don Giovanni* reflects Kierkegaard's own views.[19]

Loving unreflectively: Mozart's Don Giovanni

Mozart's *Don Giovanni* is a legendary libertine and a womanizer who enjoys a fast turnover. As soon as he has seduced one woman, he moves onto the next conquest. He confidently boasts that he has loved over 2,000 women, recorded in his not-so-little black book. "A" chooses Mozart's *Don Giovanni* as the ultimate representative of the aesthetic life because he exists only in music, embodying his living in the moment. Moreover, he loves pleasure, is highly erotic, and focuses entirely on sexual gratification. As a force of nature, "A" proposes that Don Giovanni is prisoner to his natural urges and primitive drives, to which he responds unreflectively. According to "A", Don Giovanni is selfish, egoistic, and child-like because he wants his desires to be satisfied *now*, with little or no regard for others. This puts him outside the realm of the moral and the ethical, unconcerned about the consequences of his actions. Owing to Don Giovanni's amoral status and lack of reflection, "A" suggests that calling him a seducer gives him too much credit, and he deserves to be called a deceiver.[20]

There are dozens of interpretations of the legend of Don Juan, but all are concerned with loving and seducing women and do not fit into the structure and rules of the society in which they live. Despite the interpretation, Don Juan usually ends up dead or bored. The main point of difference in interpretations usually pivots on Don Juan's relation to women: sometimes he is the seducer, sometimes the seduced, sometimes libertine, and sometimes henpecked.[21]

According to "A", Mozart's Don Giovanni finds himself condemned as a moral villain as a result of his relentless quest to fulfill his sexual desires. Choosing hell over repentance and an absurd and meaningless existence, the stage collapses around Don Giovanni. Even when he finally faces the consequences of his actions and descends into hell, he does not despair or apologize, since doing so would betray the character that Mozart and his librettist construct.

The main problem that "A" has with most interpretations of Don Juan is that in plays, novels, and poems, the protagonist speaks, which makes him reflective. The sensual erotic life, according to "A", is best expressed in music because it is continually immediate and energetic. Mozart has found the ultimate expression of Don Giovanni's elusive but vivacious, powerful, and exciting existence. Just like Don Giovanni, Mozart's music effervesces like freshly poured champagne. No other medium portrays this quite so well.[22]

Although Don Giovanni's passion is admirable, "A" suggests it is a life void of true meaning. It is a shallow existence because his passion is frivolously directed at satisfying sexual urges. The vibrating music reinforces the ambiguity of his existence.

Moreover, "A" has a problem with the way in which Don Giovanni loves women. He loves sensually, repetitively, and hence deceitfully. The Greek legend Hercules was famous for loving 50 daughters in one night. Hercules could doubtless produce a list of lovers to rival Don Giovanni's, but, according to "A", Hercules and Don Giovanni are completely different. Hercules is not a seducer, because he truly loves and appreciates each and every individual woman. The fact that it is only for a few minutes per woman is, for "A", irrelevant. The individual woman does not matter for Don Giovanni. Anyone in a skirt will do.[23]

Anxiety is the key element that distinguishes Don Giovanni's sensual love from Hercules' faithful and soulful love. Hercules is anxious about whether his love will be requited and consummated. Don Giovanni lives from moment to moment, so there is no time for thinking about possibilities from which anxiety arises. Kierkegaard disapproved of being busy precisely because it distracts from reflecting, that is, from consciously choosing one's life. In fact, Kierkegaard advocated focusing on a single goal that unites one's existence: *"Purity of heart is to will one thing"*, lest one's life become fragmented and unstable.[24] In a journal, Kierkegaard said he admires those who find something they can dedicate themselves to:

> So it is with joy and inner invigoration that I contemplate great men who have found that precious stone for which they sell everything, even their lives, whether I see them intervening forcefully in life, with firm step, without wavering, going down their chosen paths, or run into them off the beaten track, self-absorbed and working for their lofty goals.[25]

Love is the key to such passion. Kierkegaard likened life without love to the danger of an ancient Greek myth: those who enter the labyrinth without Ariadne's thread will not survive the Minotaur's lair. One interpretation of the ending of Don Giovanni is that being dragged to hell was appropriate "comeuppance" for a philandering failure who does not influence anyone.[26] However, he can also be seen as a great hero who died fighting for his principles. Since a fulfilling life involves "willing one thing", as Kierkegaard suggested, then Don Giovanni can be said to have done so, preferring to die for his self-chosen principles rather than repent. The final scene of the opera decries herd morality because the other characters go back to their mundane lives without "an idea to live and die for" and without Don Giovanni's exuberance. If Don Giovanni did not influence anyone else, it would not have mattered to him since the only influence he valued was that of temporarily dazzling women in order to have his way with them. Moreover, there is no such imperative in Kierkegaard's philosophy to influence others.

Loving reflectively: Johannes, the sophisticated seducer

According to Victor Eremita, *how* the reflective aesthete seduces is more important than *how many* (as in the example of Don Giovanni). Whereas Don Giovanni represents unbridled lust, Johannes is portrayed as more sophisticated since he is introspective and strategic. They are both serial lovers, but while Don Giovanni loves for a night or two, Johannes covets one woman for six months. Sensuous pleasure is enough for Don Giovanni, but not Johannes. Johannes loves intellectually. He sees himself as an artist or scientist of love and is more evolutionary than Don Giovanni because he strives to improve his art.

In the *Diary*, Johannes recounts in meticulous detail the seduction of a young and beautiful woman named Cordelia. Johannes made a hobby of seducing women without saying "I love you" and then leaving them when they were on the verge of sacrificing themselves to him. Johannes' manipulation revolts "A". He says that Johannes' lovers were unlucky victims of a conniving, sick parasite because he treats them as pieces of his own personal chess game, using them to construct interesting scenarios as long as they serve his purpose. He plucks women like fresh flowers, rejuvenates himself with them, and then discards them.[27] Highly aware of his duplicity, Johannes feebly vows to himself to make it up to her.[28] His atonement turns out to be giving her an interesting experience and a broken heart and highlights, like Stirner, that he rejects accountability to others.

Johannes is also portrayed as detached from reality. While he physically runs around in the world, he is intellectually beyond it. He is free because he is not bound by societal norms or ethical considerations for others. He is so elusive and uncommitted in his relationships that others never know where they stand. At the end of the *Diary*, Cordelia is completely confused and left wondering if she was the seducer. She has called off the engagement but is bewildered as to how it happened and why. Johannes says that he surreptitiously convinced her to do so. Perhaps she realizes that she has been deceived. Even so, she still loves him and forgives him, but to no avail.[29]

There are three key features of aesthetic loving that Johannes brings to our attention: love is an art form, love is intoxicating, and love is war.

Love is an art form

Johannes wonders if he actually loves Cordelia and convinces himself that he does indeed. Yet, he poses the caveat that he loves her aesthetically but is unsure what that implies.[30] Immanuel Kant, one of Kierkegaard's philosophical forefathers, proposed that aesthetic judgment is about imagination, pleasure, beauty, and art.[31] Johannes is an artist of love. He has a hyperactive imagination and uses it to fashion the world around him to make people and situations more interesting. Johannes loves loving Cordelia, ignited by his appreciation of her beauty.

The biggest problem for the aesthete, however, is finding someone worth seducing. Like champagne that froths then quickly goes flat, the excitement of first encounters fizzles fast.[32] His first criterion for picking out a girl is that she must enchant him from the very beginning. Otherwise, a relationship is not worth his time.[33] As an early exponent of speed dating, Johannes is convinced that first impressions are everything.

This highlights the ambiguous relation between loving as a choice and as an innate attraction. Johannes acknowledges that, on the one hand, he wants to choose a lover who will challenge and motivate him. This is why he carefully chooses his target, unlike Don Giovanni who is less discriminating. However, he also acknowledges that there must be some attraction to spark his interest in the first place.

For Johannes, seducing is easy and is not an art in itself. The artistry is in enchanting and beguiling a woman. Bringing her into his power and being loved is the most enjoyable thing in the world. Not only does he use Cordelia to create an aesthetic loving experience, but he also uses her to fashion himself into a kind of art form, exalting himself as an ideal lover in a utopian relationship. This is consistent with Climacus's explanation in *Concluding Unscientific Postscript* that existence is an art and not a science because it cannot be understood objectively or without passion. It can be understood from the perspective of the existing individual only. It is up to the individual to create oneself, and this action of constant creativity is an art form. For Climacus, as for Victor Eremita, it is not what but how one says or knows something that is important.[34]

Johannes – at least in his own estimation – manipulates Cordelia like a puppet. Perhaps not accidentally, Cordelia's last name is Wahl, which means "choice" in German. Johannes was so confident of his ability to make Cordelia fall in love with him that he did not recognize her as a choosing subject. She is presented as a victim under Johannes' love spell. For him, she is no more than a sexual object.[35]

However, why should Cordelia not have chosen to love him? He presented himself as confident, charming, mysterious, and sensitive. He was a man who took a particular interest in her, made her feel special, and declared his undying devotion and love for her in beautiful love letters. Perhaps one might be suspicious of such eloquent and exuberant expressions of love. However, to a nineteenth-century 17-year-old girl whose only other option at the time was a lovesick young boy called Edward, it seems obvious that she should choose the exciting, interesting, and unique alternative. Moreover, Cordelia may well have been seeking in Johannes the same as he was seeking in her: the interesting experience, but with the difference that she was unaware of Johannes' time limits.

Johannes loves the beauty of the objects of his desire, the fascinating experience of plunging into the depths of passion, and exercising his skills of seduction. To use a cliché, he prefers the journey rather than the destination, that is, seduction rather than sex.

Love is intoxicating

Two things intoxicate Johannes: Cordelia's beauty and his power. First, Cordelia is very beautiful. Assuming that there is some truth in the letters that he wrote to Cordelia in which he described his feelings, loving her transforms the meaning of everything in his life. He lets the enjoyment of her beauty consume him and exalt his life to a euphoric and mythological level.[36] The analogy of a myth is interesting in two ways: not only because the myth in this instance is an art form, but also because his loving relationship with Cordelia is a myth in itself – that is, an illusion, albeit one that is built upon truth.

Second, the idea of having power over Cordelia intoxicates Johannes, although he claims to be in control of his passion. Johannes seems to align himself with Stirner's construction of loving whereby he loves the experience of Cordelia; he finds himself exhilarated in her presence; and he loves himself in the state of loving. She nourishes his passion. His sense of power comes from maintaining control of the situation by planning the end of the relationship. It is possible that after six months, there is a greater risk of Johannes' becoming attached to her or tired of keeping up the appearance of being interested. Possibly, he worries that he will let his guard down and reveal his flaws, that Cordelia will become bored, or that being too intimate with her means she will find out what he is really like and lose interest in him. These remain speculations: he does not take the risk, so we will never know. If he does limit himself to six-month relationships for any of these reasons, then he is purposely closing possibilities to himself, which would contribute to his boredom.

Nevertheless, Johannes is a master of love, and he writes of applying strategic principles, launching campaigns, sitting in ambush, spying Cordelia out, gathering intelligence from her friends and family, stealing after her, attacking, and assaulting psychologically. Involving her in interesting situations is Johannes' main strategy. Judge William, the representative of the alternative ethical sphere in *Either/Or*, describes an aesthete as being like a spider waiting for prey. The Judge chastises the aesthete for his obsession with observing other people, thereby making a spectacle of himself.[37] Freely, Cordelia flies over to Johannes to observe him. Too late, she is psychologically trapped. Pre-empting the damage he knows he will create, Johannes says, "it is a matter of life and death".[38]

While gaining psychological power over a woman is the ultimate aphrodisiac for Johannes, in a broader sense there is the possibility that he becomes beholden to his own desire to pursue interesting loving experiences. If he is addicted to his aesthetic endeavors, then this is true. Like Stirner, one of Kierkegaard's lessons is not to be prisoner to one's immediate desires. Yet if he remains in control of his passions and actively chooses them, it cannot be said he is beholden to them.

Johannes thinks he knows everything about love.[39] However, there is a contradiction here. If he is an artist creating new loving experiences, how can he claim to know everything before it has happened and if it has not yet been defined? He seems to believe that women are totally predictable and malleable. However, seeing something new, different, and interesting in each woman he chooses to take on as a challenge suggests that he does not know everything. We do not really know whether he has ever been rejected or encountered an unpredictable woman. That would be his ultimate challenge.

Love is war

Johannes fights two wars of love. The first war is to liberate his lover, by which he means to educate her to realize her psychosocial freedom. He wants her to choose him, not because she thinks she should but because she wants to. Although Johannes thinks he has total control over her, he also says that unless she gives herself freely, it is not fun.[40] Like playing a game of chess, his enjoyment lies not in a quick and easy win but rather in engaging with a worthy and challenging opponent. The more resistance, the more interesting is his experience because the greater is the demonstration of his power over her.

Johannes' dream-girl is independent and self-sufficient. Revealing the extremities of his chauvinism, he says that women are free in only a superficial sense. Like a flower, he thinks that they are essentially unreflective. This is, however, part of their attraction since he considers too much thinking to be unfeminine.[41] This is why Johannes prefers a woman without friends. Since women like to talk about their relationships, cynical friends have the potential to undermine his spell and ruin his plans. For Johannes, critical thinking destroys a girl's innocence, beauty, and quality of being interesting.

At best, in Johannes' view, woman is "being-for-another".[42] While there appears to be a contradiction between woman defined as being-for-another and his battle to liberate Cordelia, this is not necessarily so. That he thinks he can liberate her means that women are capable of being free, but she is neither aware of it nor encouraged to be in nineteenth-century Europe. However, the problem for Johannes is that once he has liberated her, he does not want her. He is no longer attracted to her, because he finds freedom to be unfeminine.[43]

Whether Cordelia even stood a chance of resisting this master of seduction is another question. For example, Johannes fancies himself as a doctor of love: he observes her symptoms and diagnoses with pleasure. He amazes himself at how good he is in predicting her behavior. He also takes this a symptom of Cordelia's health since she behaves as he expects.[44] This implies that if there were a woman immune to Johannes' charm, he would cast her as sick rather than admit his failings. Johannes certainly did not doubt his ability to gain power over Cordelia, not only because of his confidence and his expertise in knowing what women want from love but also because he does actually love her. It is, therefore, not a complete lie.

The second war for Johannes, after liberating a woman, is to conquer her. However, her surrender signals the pinnacle and demise of the relationship. Johannes grumbles in disappointment about the short-lived nature of the experience. While Johannes wishes that romantic love would last forever, he constructs a self-fulfilling prophecy, and her submission forfeits the game. The game is interesting and beautiful only while there is resistance. The seduction is finished when she "gives herself" totally. While there is ambiguity about the meaning of "giving herself", Johannes seems more interested in courting than in consummation.

Once a freshly plucked flower, Cordelia grows weak and loses her fragrance. Then, love dies. The suggestion is that Johannes decides that he and Cordelia cannot grow together. She bores him, the experience becomes stale, and he wants a fresh flower. He convinces Cordelia to break off the relationship and feels no anxiety or remorse about it. He has never experienced "lovesick fear and trembling" and wonders if that indicates that he has never really loved anyone.[45] The answer remains ambiguous.

Notwithstanding Johannes' deceptive and manipulative behavior, Cordelia continues to proclaim her love for him, declaring herself his slave in the very same letter that she attacks him for being deceitful and making her miserable.[46] Heart-broken and despairing, she appears to have denied responsibility for her own choosing of Johannes and, disappointingly, confirms to Johannes his belief that her surrender was inevitable. Declaring herself his slave not only is emotional blackmail but also signals that she has lost her self-respect and is avoiding responsibility for her own life. She realizes her freedom, and then throws it away. While Johannes understood the kind of charming and mysterious man she was interested in, she did not understand the type of woman he wanted: strong, independent, interesting, refreshing, perpetually combative, and – paradoxically – ultimately unattainable.

Kierkegaard's critique of loving aesthetically

Either/Or begins with a collection of "A"s' poetic musings in the chapter entitled "Diapsalmata". The musings highlight the aesthete's pleasure and pain when he recognizes the vacuity of his life. It acts like a siren: beware of the enchantment of the aesthetic sphere; danger lies ahead. This danger is the risk of the aesthetic life dissolving into melancholy, loneliness, and boredom, fueled by despair and meaninglessness. Indeed, Johannes does start to show signs of boredom when he laments the brevity of romantic loving. The suggestion is that anxiety lurks around the corner for both Don Giovanni and Johannes.

For Don Giovanni and Johannes, pleasure exists in the power they have over others, demonstrated by getting their own way. Yet, this attitude – particularly the treatment of women as sex objects – is painted as immunizing the aesthete from meaningful connections to others and rendering him alone and sad. "A" describes his sorrow as a refuge from engaging in life and likens it to death.[47] Melancholy is such an intimate feature of the aesthete's life that "A" takes great solace in it and talks about it as if it were his best friend.[48]

The message is that sooner or later an aesthete will become bored with such a superficial and empty existence and lose the motivation to live. He feels like a spider plummeting into a void, scrambling for something to hang on to, and finding nothing.[49] It is excruciating for him. Similarly, Don Giovanni naïvely dances over the abyss, blissfully ignorant of the meaninglessness of his existence and the inherent danger.[50]

Johannes also dances over the abyss. Like Stirner, Johannes commits to his chosen way of life at the expense of commitments to others. Although Cordelia breaks off the engagement, strictly speaking, it is clear that Johannes had no intention of marrying her. There is little evidence within the *Diary* as to what Johannes does next, but he hints that he goes searching for his next muse. Another chapter in part one of *Either/Or* suggests that in order to avoid boredom, one "rotates crops". Like sowing seeds in preparation for the next season, the suggestion is that it is prudent constantly to develop a pipeline of prospective lovers.[51] Marriage is, therefore, to be avoided because it binds one to a single pasture for life.

The source of anxiety in the aesthetic sphere, as suggested in *Either/Or*, is frustration and disillusionment with the finite world and a longing to belong to something more than this life. The despair about the meaninglessness of such a lifestyle is the fuel for transitioning to the higher spheres: ethical then religious.

Kierkegaard's solutions

Loving ethically

The ethical lifestyle is one in which the individual recognizes the meaninglessness of the aesthetic life and takes a definitive leap into making active reflective choices, accepting social norms and morals and recognizing the corresponding duties and obligations to society. While the aesthete's life is filled with possibilities, experimentation, and living in the present, the ethicist sees his future filled with concrete goals.[52] Kierkegaard suggests that this means turning away from Don Juan's trysts and Johannes' seductions, instead choosing despair and marriage.

Choosing despair is important because it is synonymous with courageously creating a concrete existence for oneself.[53] According to Judge William, despair is the necessary atonement for exploiting others in the aesthetic sphere. Responding ethically allows for deep and meaningful connections to others. It does this by addressing two major issues in aesthetic relationships: fleeting sensuality and dependency.

First, both the criteria and the problem with romantic loving, as discussed in *Either/Or*, is that it is sensuous. Since it is based on instant satisfaction, it is likely to evaporate at any moment. In the ethical mode of life, one controls one's aesthetic impulsive behavior. Reflection on one's moods allows one to master one's desires and, like Stirner, gives one the ability to say: "Now I own myself".[54] While "A" charges Don Giovanni with impulsiveness, the same cannot be said of Johannes, who is very strategic.

Kierkegaard wants to find a means of making love more secure, and marriage is a neat solution because it is a difficult, meaningful, life-changing, and irrevocable decision that provides reliability without eliminating the possibility for sensuality and romantic loving (allegedly). While romantic loving thrives only in the moment, married loving continually revives itself between the same two people, thereby overcoming the fleetingness of romance.

Second, ethical living addresses the issue of dependent loving. In a letter to his fiancée Regine Olsen, Kierkegaard wrote that lovers want to unite and strive to possess each other, but it is impossible.[55] The suggestion in *Either/Or* is that marriage overcomes possessive games because it assumes that lovers have already conquered one another.[56] In *Works of Love*, Kierkegaard further elaborates that truly free and independent love does not change if the object of affection changes. The attitude "If you don't love me anymore, then I won't love you" demonstrates dependent love. Free and independent love would love the other regardless of whether one's love is reciprocated. This might seem irrational at first, but Kierkegaard argued that it is a way to avoid disappointment in loving relationships because lovers can do or say anything and the lover will not cease to love them. Thus, Kierkegaard advocates unconditional love. For Kierkegaard, married loving is bound by a duty, which ironically frees an individual in the same way that law gives freedom. However, it also implies that the object of affection is irrelevant; one's choice resolutely to commit to love and marriage is paramount because it is within one's control. Love that depends on reciprocation is not within one's control.

Nevertheless, the ethically endorsed married life also has its obvious drawbacks. Even the Judge admits that the risk of married life is habit: "Its uniformity, its total uneventfulness, its incessant vacuity, which is death and worse than death".[57] Kierkegaard developed this theme in *Works of Love* when he proposed that love naturally stagnates over time and decays into miserable exhaustion. Moreover, married couples can be just as anxious as aesthetic lovers, according to Kierkegaard, because neither guarantees lasting love or security. This is why lovers are compelled to test each other's love. Even if people love each other their whole lives, their love is underpinned by anxiety and is unstable.[58] Although lovers feel as though they unite, the mere awareness of death – the awareness that love comes with a stopwatch – separates them.

In his own copy of *Either/Or*, Kierkegaard wrote that he had thought about including a narrative to contrast with the Seducer, entitled "Unhappy Love". In this alternate version, the man behaves exactly as the Seducer did, but for different reasons. The Seducer had no scruples, but the unhappy lover was melancholy whenever he thought about time.[59] Such an example would have emphasized the tension between the joy of romantic loving and the anxiety about its duration.

Judge William not only concedes that the ethical life of duty-bound actions can be very boring but also justifies the aesthetic life, highlighting that both modes of living are flawed. At the end of *Either/Or*, there is a sermon on the religious life, which suggests that neither the aesthetic nor the ethical life is satisfactory. The religious sphere is indeed Kierkegaard's solution to the problems of erotic love. Security and escape from despair will not truly exist, and anxiety will continue, until the loving relationship has been eternally secured through God.

Religious love

In his journals, Kierkegaard noted that the romantic novel that culminates in marriage falls very short of the necessary passion to lead a vigorous life. After a royal struggle to overcome all obstacles, the lovers end up living tediously every after. Instead, Kierkegaard envisioned that a great relationship would awaken "a new growth in love, an intimate, mutual mirroring in each other".[60] He was talking about forming a new relationship with God, but it is also relevant for romantic lovers.

Kierkegaard thought that the goal of life is to create oneself as an authentic individual and to be as good a human as possible before God. Kierkegaard's religious perspective gives God the role of "other". The reason for this, according to Kierkegaard, is that God is the only one who can really know an individual to the core and therefore is the only one who can be a judge of an individual's true character. Although there are no empirical facts to support his belief in God, Climacus says in *Concluding Unscientific Postscript*, "If I wish to preserve myself in faith I must constantly be intent upon holding fast the objective uncertainty, so as to remain out upon the deep, over seventy thousand fathoms of water, still preserving my faith".[61] Abraham's intent to murder his son Isaac at the command of God, in Kierkegaard's *Fear and Trembling*, illustrates such passionate loving faith, beyond the ethical realm.

There are three key advantages of religious loving, in Kierkegaard's estimation: it is unegoistic, it is secure, and it is a panacea for the anxiety of love. One, Kierkegaard accused erotic love of selfishness because even lovers who are selfless toward each other tend to be selfish with respect to others outside the couple. Through loving everyone equally, religious love overcomes the exclusivity of erotic love and jealousy will not be an issue because there are neither comparisons nor preferences. As if in response to Stirner, Kierkegaard proposed that although Christianity advocates loving one's neighbor as one loves oneself, loving oneself without loving God is simply "egotism".[62] Sharing one's life with others brings happiness, self-esteem, and purpose, and yet without God, it is reduced to self-love.[63] True love, on the other hand, is unegoistic, and it requires loving others even if they make you unhappy.

Two, in *Works of Love*, Kierkegaard asserts that the religious sphere, in which one loves thy neighbor, is the highest sphere of existence. Kierkegaard generalizes loving to a universal love for all humanity, as opposed to specific human erotic loving.[64] However, by definition, love for that special someone is encapsulated in one's love for all. This is the secret to peaceful, happy, and eternally secured love, according to Kierkegaard, because as a divine commandment, thy love must not change. Even if the attraction withers, the previously coveted object loses all its loving qualities, its love is unrequited, or it bestows its interest upon someone else, one's love must not wane. Thus, it is steadfast in its security and overcomes the temporal nature of erotic loving. This unwavering commitment to loving everyone, according to Kierkegaard, demonstrates a supremely developed human being.

Three, a further benefit of eternal security that Kierkegaard outlined in *Works of Love* is that it protects against the pain of breaking up. If one loves abstractly rather than individually, then it does not matter if one's love is requited. Instead of relating to the beloved, one relates to love, and thus the beloved cannot break the relationship, because it does not depend on the beloved. The one who "falls away from love" is not only guilty but also worse off by missing out on love. The religious lover becomes richer with every new person loved even without reciprocity. Thus, religious love addresses the anxiety inherent in aesthetic and ethical loving.[65]

Leaping

Now that Kierkegaard's three phases have been canvassed, the traverse between the spheres shall be revisited. At the precipice of each of Kierkegaard's "stages on life's way" (i.e., aesthetic, ethical, and religious) lie either/or choices. These are momentous and life-changing possibilities that cause anxiety (also known as dread, angst, or anguish). For Kierkegaard, the anxiety inherent in the lifestyles of the lower spheres is the impetus for leaps to higher realms because passionately committing oneself to a freely chosen path gives stronger meaning and purpose to individual existence. For Kierkegaard, this is ultimately how one is judged before God.

In *The Concept of Anxiety* Kierkegaard's pseudonym Vigilius Haufniensis says anxiety stems from awareness of one's possibilities and potential. For example, Adam became anxious when he realized the possibility of disobeying God by eating the apple from the tree of knowledge. Anxiety occupies the chasm between possibility and actuality, that is, between Adam realizing that he could eat the apple and actually eating it. The leap is then the decision to turn the possibility into actuality. Life is a series of leaps between states, and in every state possibilities lie in front of it and give rise to anxiety. We fashion ourselves through leaping because, Kierkegaard suggested, we create ourselves through our commitments.

There are some peculiar things about anxiety noted in *The Concept of Anxiety*. First, it is unavoidable because awareness of one's possibilities draws one in like a moth to a flame. Second, anxiety is quite different from fear. One is a passive victim of fear. On the other hand, anxiety is active because it is inherent in assertively choosing oneself. To use an example that Sartre developed in *Being and Nothingness* from Kierkegaard's analogy: one *fears* being pushed off a cliff by another person, but one is *anxious* about the possibility of throwing oneself, actively and freely, over the edge. If it were anxiety *of* something, all that would be required is a transition. The suggestion here is that if the decision is, for example, stepping back from the cliff to safe ground to avoid being pushed off by someone, it is not a leap, because it is a reaction to an external influence. The leap, on the other hand, is the decision not to throw oneself off the mountain path, because one wants to live. In this sense it is self-assertion.

Anxiety has a similar effect to vertigo: it is the "dizziness of freedom", and "He whose eye happens to look down into the yawning abyss becomes dizzy".[66] Yet it is not the abyss (the possibility) that creates the anxiety but rather the individual who looks upon it: some do not look down, subjective perceptions about the size of the chasm differ, and the passion with which individuals approach the abyss and leap differs enormously.

Anxiety has both a dark and a bright side. On the bright side, anxiety can be an adventure. Haufniensis correlates anxiety with greatness because more intense anxiety indicates that one is more highly attuned to one's options.[67] The dark side of anxiety is that "one feels in one's bones that a storm is approaching... the individual trembles like a horse that gasps as it comes to a halt at the place where once it had been frightened".[68] It risks turning into "bestial perdition", "horror", and "wretchedness",[69] and it can be the scariest thing in the world:

> And no Grand Inquisitor has such dreadful torments in readiness as anxiety has, and no secret agent knows as cunningly as anxiety how to attack his suspect in his weakest moment or to make alluring the trap in which he will be caught, and no discerning judge understands how to interrogate and examine the accused as does anxiety, which never lets the accused escape, neither through amusement, nor by noise, nor during work, neither by day nor by night.[70]

Leaping requires bravery and effort, and nothing can make it easier. Another person cannot help. One cannot stumble into it by accident, make a transition to it, or just let it happen. Moreover, if one perceives it as impossible, then nothing will help. The only way to conquer anxiety entirely, Kierkegaard suggests, is with faith where one finds "rest in providence".[71] It is a matter of confronting the abyss and making a brave decision beyond rationality in the face of absurdity.

It would appear that Kierkegaard knew all too well the problems with leaping. He wrote in a journal that "It takes courage to get married", and yet he never had the courage to marry.[72] There are stark similarities between Kierkegaard's own situation and the story of Johannes the Seducer. At the age of 21, Kierkegaard met and fell in love with the 14-year-old Regine Olsen. However, Regine already had a boyfriend, Fritz Schlegel. At the time, the legal courting age for women in Denmark was 17, so Kierkegaard waited. During that time, he studied her and made himself well known to Regine's family and friends, including Fritz. As soon as Regine was legal, Kierkegaard wooed her, and they became engaged.

Kierkegaard imagined that with Regine he would have been happier than he could have ever dreamed. However, the day after they were engaged, he changed his mind. He was melancholic, felt guilty, and wrote in his journals that he thought God was punishing him. He understood it to be "a divine protest".[73] He did not tell Regine right away, and although she noticed he was unhappy, he encouraged her to continue to surrender to him. He did not want to have to explain to her why he was melancholy and thought his anxiety would have ruined the relationship anyway. Thus, he convinced himself that it was in her best interest not to marry him, and he broke off the engagement via a letter accompanied by the engagement ring.

Regine's father told Kierkegaard that she was in despair, utterly desperate, and her father pleaded with him not to break up with her, but to no avail. The two months that followed the breakup were agonizing for both of them. He loved her but he thought he had to be cruel to be kind. He thought it would be easier for Regine to accept the end of the relationship if she thought he was malevolent, so he tried to make her hate him. When she asked if he would ever marry, he replied, "Yes, in ten years, when I have had my fling; I will have to have a lusty young girl to rejuvenate me".[74]

After his cruel discussion with Regine, he cried all night, but the following day he behaved as if he were happier than ever, even though he thought of and prayed for her every day thereafter. Although he could not be faithful to Regine through marriage, he suggested he was faithful to her by never loving another woman as he loved her. Regine subsequently married Fritz. Kierkegaard was eternally grateful for his relationship with Regine since through her he discovered both how happy he could be and how melancholy he was.

In a journal Kierkegaard wrote that *The Seducer's Diary*, written shortly after his engagement to Regine, was for her benefit. He wanted to repulse her and to make it public that he was to blame for ending the relationship.[75] The difference between his situation and Johannes' was very little from an outsider's perspective, but their personal reasons were poles apart: Johannes was a scoundrel, but Kierkegaard was depressed.[76]

Kierkegaard was so desperate to hide the truth that he threatened to kill his brother if he breathed a word of it to Regine's family and begged a friend not to defend him.[77] He felt called to the service of God, and that precluded his having any relationship with Regine. It would seem that Kierkegaard's search for truth and meaning in life was to him inconsistent with the state of marriage, and yet he advocated marriage as a stage on the existential path to a fulfilling life. Thus, the way he lived his life would seem to contradict his philosophy.

Later, Kierkegaard acknowledged that he could have made the same journey if he had married Regine by reconciling his love for her and God in his religious sphere.[78] In *Either/Or* Judge William argues that faithful love is demonstrated in and by marriage. Nevertheless, in a draft letter of 1849 that never reached Regine, seeking reconciliation, Kierkegaard wrote that even if she were still available, he could not marry her. His journals reveal that for the rest of his life, he still loved her obsessively. He wrote extensively about passing her on the street or seeing her in church and drafted multiple letters that never reached her. He was conscious of the suffering and humiliation he caused her but thought that he suffered more than she did.[79] He longed to explain his actions to her, but he dared not to since he thought that she would regret marrying Fritz and wanted to save her from more distress that he thought such knowledge would cause.[80] However, it would seem that he wanted to save himself the risk of complications to his own life if Regine decided she wanted a relationship with him despite his melancholia.

Kierkegaard considered himself to be the exception to his rule about marriage since God had granted him special status.[81] Thus, through what could be construed as an inflated sense of self-importance, Kierkegaard justified not being married, even though he advised others to do so. He thought himself to be like Diana, the goddess of birth, who would never give birth herself.[82] Even though he thought that God would approve of his teaching, he acknowledged that his life was his choice and sacrificed himself for others not because he thought he was better but because he felt more wretched, sinful, and melancholic.[83]

Key considerations

Problem with the aesthetic sphere

One question at the heart of Kierkegaard's philosophical spheres is the relationship between existential development and intellectual development. For example, Kierkegaard suggested that Don Giovanni is neither intellectually nor existentially developed and that Johannes is portrayed as intellectual but not existentially developed.[84] Nevertheless, this representation confuses the issue, which I see as Kierkegaard's relegating Don Giovanni and Johannes to an "aesthetic" sphere, characterized by immaturity and immediacy and placed at the most primitive stage of life. I argue that (a) Kierkegaard was wrong to categorize immature childlike behavior in the same mode of existence as appreciation of beauty, creativity, and passion, and I argue that (b) the aesthetic sphere to which Johannes belongs is characterized by the latter description and not the most primitive mode of life.

Let us consider the situation where an aesthete becomes aware of the choice between the aesthetic and the ethical and yet still chooses the aesthetic. Kierkegaard criticized the aesthetic sphere primarily because of the lack of commitment to meaningful moral decisions. Judge William discounts the aesthete's choice as superficial because it is either impulsive or changeable. For example, a young girl following her heart is not really choosing, because her actions are impulsive and her decisions are whimsical.[85] A real choice, for the Judge, is that of either/or: one stands at the crossroads in life and makes a meaningful, absolute, and essentially irreversible decision. The quality of one's choice divides the aesthetic and ethical spheres. Don Giovanni and Johannes, in the Judge's estimation, do not make any proper moral decisions. Judge William also criticizes the aesthete for lacking seriousness and drifting through life. Thus, an aesthete, as Kierkegaard suggested, is still immature and has a very long way to go on the existential road to becoming a fulfilled human being alone before God.

Don Giovanni and Johannes do not deserve these criticisms. Johannes is intellectually very highly developed. Both have deliberately chosen their lifestyle, are unwaveringly dedicated to it, and are successful.[86] They are not, as Judge William asserts, indifferent to their life choices. On the contrary, Don Giovanni strives for as many loving experiences as he can manage; Johannes strives for ultimate enjoyment through creating and perfecting loving experiences, making them as interesting as can be, and has high standards for the women he chooses. Both characters' commitments to their chosen lifestyles are demonstrated by their extraordinary seductive skills and strategies: to evade being captured by authorities and jilted lovers in Don Giovanni's case; and to beguile women into surrendering themselves to him in Johannes' case. Both actively choose their lifestyles and commit to their self-chosen principle of sensuality, and they are willing to die for it.

"A"s' conclusion – that Don Giovanni is oblivious to the consequences of his actions – is not the only conclusion to be drawn. Don Giovanni has to deal with others and their ethics in order to achieve his ends. He is not completely detached from the world but engages with society on his own terms. Don Giovanni and Johannes are extraordinary human beings who excel at their chosen pursuits, create their own life, and are not determined or restricted by society and law. They are not beholden to the ethical realm. Kierkegaard implies that these two men are *under*socialized because Don Giovanni is child-like and immature, acting impulsively and unreflectively to satisfy his biological urges, and Johannes does not make any meaningful decisions. However, there is support for the argument that this is not the case. For example, Don Giovanni can be portrayed as a romantic hero, living and loving as he chooses. It was not simply good fortune or luck that he evaded capture for so long. In the end, a dead man reincarnated as a statue sent him to hell. Both Don Giovanni and Johannes chose not to conform to socially accepted norms or the law (which, according to Kierkegaard, characterizes ethical individuals).

They commit to celebrating and enjoying life and love, are powerful beings, and are not as immature as suggested in *Either/Or*. Self-development and Kierkegaard's spheres are not simultaneous, meaning that an advanced person could take up residence in the aesthetic sphere and still become a fulfilled individual, albeit not before God. This then brings into question the definition of Kierkegaard's aesthetic sphere. If we consider the aesthetic sphere to be characterized by appreciation of beauty and artistic creativity (which Kierkegaard includes in his definition of the aesthetic), then it is not justified to paint it as if it were undeveloped.

While doubt can be cast upon whether Don Giovanni is undersocialized and child-like, there is little question that he is sensual. The main point of difference between Don Giovanni and Johannes, as pointed out in *Either/Or*, is reflection. Don Giovanni actively chooses his lifestyle and is very successful, but this does not mean he reflects upon it. He has no interest in becoming a better seducer. For example, he does not reflect on how he could have better avoided Donna Anna, a woman scorned, who spoils his seduction of Zerlina. Don Giovanni is pure libido, and there is nothing cerebral about his lifestyle. Don Giovanni is also not romantic in the traditional sense of the word, because the relationships he created were purely sensual. He did not show any hope that the relationship would endure. Moreover, since he loved so many women, it is dubious that he was interested in the individual woman, suggesting that his love was impersonal. He shows no concern for his beloved's welfare. Sexual desire alone is insufficient to classify Don Giovanni as a romantic lover, and since he shows no interest in anything more than sex, not even appreciation of beauty (the only criterion in the original aria, according to the character Leporello, is that she wears a skirt), relegating him to an aesthetic sphere is problematic and a more appropriate name for it would be "sensual" sphere. He leads a hedonistic lifestyle, one in pursuit of sexual satisfaction and guided by sensuality.[87]

Johannes, on the other hand, is interested in more than sex. He sublimates sexual desire into a romantic relationship. He is passionate about particular women and reflects. However, his enforced six-month time limit on relationships renders his activities unromantic since it eliminates the hope that the relationship will endure. Nevertheless, Johannes also laments about the brevity of romantic loving, which raises the possibility that he would have liked his relationships to last longer, and instead of taking the risk, he creates a self-fulfilling prophecy. He does show some concern about his beloved's welfare, even if it is somewhat superficial, when he writes about wanting to compensate Cordelia.[88] Nevertheless, he is in a very different realm from Don Giovanni's realm. He is authentic, self-determining, and committed to his chosen lifestyle, and he refuses to be subordinated to external influences or his base desires and chooses his own values, morals, and actions. If the existential leap is equated actively to deciding and committing to a lifestyle, which is consistent with Kierkegaard's description, then a leap into an aesthetic sphere, beyond a purely sensual realm, is valid and need not result in anxiety, as Kierkegaard would argue.

Problem with the ethical and religious spheres

As a result of reflecting and thinking, one enters into the realm of the rational. The reflective sphere is pragmatic. In such an ethical/rational sphere, one marries for money or fame or in order to have children. It is a terribly sensible sphere but potentially very dull and boring, as the Judge in *Either/Or* knows all too well. His relationship with his wife is characterized by respect, and excitement in his life is limited to armchair philosophizing.

The problem with loving in the ethical sphere is that it ceases to be romantic because sexual passion is irrelevant, and it becomes impersonal since it is no longer an appreciation of the beloved and their unique qualities. While marriages can be romantic, it is not a necessary feature. Rather, the focus is on upholding one's obligations and tasks, as established by society. The duty to love does not necessarily involve the choice to be passionate about one's beloved. Even though the aim of marital love is to establish a permanent union, Kierkegaard suggested that it is still based on erotic love, which depends on the beloved to reciprocate. He sought to find a way to love another that does not depend on the beloved – hence his leap to religious faith.

Kierkegaard's religious mode of existence is based on the idea that we use reason as far as it will take us, but at a point, reason becomes insufficient for existing, and a leap into something suprarational is then required. While faith in God can require such a leap, it is not necessarily so, since many religions base their doctrines on rational grounds (even if questionably rational). Thus, religion can be pragmatic.

A leap to faith was Kierkegaard's unique prescription for anxiety. Yet, if one is not anxious about the abyss, then there is no imperative to change and no need to find something to leap to. Kierkegaard had already decided that one is going to have existential problems if one does not have faith in religion, and therein lies the difficulty with his argument. Haufniensis and Climacus suggested that anxiety grows in the space between possibility and actuality. Yet, as Stirner showed, awareness of one's possibilities need not necessarily result in anxiety. I may not know what lies ahead and may be nervous or have reservations about what to choose, but that does not mean I am anxious. Rather, I may be bursting with excitement about what to choose and what to do. Haufniensis recognizes this more positive aspect of anxiety, but he suggests, unconvincingly, that it is possible only with the support of one's faith in God. Kierkegaard suggested it is only a matter of time before Don Giovanni and Johannes do experience anxiety, and yet Don Giovanni shows no such signs before descending into hell. Certainly, Johannes seems bored after Cordelia, but boredom does not equate to anxiety, and he admits he has never experienced the "lovesick fear and trembling" that is associated with anxiety. And who is to say that he ever will? The imperative to leap – anxiety – does not exist for either of them.

Even if one does face anxiety, what is the imperative to leap to spheres of ethics and religion, that is, to marry and to love everyone equally? Kierkegaard suggested Don Giovanni and Johannes are immature because they make a welter out of the aesthetic sphere and do not make the required leap to higher modes of existence. However, these are not the only options. Another option is a leap into an existential sphere of self-chosen principles based on neither religious faith nor ethical considerations.[89]

For example, it could be argued that Don Giovanni and Johannes leap beyond rationality into suprarational principles. They know how the world works and what women want. They are not oversexed teenagers, because they are enlightened by knowledge and experience. They are confident, capable, and aware. They throw themselves into what they find beautiful and enjoyable, something they "lived and died for" – that is, loving relationships. They would not die for their beloved, but they would rather die than give up their passions.

Kierkegaard would have argued that the highest form of passion is meaningful in only the religious sphere. For example, in *Concluding Unscientific Postscript*, Johannes Climacus proposes that pursuit of eternal happiness through religion is the "highest good".[90] He did not consider the possibility that one would be able to achieve eternal happiness without the intensity and transformative powers of the desire for what he referred to as the absolute or infinite. Furthermore, he did not deem any goal other than eternal happiness to be meaningful or the possibility that one might strive to become complete without eternal happiness. Such an attitude demonstrates Kierkegaard's determination to create a spiritual solution to existential anxiety. The other existential philosophers in this book propose secular alternatives.

The implication of adopting Kierkegaard's religious sphere is that lovers are objects of love and used as stepping-stones on the path to the religious person's fulfillment, and, in this sense, his higher spheres are no more honorable than his lower modes of existence. Moreover, Kierkegaard is endorsing the view that one should never stop loving so as never to be hurt in any relationship, even despite abhorrent acts. The nastiness of a relationship breakdown can be prevented through defiance. The one who is dismissed simply refuses to "fall away" from love. Kierkegaard did not endorse denial as such (although I think this is the effect), but rather because one has a duty to love everyone, it does not matter if the love is reciprocated. Kierkegaard is essentially recommending: "don't think; just love". In fact, the more terrible others are, the more a lover can prove goodness to God by resolutely adhering to God's commandments.[91] Yet, an insecure love relationship is not such a terrible thing. To know that the relationship could change means that lovers must work harder at making it extraordinary and must not take each other for granted.

While Kierkegaard criticized Hegel for being abstract, Kierkegaard is himself guilty of abstraction in his support of the duty to love thy neighbor.[92] The neighbor is an abstraction and represents anyone and everyone that the individual may happen to encounter. Kierkegaard referred to them as "Those We See".[93] The object of affection would appear to be irrelevant in Kierkegaard's doctrine of love because one loves a generalized other.[94] And this element is at odds with romantic love. Kierkegaard came to argue that romantic love could still exist at the religious level because one loves everyone. However, romantic love is personal, and religious love, which loves everyone equally, devalues the personal element of the romantic. In Kierkegaard's religious sphere, he recommends that one become blind to individual differences in order to ensure that one loves all humans equally. For a philosopher who defends subjective truth so magnificently, loving everyone despite individual differences would appear to contradict his defense of the individual, and there is nothing meaningful left of romantic loving. It is precisely because religious love is not preferential that it cannot be romantic.

In sum, Kierkegaard was wary of the frivolity of sensual loving. He described the appeal of wanting to give up one's freedom and devote oneself to the beloved and the struggle to control one's passions in light of the overwhelming nature of romantic loving. He suggested that freedom is incompatible with romantic loving because it is dependent on one's desire and the other's qualities and is void of choice. Actively choosing and committing oneself ethically to others overcomes the spontaneous nature of sensual loving and allows for meaningful connections. However, it takes a leap to faith to achieve purpose, constancy, and stability in order to overcome the anxiety of preferential loving and free oneself from dependency on the object of affection for reciprocation. Nevertheless, doing as Kierkegaard suggests means that lovers are freeing themselves from what makes love romantic.

4
Friedrich Nietzsche and Loving Powerfully

Nietzsche admired the ancient Greek model of relationships, where friends were great, men were warriors, and women were for their recreation. He saw the fact of loving relationships as another example of the collapse of standards in a hedonistic world that is heading for nihilism. We have forgotten what it means to be courageous and strong. A great life should be challenging, not comfortable and secure. Nietzsche advocated a philosophy of "aristocratic radicalism",[1] where a few brave human beings take up the challenge of striving toward the ideal of the *Übermensch*. Sometimes tenuously translated as *superman* but meaning *overperson*, the ideal of the *Übermensch* is not a goal that can be achieved but is instead characterized by striving passionately and creatively to overcome oneself, living life to the fullest, constantly combating and overcoming obstacles to become greater, or in existential terms, transcending.

Loving relationships appalled Nietzsche because he thought that they were all too often based on sacrifice, weakness, and disappointments. He identified at least four key developments as the source of relationship problems, including warped ideas about femininity, unwarranted popularity of agape, Christianity's demonizing of sex, and the malfunctioning institution of marriage.

Scattered throughout his works, Nietzsche proposed suggestions about how to strengthen relationships. Ultimately, for loving relationships to be compatible with his ideal view of being with others (that contributes to *Übermensch* striving), they need to overcome these primary issues listed above. While Nietzsche comes close to rejecting romantic loving, such a relationship remains possible, albeit extraordinary, within his thinking.

Nietzsche often wrote in aphorisms, which provide a variety of fragmented perspectives that can appear contradictory or overgeneralized. Moreover, Nietzsche's ideas are often so impregnated with possible meaning that it is difficult to conclude definitively what he is trying to communicate. Like Kierkegaard, Nietzsche encourages readers to create their own interpretation. Also, like Kierkegaard, Nietzsche was unsystematic. Although he said that he was highly suspicious of system-builders,[2] some writers have argued that Nietzsche is indeed systematic because, for example, he aims to overcome nihilism in a logical manner.[3] Nevertheless, if he attempted a systematic approach, the contradictions within his writing invalidate it. However, I intend to take a generous approach and assume that he was not trying to be systematic. The implication of this is that the contradictions are less important and the point is not to try to reconcile them but to look for key messages and themes. Even though Nietzsche's views on love are fragmented, love is a recurring theme in his writing, and he has addressed it in enough detail to warrant examination. In light of this, the purpose of this chapter is to gain insights into Nietzsche's views on romantic loving by canvassing emerging themes across a variety of his works. Due to such reasons as these, this chapter is structured slightly differently to the others in this book; that is, the possible solutions are presented in response to each of the problems in turn.

While Nietzsche's vitalism differs from existentialism, he contributes significantly to existential ideas. Many of the existential philosophers agreed with Nietzsche that there is no inherent meaning in life. Since God is dead, Nietzsche argued that it is up to individuals to create their own morality and values. It is this focus on individuals as creators, "who are new, unique, incomparable, who give themselves laws, who create themselves!"[4] that opens his thinking to be aligned with, if not officially classified as, existentialism.

Nietzsche might seem to be an odd authority on the subject of love. This is not only because his writings about love are fragmented but also because, as far as we know, Nietzsche's romantic aspirations were never reciprocated. Nietzsche tended to love women who were already married, in love with someone else, using him to become famous, or put off by his walrus moustache and awkwardness.[5] Nietzsche's life was so void of romantic involvements that his interest in women has been brought into question. In *Zarathustra's Secret* Joachim Köhler asked "What love life?" highlighting that "So little was known about it that people had concluded that he had none".[6] Or perhaps, Köhler argued, he was discreet about it because he was homosexual. Since homosexuality was illegal at that time, if Nietzsche was homosexual, Köhler implies that he may have been writing about loving relationships in a form of code. Others argue that evidence for this is inconclusive,[7] so this chapter proceeds on the basis that when Nietzsche wrote about the relationship between men and women, he means heterosexuality and that it is not coded homosexuality.

Regardless of Nietzsche's sexual orientation, it is clear that he had difficulties in his relationships with women. He seemed to have romantic hopes, reportedly proposing to Mathilde Trampedach after three conversations. She declined. Then, in 1882 Nietzsche's friends introduced him to Lou Salomé, thinking that they would be well matched intellectually. They were right. Salomé was young and outgoing, and she had both brains and beauty. On their first encounter, Nietzsche reportedly said to Salomé: "From what stars have we fallen to be brought together here?"[8] By some accounts, Nietzsche was smitten and proposed twice, the first time only a few days after they met, but she refused.[9] Nietzsche was also infatuated with Cosima Wagner, wife of the composer Richard Wagner, and raved about how captivating, noble, intelligent, and classy she was.[10] Nietzsche might have conceded that her only flaw was her taste in men. He was dismayed when Richard Wagner developed religious themes in his compositions and the once great friendship between the two men never recovered.

Nietzsche's writing suggests that he loved and honored women yet was critical of much of their behavior. Some Freudians and feminists blame his growing up without a father as the source of his apparent misogyny and failure to find a wife or lover.[11] Nietzsche may have been persuaded: he grew up in a dominating matriarchal family, and he wrote that one's view of women is largely determined by one's relationship to one's mother.[12]

Nevertheless, Nietzsche's work does provide valuable insights into the nature and problems of romantic loving. Although he often spoke critically of love, perhaps not surprisingly given his difficulties in finding it, he also described it in *The Will to Power* as "the most angelic instinct" and "the greatest stimulus of life".[13] In *The Gay Science*, he likened learning to love with learning to hear music: once we learn how to hear it, it enchants us, and we want more.[14]

Although Nietzsche's lack of romantic involvements meant that he was not able to personally test out his own advice in practice, it does not mean that he was unaware of the problems and pitfalls of romantic relationships. One would not expect doctors to have experienced firsthand the conditions that they treat. It is possible that Nietzsche's longing for romantic loving made him even more highly attuned to its importance. Nietzsche's personal letters suggest that he was insufferably lonely and longed for someone to love.[15] In both his letters and philosophy he salutes love as a critically important part of life: without it, one's "soul will grow dry".[16]

Problems of romantic loving and Nietzsche's advice

According to Nietzsche, the basis on which Western society's values were built – Christianity – is crumbling because with the Enlightenment, religion ceased to be the dominant framework for regulating moral values. Like Stirner, Nietzsche declared, "God is dead!"[17] By this, he meant that the Christian value structure had been destroyed by science, but no one realized it or knew what to do about it. Science cannot penetrate value, and thus spirituality was lost, but the world had, by default, kept a Christian-style ethical system. Now we have a society with stale foundations.

Nietzsche thought that this meant humanity was heading toward nihilism because the Western lifestyle is based on decadence and hedonism, and it wallows in a moral void. Questions arise such as: how should we regulate our lives? Nietzsche thought that to avoid nihilism, it was time for a revaluation of values. Instead of accepting life as dictated by an obsolete deity, we ought to accept life on its own terms – *amor fati*. This was his "formula for human greatness", that is, to love life and "not want anything to be different, not forwards, not backwards, not for all eternity".[18] Nietzsche thought that if Arthur Schopenhauer, one of his favorite philosophers, was right when he said that the world is inherently meaningless, then the best thing to do is to strive to change it for the better. Rather than reject reality, Nietzsche urged creative action and a striving toward the ideal of the *Übermensch*.

The next section addresses four fundamental issues that Nietzsche identified with respect to romantic loving that should be revalued. The first issue springs from a creation myth, that is, that Adam idolized Eve and she complied. Nietzsche did not propose that men stop idolizing women but instead attempts to remind women of their power over men. Second, Nietzsche accuses Christians of being guilty of first-degree propaganda with respect to "agape". It shall be seen that his favored antidote involves self-mastery. Third, with the aim of thwarting Christian misinformation regarding the demonization of sex, Nietzsche's advice to celebrate sensuality and sex education is outlined. Finally, what happens when Nietzsche's gaze turns toward the value of marriage, which is often confused with romantic loving, is explored. Nietzsche's attack on romantic loving as a basis for marriage is dispersed but sustained, and so in the final section I analyze his musings on the issue.

Problem 1: idealizing women

The myth of Adam and Eve has created major difficulties for women, according to Nietzsche. He suggested the problem started with the story that man created woman "out of a rib of his God, of his 'ideal'".[19] In love, women fulfill such ideals.[20] A "wise man" in *The Gay Science* explains it as a function of the law of the sexes: "the way of men is will; the way of women is willingness".[21] The effect of this is that women are unwittingly coerced into conforming to the ideals or images that men have about them, so that men hold the advantage. Men have been idealizing women and women have been shaping themselves to fulfill this ideal. In a passage that suggests Nietzsche was sympathetic toward women's historical, socio-cultural predicament, he said women, being "doubly innocent", have not realized that men have been corrupting them.[22]

In *The Will to Power*, Nietzsche discussed a similar point in relation to the perfection of women in art: women are aware that men idealize them, and women instinctively facilitate it. Here Nietzsche emphasized two seemingly contradictory perceptions: pre-reflective and conscious. Being conscious of their behavior implies that women are complicit and use it as a form of power. Women know that their innocence and naïvety is seductive. Yet, since women's instincts are so subtle, it is not hypocrisy but rather "A deliberate *closing of one's eyes to oneself*".[23] He also addresses this point in *The Gay Science*: with women conforming to men's ideals of them, they have also instinctively learned to be actresses as a defense mechanism.[24]

While he sympathized with women who have ended up in such a position, Nietzsche is also scornful of women for perpetuating it and for their tactics in dealing with the situation. In *Human, All Too Human*, he suggests that women have cleverly figured out what men want and have played up to the ideal in order to attract and gain power over men. Women who use their youthful charm and cunning for seduction purposes are just like prostitutes, according to Nietzsche, except that prostitutes are more open and honest. He distinguishes between women who are aware of these dynamics and use it to their advantage from those who forget they are acting. The former are to be respected but the latter are vacuous women who are no more than a façade. The effect is that such women appear mysterious and elusive but are actually just empty shells.[25]

The problem, Nietzsche contends, is not acting. It is relying entirely on others for one's self-definition and believing one's own false performance.[26] Not consciously to reflect on one's behavior is a sign of a weak, undeveloped, and inauthentic individual. Such women, after playing a part to seduce a man, face a dilemma because they have won their battle on false grounds. It would be a mistake to stop acting at that point because they would lose the power they had gained.[27]

Nietzsche did, however, appreciate feminine charm, mystery, and allure. His solution to the problem of men's idealizing women was not emancipation, because he feared that the illustrious feminine mystique would be shattered. Women's tactic in revealing the truth about themselves in order to scare and gain mastery over men is absurd, according to Nietzsche, since the source of women's strengths is their beauty and ability to lie. He advised women not to emancipate, not to lose their femininity, and not to give up their strongest weapons, such as charm, comfort, and affection. He referred to modern women as boring and sterile, and he decreed that through emancipation, women are "*retrogressing*".[28]

Another consequence of women's forgetting how to charm is that Nietzsche feared that they would end up hating men. Nietzsche did not want to encourage this for two reasons. One, he saw it as a function of women's losing modesty, charm, taste, and femininity.[29] Two, he believed women could be much more dangerous and hostile than men when it comes to love: their "dagger-pointed intellect renders them excellent service".[30] Women do not play fair: they know how to find Achilles' heels, and rather than fighting back, men prefer to seek a truce.

Assuming that women are trying to gain mastery over men rather than equal rights, Nietzsche did not understand emancipation. He seemed to fear that women would free themselves from a male-dominated society but had not created their own, new rules. By his own account, he did not have a problem with women's freeing themselves from oppression, but questioned what they were gaining freedom to do. Nowadays, we understand it as freedom to participate in the same activities as men. Nietzsche thought women could do most things that men could do, but he could not understand why they would want to. In *Beyond Good and Evil* he proposed that women are more respected than ever before. He believed that a system that enables women to raise children while supported by working husbands is a good system. From Nietzsche's perspective, emancipation distracts women from the more worthwhile endeavor of raising strong children.

Advice: leverage strengths

It is difficult to pinpoint what Nietzsche thought women ought to do. He criticized women for being actresses and lying, but he did not want women to reveal the truth about themselves to men. He blames women for being complicit in their subordination but advises against any change in their situation. Such comments as these have earned Nietzsche a reputation for misogyny.[31] However, looking into his comments across a range of texts, the jigsaw can be understood differently. Nietzsche explored and reported on his view of sex roles and women's cultural conditioning. Although men have indeed idealized women, he pointed out that women have tolerated their subordination to men. He admired women's ability to adapt and gain power and mastery over men while maintaining their femininity. Indeed, Nietzsche's perfect woman, he said, "is a higher type of human being than the perfect man: also something much rarer".[32] Yet, vacuous women who have forgotten that they are actresses disgust him because they lead empty lives, void of their own goals. He also disdains shrewd women whose aim in life is to entrap men with their youthful charms because their success is short-lived. He loved women to be feminine. He appreciated their mystery and did not want things to change because he thought this could only be for the worse. He considered women's strength to come from their femininity, and losing their femininity means becoming masculinized, which means that they lose their power because they do not play to such strengths as intelligence, cunning, and beauty.

Problem 2: Christian morality

Nietzsche credited Christianity not only with starting the problem of men's idealizing women but also with turning morality upside down. Nietzsche's two main criticisms of Christian morality were that it was sourced from outside this world (God) and it glorifies the meek while dragging down the strong because it helps and aids the herd at the expense of the heroic and noble. The purpose of this strategy was to control the resentment of the weak by making them feel less weak.[33] In doing so, it destroyed the ancient Greek doctrine of power – an aristocratic code of warriors – and replaced it with a doctrine of subordination and emotional repression. Nietzsche worried that by sheer majority the weak would dominate the strong.

In attacking Christianity, Nietzsche also attacked its core: love thy neighbor. Like Stirner, Nietzsche criticized agape's impartial and indiscriminate nature as foolish. Through love of, and sacrifice to, one's neighbor, we bestow value on unimportant things.[34] Nietzsche portrayed agape as the lowest form of love because he saw it as a herd-animal strategy to achieve safety in numbers. He saw it as an excuse to be lazy because one pursues such a strategy to avoid conflict and enemies.[35] A higher type of person does not fear life or rely on the masses for protection but instead embraces battles in life, and thus Zarathustra, the protagonist of Nietzsche's *Thus Spoke Zarathustra*, encourages neighbor-flight.[36]

Advice: self-mastery

Nietzsche's antidote to the hypocrisy and weakness of agape is self-mastery. In one of Nietzsche's later works, he highlighted that the prerequisite for being capable of loving another is self-mastery: "to be firmly grounded in *yourself*, you have to stand bravely on your own two feet to be *able* to love at all".[37] Self-mastery is required not to let oneself become addicted to, and deceived by, the unproductive trappings of devotion, greed, and jealousy that can be a part of loving. Nietzsche presented a similar idea in *The Will to Power*, where he proposed that it is a crime to understand love as surrender and sacrifice. Rather, the greatest lovers are those who are the most fiercely independent and passionate about life.[38]

Scoffing at Christianity's advocacy that we should love others at our own expense, Nietzsche asked why people should expect to be loved if they do not think themselves worthy of it. Using Christianity's argument against itself, Nietzsche suggested that if Christians advocate clemency toward neighbors, then why not "go a step further: love yourselves as an act of clemency".[39] In *Ecce Homo* and *The Will to Power*, Nietzsche maintained that it is absurd to talk about egoistic and unegoistic actions; there is only egoism with varying degrees of willing.[40] Like Stirner, Nietzsche annihilated any possibility of disinterested charity and emphasized the hypocrisy of altruism.

However, Nietzsche is also wary of egoism because it depends on the kind of ego in question.[41] In *Twilight of the Idols* he proposed that selfishness must be assessed in terms of ascending and descending lives. Selfishness has extraordinary value in ascending individuals since they are the ones who advance life as we know it. However, descending people are ugly, parasitical and decadent and drag others down with weakness and sadness.[42]

Sexual loving is the "most candid expression of egoism", according to Nietzsche, because it is really about loving one's ideal self and a means to satisfy one's passions.[43] Like Stirner, Nietzsche held that when one loves another person, one loves the feeling of love.[44] Nietzsche had already been laying the foundations for this idea in earlier works. In *Daybreak* he indicated that sex is a natural arrangement of simultaneously receiving and giving pleasure.[45] Nevertheless, while erotic loving *can* result in interpersonal pleasure, the other's happiness and well-being is a function of one's own. Socializing opens up possibilities for new pleasures that one cannot experience on one's own, and this explains why men and women are so interested in one another. In *Human, All Too Human*, he noted that another's pleasure enhances one's own because it generates feelings of prosperity, security, and trust.[46] This is an idea that is not dissimilar to Stirner's perception of the value of relationships: we are social because it furthers our pleasure in life.

Nietzsche saw love as ultimately narcissistic because it is the search for one's idealized self. This is a strong theme repeated throughout his writing. For example, in *Beyond Good and Evil* Nietzsche suggested, "fundamentally they love and honour only themselves (or their own ideal, to express it more pleasantly)", and in *Human, All Too Human*: "what they are seeking...is not a complement but a perfecting of their own best qualities".[47] This is also consistent with *Daybreak*, where Nietzsche emphasized that love is the search for a means of resolving personal shortcomings and excesses (reminiscent of Aristophanes' myth) by finding a partner that can even out one's imbalances.[48] The implication of these statements is that loving is a means to an end, not an end in itself.

One problem with searching for one's perfected self is that it is easy to become delusional. In an idea reminiscent of Stendhal's crystallization process whereby lovers discover – and possibly even create – new perfections in each other that (for them) are as mesmerizing as shimmering crystals, Nietzsche suggested that lovers overestimate each other's virtues. He was quite convinced that love is delusional, repeating similar ideas in *Daybreak, Beyond Good and Evil,* and *The Anti-Christ*. It is not only natural but also an absolute pleasure for lovers to put each other on pedestals to marvel about how beautiful and exceptional each other is.[49] So strong is the desire to unearth and worship such rare treasures that it is all too easy for lovers to deceive themselves about how great the other person is. Lovers desperately want to ignore each other's flaws, and Nietzsche suggests that this one of the justifications for Christianity: "A religion had to be invented where people could love: it gets them through the worst in life – they stop noticing the bad aspects completely".[50]

In *The Gay Science*, Nietzsche pointed out that "Love forgives the beloved even his lust",[51] suggesting not only that lust is a normal part of love but that it is not one of its admirable features, since lust is a primal instinct in which unrestrained indulgence is decadent. Moreover, lovers are quite willing to support each other's imagination in bestowing undeserved or delusional merits upon each other, not out of vanity but instead because they want to protect each other from their defects.[52] The theme is that lovers love to overlook vices.

The deceptiveness of love is so powerful that it also transforms the lovers' understanding of themselves. In *The Will to Power* Nietzsche suggested that lovers tend to be overwhelmingly flattered by the way they appear through each other's loving gaze. On the one hand, the delusion becomes more than imagination since it has a psychosomatic effect: lovers understand themselves to be stronger, more capable, and more adventurous. In a passage strikingly reminiscent of Stirner, Nietzsche described the perspective of a man in love: "His whole economy is richer than before, more powerful, more *complete* than in those who do not love. The lover becomes a squanderer: he is rich enough for it". And yet, on the other hand, Nietzsche described such a lover as foolish since such perceptions are based on a fantasy.[53]

Nietzsche also warned against yielding to one's impulses immediately, lest one become a slave to them. Taking the view that beauty is in the eye of the beholder, Nietzsche explained that all instinctive judgments, including beauty, are persuasive but shortsighted because they appeal to our impulsive nature at the expense of careful deliberation. To focus on immediacy is a feature of decadence, hedonism, and a weak will that Nietzsche scorned as the ugly side of humanity. "To experience a thing as beautiful means: to experience it necessarily wrongly", because long-term ramifications are ignored; yet love is such a powerful passion, like a narcotic drug, that it seriously impairs judgment, and it is difficult to avoid becoming overwhelmed by it.[54] Love is not blind, he said, but is "dazzled" by its own fire.[55]

Advice: self-mastery ... in moderation

Notwithstanding his advice for self-mastery, Nietzsche lobbied for expressing one's passions and admired the power of loving. He refers to love as a precious panacea for the unbearable pain of reality: "love as the only, the *final* possibility for life".[56] He also endorsed intoxication and sexuality not only because they are enjoyable but also because they infuse individuals with tremendous feelings of power and galvanize people to accomplish great things. Thus, "how wise it is at times to be a little tipsy!"[57] However, a strong will coordinates desires and passions in concert with reason. Everyone can be impulsive and indulge blindly, but mastering them reveals great character.

Yet, loving is all too often an unrestrained desire for possession, and both women and men are guilty of treating it as such. In *Human, All Too Human*, Nietzsche accused women of being prone to locking up their lovers possessively. Nevertheless, he also said that their vanity usually stops them since women enjoy flaunting a lover if he is a good catch.[58] Later, in *Beyond Good and Evil* Nietzsche accused men of doing the same. Being territorial and prone to jealousy, men tend to treat lovers like exotic birds that need to be caged so that they will not escape.[59]

In *The Gay Science*, Nietzsche expands on the ways that egoism manifests differently in relationships for men and women. For men, sexual loving manifests as a voracious hunger to vanquish and exclusively own a woman's body and soul and to be worshiped and adored by her. This also explains, at least in part, jealousy. Coveting his sexual trophy, Nietzsche described a man in love as a selfish and zealous "dragon guarding his golden hoard".[60]

Nietzsche took this idea further in *Beyond Good and Evil*, suggesting that there are different ways in which men like to possess women. While some men are happy with sexual satisfaction as evidence of their ownership over a woman, other men want her to give up everything for him. Even more ambitious men want to ensure she truly knows him to the core and loves him for both his virtues and vices. Notwithstanding women's willingness to love in this manner, Nietzsche was skeptical that it would be possible.[61]

In *The Gay Science*, Nietzsche also proposed that romantic loving is always unequal in terms of what a man and a woman put into – and get out of – the relationship. For women, love means unconditional devotion. A passionate woman who unconditionally sacrifices herself for love becomes "a *more perfect* woman".[62] A real man would never do the same for a woman; he would want to possess her devotion. Women want to submit and men want to dominate. Each partner's life is enriched in its own way through the unequal elements. If both lovers were to renounce themselves, Nietzsche suggested that nothing would be left. It is precisely the nature of romantic loving relationships to be unequal, and a logical conclusion might be that the differing approaches are compatible.[63] However, this is not Nietzsche's main conclusion because, he proposes, love is egoistic for both men and women.

Further to the notion that women give themselves up (or in existential terms, compromise their authenticity) in loving relationships, Nietzsche proposed that they do so in order to satisfy their passion. In *The Will to Power*, he insinuated that they sacrifice themselves not to their lover, but rather to their "unbridled urge".[64] Even if it benefits others, sacrificing oneself is egoistic. He raised a similar point in *Human, All Too Human* when he suggested that sacrificing oneself to another is egoistic because it is giving in to one's desires.[65] Since succumbing to one's immediate desires is characteristic of a weak will, lovers who succumb to their urges are also weak willed.

Nevertheless, he proposed later that women also gain power through their subordination by portraying themselves as weak, clumsy, and fragile.[66] It tends to be a successful strategy because, he suggested, men are fascinated by such qualities.[67] Herein lies the paradox of women: their will to power is satisfied through their will to slavery. Since women can achieve power by using their will to slavery, it is still an expression of their will to power. The point is that all actions are an expression of the will to power.

Thus, love is a form of possessiveness for both sexes, but while men gain power through domination, women gain power through submission. This relationship is not complementary, however, since both are forms of attempting to gain power over the other, and a battle ensues. The different understandings of men and women about love are possibly one of the most important reasons for frustrations in romantic relationships. Hence, Nietzsche praises Bizet's *Carmen* for its insights into love as war, since it is a *"deadly hatred between the sexes!"*[68]

Advice: embrace risks and cherish obstacles

The sexes' differing attitudes to life presents another potential source of problems in loving relationships. According to Nietzsche, whereas women naturally like peace and comfort, men want quite the opposite: men welcome challenges and obstacles. Women do not like to see their lovers suffer and try to help them to have easier lives by removing obstacles. Doing so is very frustrating for men since they intentionally seek out challenges: "Without realizing it, women behave as one would do who removed the stones from the path of a wandering mineralogist so that his foot should not strike against them – whereas he has gone forth so that his foot *shall* strike against them".[69] While women might think that they are concerning themselves with their beloved's welfare, their concern is misdirected since it would be in the man's best interest not to remove obstacles. Nietzsche claims that women who try to make their lover's life easier do so for their own sake since they prefer calm lives. Alternatively, women see men's ambitions and passions as rival projects to their affections, so unless men's activities are beneficial to women, they would prefer men had none. Nietzsche resented the motherly women in his life who spoiled and oppressed him, and he blames loving women for interfering with men being great in the same way that vines smother trees.[70]

Nietzsche suggested that one could appreciate the heights of the mountains only after experiencing the depths of the abyss. Zarathustra explains the phoenix-like rebirth that comes from the most harrowing experiences: "You must be ready to burn yourself in your own flame: how could you become new, if you had not first become ashes?"[71] Like giving birth, great creations and achievements are painful.[72] This idea is something of which Nietzsche had firsthand experience, since he was sick most of his life and probably died from syphilis. His illness was excruciating and exhilarating, crippling and propelling his ability to work. He found intellectual ecstasy through his physical agony.[73]

One of Nietzsche's most enduring maxims, "What does not kill me makes me stronger" seemed to inspire him.[74] Comfort and happiness is characteristic of a weak will, whereas dissatisfaction, constantly taking risks, pushing limits, challenging oneself, and striving to overcome obstacles indicates a strong will, proves strength of character, and brings the greatest rewards and creativity.[75] Zarathustra urges, *"Become hard!"*[76]

Problem 3: demonizing sex

Although Nietzsche champions mastering one's passions, he also celebrates the passions and condemns Christianity for demonizing them. Christianity's position on sexual loving has not helped the battle of the sexes because it turned sexual loving into a taboo.[77] The reason it originally did this is because, as Nietzsche highlighted in *Twilight of the Idols*, lovers tend to behave foolishly. To prevent this stupidity, Christianity sought to destroy passions and successfully transformed popular perceptions of sex – a completely natural and normal function – into something evil and mysterious, something to be hidden away in bedrooms, and thus it became a source of guilt, shame, and misery.[78]

Nevertheless, just as it is absurd to pull out a tooth if it hurts, Nietzsche proposed that is it absurd to ban passions just because they can have foolish consequences. In a strikingly pre-Freudian analysis, Nietzsche argued that because the sex drive is natural, turning it into something evil means that people have to try to suppress their desires. Unfulfilled sexual desire fuels the "demons raging within", and like a full vessel, one more drop of water will cause it to run over, spilling into "devastating torrents" of violent passion.[79] Similarly, Zarathustra warns of the havoc that suppressed sexual desires can create: "These people abstain, it is true: but the bitch Sensuality glares enviously out of all they do... And how nicely the bitch Sensuality knows how to beg for a piece of spirit, when a piece of flesh is denied her".[80] Thus, denying and suppressing passions encourages becoming slaves to them and makes them much more difficult to control.

Advice: celebrate bodies and passions

Nietzsche offered two resolutions. First, he proposed "de-demonizing" Eros, or in other words, revitalizing and celebrating the body and passions. Reprimanding Christianity for castrating the passions, he also accused the Church of never asking the obvious alternative: "how can one spiritualize, beautify, deify a desire?"[81] Nietzsche's frustration with Christianity, and any religion that turns sexuality into something shameful by making it secretive, is that it is a "crime against life" and this "anti-nature" is the true vice.[82]

Although often critical of romantic loving, Nietzsche respects its role in reinvigorating sensuality and passion from Christianity's attempt to eradicate them.[83] By denying the passions, Christianity unwittingly turned sexual love into romantic love. The scorpion stung itself with its tail because demonizing the erotic and making it dark and secretive made it more interesting and intriguing, and this is why Western culture has come to overvalue romantic love.[84]

In an attempt to overthrow Christianity's demonization of sex, Nietzsche extols Eros. He acknowledged that sex is a natural part of being human and lobbies for it. Instead of educating people about sex, Christianity began a smear campaign, a strategy aimed at keeping the meek uninformed and under control. One antidote, Nietzsche proposed, is regular sex.[85] Indeed, as soon as a fantasy is realized, it stops being a fantasy. However, Nietzsche realized that regular sex alone is not going to solve the problem. Ironically, both Nietzsche and Christianity want to avoid unbridled, naïve, and hedonistic sex, but in opposite ways: Christianity through abstinence and Nietzsche through indulgence.

Advice: sex education

Nietzsche's second suggestion to overcome the clandestine phenomenon of sexual loving is sex education. Part of the process of de-demonizing sex is empowering people, particularly women, with knowledge. Revealing a sensitive side in *The Gay Science*, Nietzsche said he thought it to be "amazing", "monstrous", and "paradoxical" that men keep women ignorant about sexual matters and concludes: "one cannot be too gentle towards women!"[86] Nietzsche was disgusted that men have not thought enough about the effect on women of keeping sexual discussions taboo.

Nietzsche took a similar outlook in *Beyond Good and Evil* when he suggested that because of their naïvety, women are in an awkward place from the very beginning, perplexed by the mystery, shame, and expectations of sex.[87] Comments like this suggest that Nietzsche was not as misogynistic as he is sometimes made out to be.[88] Similarly, earlier in *Daybreak*, Nietzsche implies that the ignorant are always victims. The more educated one is, the better decisions one will be able to make, and the more fully one will be able to live.[89] While Nietzsche was not specifically referring to sex education here, it certainly could apply in this situation. By Nietzsche's own account, it seems logical that sex education would help women to deal with the shock of sex.

However, Nietzsche also has a problem with education of women. In *Human, All Too Human*, he proposed that women are just as intelligent and capable of being educated as men.[90] However, later in *Beyond Good and Evil*, Nietzsche warned against women becoming too enlightened because he associated education with masculinity, which is unnatural for women: "When a woman has scholarly inclinations there is usually something wrong with her sexuality".[91] There is an inconsistency here. Nietzsche suggested that sex education for women would be prudent, but not so much education that they become masculine. It is an invalid inductive inference that if women become educated and scholarly they will become masculine or will have to become masculine to be educated. Another possibility is that Nietzsche considers being educated and being scholarly to be two different characteristics, but if so, his point is unclear.

Problem 4: marrying for love

On the one hand, Nietzsche praised the fact that marriage had become the culmination of romantic loving. He appreciated that there is value in the belief that marriage can secure love for a lifetime since marriage has made romantic loving more meaningful than a fleeting encounter: "marriage has bestowed upon love a higher nobility...raised it to a new rank...[and] introduced a new *suprahuman* concept which elevates mankind".[92]

Yet, on the other hand, Nietzsche recognized that romantic loving has created problems for the institution of marriage, two of which will be addressed in this section. One, romantic loving is ephemeral because loving feelings wane over time and lovers change, and two, romantic loving that culminates in marriage often does not lead to an ascending life, because procreation is accidental and lovers are distracted by the urge to merge. A solution that can be derived from Nietzsche's musings is based on lovers being great friends too.

Advice: make promises that can be kept

In a statement reminiscent of Kierkegaard's view, Nietzsche proposed that the key problem with romantic loving is that it is ephemeral: "Sensuality often makes love grow too quickly, so that the root remains weak and is easy to pull out".[93] Since such a key feature of love is fleeting, Nietzsche thought it to be ridiculous that people believe marriage will make love stay.[94] Zarathustra says that marriage based on romance is stupid, and in both *Human, All Too Human* and *Daybreak*, Nietzsche warns that it is a mistake bound to end in misery and ennui.[95]

Such factors have contributed to the meaninglessness and disappointment of modern marriage. Nietzsche thought marriage had become absurd, banal, irrelevant, and irrational because it is based on something so shallow.[96] In *Daybreak*, Nietzsche contends that marriage has become a sham because more often than not, couples default on their promises and make hypocrites and liars of themselves.[97] People rush amorously into marriage, and when it goes wrong, it causes them – and everyone around them – a lot of aggravation. A woman says to Zarathustra, "True, I broke up my marriage, but first my marriage – broke me up!"[98] Zarathustra insists that the pair ought to end their relationship quickly rather than having to endure the vengeful suffering and lying inherent in the collapse.

One of Nietzsche's suggestions is for lovers to promise each other loving actions instead of loving feelings. Since romantic loving is ephemeral, promising to love one's partner forever is absurd and a lie. It would be much more appropriate to recognize this contingency and be honest about it. To avoid deception in marriage, Nietzsche recommends vowing to continue loving behavior even if the couple falls out of love.[99] Nietzsche is convinced that this would be perfectly acceptable because the couple will outwardly appear to still love one another. It will not be misleading, because lovers will have promised something that they actually have control over, that is, their actions. Nietzsche assumed that the beloved would understand and still say "I do" to marriage when being confronted with a partner who is uncertain about how long the loving feeling will last. His rationale is that feelings are involuntary, and thus loving is not a choice, so one ought to embrace the commitment of marriage.

The latent suggestion here is that one has no control over one's feelings. However, this is at odds with his later idea that we can master our passions. For example, he said in *Twilight of the Idols* that it is characteristic of a weak will not to control one's desires, and he described freedom as mastering instincts.[100] Thus, if one is strong willed, then one ought to be able to allow one's feelings to flourish or fade, as one does with *amor fati*. Zarathustra also represents such a stance when he urges lovers to master their passion, keep their vows, and work on making love last.[101] Nevertheless, Nietzsche was right in acknowledging that, for many people, it is absurd to promise irrevocable feelings. Since romantic loving is usually not strong enough to endure a lifetime, other motivations are needed. Like in Kierkegaard's ethical sphere, Nietzsche is recommending to accept a duty to perform loving actions, irrespective of feelings. Promising the semblance of love, not the continuation of the feeling of love, will make it easier to keep the promise and to stay together as expectations have already been set. Trying further to convince the reader that romantic love actually is irrelevant in a marriage, Nietzsche wrote:

> *Sample of reflection before marriage.* – Supposing she loves me, how burdensome she would become to me in the long run! And supposing she does not love me, how really burdensome she would become to me in the long run! – It is only a question of two different kinds of burdensomeness – therefore let us get married![102]

Nietzsche acknowledged that once romance beings to wane, the foundation of a marriage built on romantic love crumbles. Romantic love does wane because too much familiarity means that people tire of each other quickly. Nietzsche used the analogy of an engraving, which when continually touched with bare fingers deteriorates to the extent that it is beyond recognizable. Living apart, he conjectured, would make marriages stronger.[103]

At the very least, Nietzsche was urging lovers to keep their promises in order to avoid what he saw as all-too-common problems and disappointments associated with waning romance in marriages. In *On the Genealogy of Morals*, Nietzsche said that promises differentiate humans from animals.[104] We just need to be careful about the types of promises we make.

Advice: serial monogamy

Romantic loving is short-lived not only because loving feelings wane but also because people change and grow apart. In *The Gay Science*, Nietzsche described a "star friendship", where two friends had a magnificent time together but drifted apart as they pursued different goals. The implication is that it is only natural for some relationships to be transitory, and friendships that do not endure should still be cherished and respected.[105]

Nevertheless, Nietzsche himself questioned whether he was strong enough for such an attitude. For example, he was completely enamored with Lou Salomé, finding in her an intellectual equal. In letters he described her as extraordinarily intelligent and enthralling.[106] He told Salomé that she was his "twin brain" and of one of the days they spent together he said: "the most enchanting dream of my life, that I owe to you".[107] The depth of her conversations with Nietzsche about his great ideas enthralled Salomé too.[108]

However, Salomé had ambitions of her own and saw him as a teacher, a critic, and ultimately just a friend. Their great friendship began to fall apart when Nietzsche's sister, Elisabeth, started to pry. She criticized Salomé for her "rabid egoism, as well as complete immorality, that tears down everything in its path" and told Nietzsche of many hurtful things Salomé allegedly had said about him.[109] Nietzsche was furious with both women. He was devastated with Salomé's comments but equally livid with his sister about her interference. Nietzsche's relationship with his sister and Salomé continued to deteriorate, and soon he never saw Salomé again.

In a letter he never sent, Nietzsche referred to Salomé as "This scrawny dirty smelly monkey with her fake breasts – a disaster!"[110] When Salomé later informed Nietzsche of her engagement to another man, he never responded but wrote to a friend that he wished her all the best – albeit with a residue of bitterness. Revealing his struggle with living his philosophy, Nietzsche said that although philosophically he was above revenge, he found himself considering it.[111]

Some scholars suggest that Nietzsche's friendship with Salomé inspired him to be so critical of women.[112] However, his own experiences and the passage above that discusses star friendships would suggest that like ships that come together for a time then go their own way, so too do lovers have their own personal goals and seek their own paths that are not always parallel. Thus, the custom of marriage where two people are bound together for life is naturally unsuitable.

As an alternative to marriage, Zarathustra proposes a trial relationship.[113] It was something that Nietzsche also considered for himself. When his friends wrote to him describing Lou Salomé before they met, he responded that he was about to start dating but would want to commit to only a two-year relationship.[114]

In *Human, All Too Human*, Nietzsche outlines the benefits of such limited-term relationships. He suggested that it would be prudent (for men) to think about the possibility of multiple marriages. The first marriage would preferably be in his early twenties and to support his education and maturity; the woman ought to be "intellectually and morally his superior".[115] He goes on to say that the second marriage, although optional, ideally would be during a man's thirties, in which it would be his turn to become a teacher to a younger apprentice. Obligations are restrictive and distracting, especially for philosophers, because they hold one back from greatness, and so a man should preferably be without a wife later in life. Elsewhere, Nietzsche cites a raft of great and unmarried philosophers as evidence for this incompatibility: "Heraclitus, Plato, Descartes, Spinoza, Leibniz, Kant, Schopenhauer".[116] Socrates is the ironic exception. Nietzsche speculated that had Socrates known his wife better, he would not have married her. Nevertheless, by being so disagreeable, Xantippe pushed him much further philosophically. Yet even when he wrote *Human, All Too Human*, Nietzsche was skeptical about whether "free spirits" could be married since they mostly like to be alone, and marriage is suffocating. Like a spider caught in its own web, marriage ends up being a trap in which the spider (free spirit) cannibalizes itself. That is the reason why free spirits frequently tear themselves free from webs of relationships that begin to stifle them, even though it is a painful process.[117]

Nietzsche wrote of breaking not only ties with other people but also self-imposed ties – and neither is easy. To Lou Salomé he wrote, "become what you are! First one needs to emancipate oneself from one's chains, and then one must free oneself from this emancipation. Each of us, though doubtless in very different ways, has to suffer from chain fever, even after he's broken his chains".[118] "Become what you are" is a line he repeated in his philosophical works, and it suggests that one is incomplete and must overcome oneself to fulfill one's potential, which he also likens to striving toward the ideal of the *Übermensch*.[119]

In order to do so, however, one must free oneself from chains such as expectations of others, herd mentality, and social conditioning. Nevertheless, freeing oneself from such pressures is only part of the problem. Such pressures constantly threaten to re-encapsulate individuals since they are comforting like a lover's arms. Moreover, it is insufficient simply to be free, but instead greatness is about using one's freedom to overcome oneself and strive toward greatness. Independence is for only those who are strong, are adventurous, seek out and embrace danger, and are willing to be "torn to pieces limb from limb by some cave-minotaur of conscience".[120]

He returns to this idea later in *Twilight of the Idols* and echoes Stirner and Kierkegaard when he indicates that the magnitude of overcoming opposition measures freedom.[121] The free spirit must constantly break free from anything that binds, traps, restricts, makes comfortable, or tempts laziness. Perhaps this is why in a letter in 1887, Nietzsche wrote that marriage would be a bad idea for him since it would compromise his hard-earned independence. Yet, he still ruminated on how he would love a companion with whom he could laugh, read, dine, and do something else that he did not want to put in writing.[122]

While Nietzsche did not address how serial monogamy could be of benefit to women, he foresaw it as a point of contention, hence the title of an aphorism in which he discusses this idea: "Opportunity for female generosity".[123] Nevertheless, Nietzsche did not specifically exclude the possibility of women's being able to strive for the ideal of the *Übermensch*.

Advice: marry for great children

Another possible option that Nietzsche, proposed in *Twilight of the Idols*, was to separate romantic loving and marriage altogether. Nietzsche saw marriage as a worthwhile institution for building strong families and communities, and ultimately a much more reliable foundation for heterosexual relations than romantic loving. Nietzsche cites ancient Greek marriages that used not to be about flight of fancy. They were rational business arrangements. Roles were clearly defined. Couples could not get divorced. Love was prudently ignored.[124]

Nietzsche wanted to encourage lovers to think twice about whether they ought to marry. For example, in *Human, All Too Human*, he thought it wise for lovers to prepare themselves for the inevitable evaporation of attraction. He speculated that having a stronger pair of glasses to be able to imagine what the beloved will look like in 20 years would be enough to deter many from marrying. Alternatively, before walking down the aisle, Nietzsche exhorts the betrotheds to ask themselves whether they will be able to bear talking to each other for the rest of their lives. While most things change in marriage, the one thing that stays the same is the need to communicate. Thus, being interested in one another is infinitely more important to the durability of a relationship than being attracted to each other. Indeed, he also suggested that men and women could not be friends unless there is "a slight physical antipathy" between them.[125] Nietzsche later advocated a law against walking down the aisle in love on the basis that lovers are not capable of taking such a decision seriously.[126]

While in most Western cultures today this idea seems archaic, arranged marriages still exist in many cultures.[127] Emphasizing the importance of choice in relationships, Nietzsche advised marrying not only because the individuals happen to be starry-eyed and sexually attracted to one another, but to consider other factors in the decision, such as the ability to communicate well and to build strong families so that future generations thrive.[128] Even popularity or fame, he advises, would be better reasons for marriage than romantic loving since the marriage would be more stable if partners use the association for other ends.[129]

Yet another problem with marrying for love, according to Nietzsche, is that romantic loving tends not to contribute to an ascending life, because it distracts lovers from striving for the ideal of the *Übermensch*. Nietzsche conjectured that people are so swept away with the frivolity of romantic loving that they do not realize their greatest achievement would be creating new generations of even more amazing individuals. With people marrying for love, mate selection is based on chance and thus, making babies is a random exercise. It is actually in the individual's greatest self-interest not to marry for love, but to create strong, healthy, and well-educated progeny.[130] While it is conceivable that when in love, partners think highly of each other and would produce fine offspring, Nietzsche's point is not to be fooled by romantic delusions.

Campaigning against marrying for love, Nietzsche advocates improvements to the human species and building great civilizations through careful mate selection. Zarathustra exhorts: "You should propagate yourself not only forward, but upward!"[131] The implication is that having babies should not be about a blind biological desire for survival of the species (reproduction) but instead about procreation in the sense of actively creating new beings. He urges: "Let the flash of a star glitter in your love! Let your hope be: 'May I bear the Superman!'"[132] Indeed, a developing market for fertility clinics where parents can create bespoke babies by choosing physical traits and screening for defects and diseases suggests that there is indeed a demand for creating stronger and more attractive children cosmetically. Nietzsche was urging a natural form of this through partner selection rather than in test tubes.

While marriage is not a necessary condition for procreation, Zarathustra proposes that the family unit would assist in building those new generations.[133] The assumption here is that two great parents will create a child who is better than they are. Yet, there is no guarantee that this will be the case in practice, and Nietzsche had already acknowledged this in *Human, All Too Human*, citing Lord Byron's underwhelming parents.[134] Conversely, it is also logical that two great parents do not create a great child and Nietzsche regretfully acknowledged that children could not be pre-determined by their parents, as nice as that would be if they were great parents. Thus, Nietzsche suggested procreation could be an authentic transcendental activity, although it usually is not. Nevertheless, his advocacy for building strong family units is incompatible with his earlier ideas about serial monogamy.

Zarathustra supposes that pregnancy is the solution to all women's problems because children are the only reason that women need men.[135] Later in *Ecce Homo*, Nietzsche reiterated this point: "Did anyone hear my answer to the question of how to *cure*–'redeem'–a woman? Give her a baby".[136] These comments, read at face value, suggest that women are no more than reproductive animals. Nonetheless, Nietzsche also held pregnancy in high regard. As seen above, Nietzsche argued that having babies can and should be creative and a great achievement, contributing to creation of a new and better humanity and therefore a form of *Übermensch* striving. Moreover, in *Twilight of the Idols*, Nietzsche links pregnancy to eternal recurrence: "the triumphant Yes to life beyond death and change; *true* life as collective continuation of life through procreation".[137] Furthermore, Nietzsche admired the ancient Greeks, who venerated procreation and sanctified the pain of childbirth since "all becoming and growing, all that guarantees the future, *postulates* pain".[138]

Nevertheless, Nietzsche also pointed out that procreating often is not an achievement, because when mate selection is based on romantic loving, it is not focused on building strong family units or bearing supermen, and it is sometimes a mistake.[139] This could be a reason that Nietzsche did not specifically discuss women striving toward the ideal of the *Übermensch* (although he did not specifically exclude women either): the latent suggestion is that women should want to focus their efforts on creating baby *Übermenschen*.

Advice: give each other some distance

A second reason why Nietzsche was suspicious of romantic loving as a distraction from striving toward the ideal of the *Übermensch* lies in the desire for lovers to merge. The temptation to merge is strong but inadvisable. For example, in one of his early works, Nietzsche painted such a desire as a longing to bridge the gap between individuals:

> there are moments and as it were bright sparks of the fire of love in whose light we cease to understand the word "I", there lies something beyond our being which at these moments moves across into it, and we are thus possessed of a heartfelt longing for bridges between here and there.[140]

Later in *Daybreak*, he also painted love as a strong desire to seek unity. The problem is that the attempt to merge is a quest to dissolve otherness, and so lovers pretend to be people they are not. Not only does this result in a false sense of connection, but also it causes a lot of confusion between the couple.[141] This insight is also consistent with Nietzsche's comments in *The Gay Science* that if both lovers renounce themselves, then all that is left is an empty space.

Nietzsche supported the idea that strong lovers master their desire to merge or make the same and instead embrace their differences. In *Human, All Too Human*, he saw love as an appreciation of otherness: "What is love but understanding and rejoicing at the fact that another lives, feels and acts in a way different from and opposite to ours?"[142] While this would appear to contradict Nietzsche's comments that love is narcissistic, since lovers look for themselves in others, it is also possible that he was talking about different levels of relationships. Narcissists look for themselves in the other or seek to compensate their excesses and deficiencies through the other. Those striving toward the ideal of the *Übermensch* celebrate their differences and frictions. In contradiction to the premise of modern dating services, they do not waste time searching for things in common.

Elsewhere, Nietzsche portrayed the temptation for lovers to merge as madness and, like Stirner, advocates distance from others to keep power over oneself. We have already touched on the idea that relationships would be more successful if couples lived apart. We have also touched on Nietzsche's comments that free spirits must sometimes break ties with others, even with people they love, since love is blinding and gives lovers the power to deceive both themselves and each other.[143]

One instrument used for keeping one's distance from others could be a whip. The following piece of advice given to Zarathustra has created a huge amount of speculation: "Are you visiting women? Do not forget your whip!"[144] Taken literally, this implies that Nietzsche would advocate physical violence against women. Nevertheless, *Thus Spoke Zarathustra* is a work of fiction and can be taken in many ways, and the context of the quote prompts skepticism about such a conclusion. A woman gave him the advice as a special gift of thanks and warns that such wise words must be kept secret because in the wrong hands, they would be misunderstood.[145]

Keeping one's distance from others, particularly lovers, is a recurring theme in Nietzsche's work. For example, we have touched on the idea that Nietzsche thought that some things about women would be best left unsaid. In *The Gay Science*, Nietzsche wrote that men prefer to admire women's beauty from a distance and distance is a source of feminine power.[146] In this context, a whip would be a self-disciplinary or self-defense tool for men to keep themselves sufficiently distanced from women so as not to give away their mystery and beauty.[147]

It is most unlikely that Nietzsche meant physical violence when Zarathustra was advised to take a whip to women. It is much more likely that the comment is metaphorical and the whip is to be used by either or both lovers to preserve distance from one another. In the context of loving relationships, the whip can also be seen as being for the great Zarathustra to give to a woman to help one or both of them to be even greater. Thus, the best type of relationship is one where the partners are brave enough to whip each other into shape, so to speak.

Advice: be great friends

Nietzsche discussed a kind of relationship that Stirner did not: one that is beyond mutual advantage, benefit, pleasure, or enjoyment. While a great friendship may include all these elements, the key difference is that great friends inspire, educate, and help one another to become better people. They push each other to live beyond what they might have thought possible alone, to extend their achievements and fulfill great ambitions. Zarathustra also urges us to strive for that future, higher ideal of human greatness. To be a good friend, Zarathustra encourages, "you should be to him an arrow and a longing for the Superman".[148]

This sort of overcoming is extremely difficult to do on one's own. Nietzsche warned: "He who fights with monsters should look to it that he himself does not become a monster. And when you gaze long into an abyss the abyss also gazes into you".[149] Thus, friends are valued not so much for their gaze as Jean-Paul Sartre later envisaged, but rather for their ability to pull one up from the depths of the abyss and be launching pads to push one toward the ideal of the *Übermensch*. Even though Nietzsche warned against marriage for philosophers, older men, and free spirits, he also suggested that they are the ones who need it the most, and this pedagogical function is perhaps why. Like the cantankerous Xantippe, a challenging partner can educate even Socrates. Similarly, in *Human, All Too Human*, Nietzsche suggested that being loved by an intelligent woman is therapeutic because it helps men to feel better about themselves.[150]

Yet being a great friend is not an easy task. The best teachers are the harshest critics and should be wary of being too sympathetic toward the friend. Zarathustra says that the best sorts of friends are actually more like enemies: they are unsympathetic and ruthless.[151] Thus, they will be best able to challenge one another. Yet, the eternal question is whether lovers can be friends. Nietzsche was skeptical. Zarathustra declares that women have no idea how to be friends. Nietzsche's criticism of women's capability of friendship is not as misogynistic as it first appears. First, he qualifies his statement with "yet", implying that the possibility exists. Second, Zarathustra is also critical of men's ability to be friends. Anyone distracted by power games – slave and tyrant alike – cannot be a good friend. Third, in Nietzsche's discussions about star friends in *The Gay Science*, he is ambiguous about the sex of the participants in such a friendship.

A fourth reason is that, earlier in *Human, All Too Human*, Nietzsche explicitly wrote that women and men could be friends.[152] Nietzsche's challenge is for lovers to be better friends. A true friendship does not entail dependency, but instead camaraderie, encouragement, and flourishing. A relationship based on great friendship between two autonomous individuals opens partners up to new experiences of, possibilities of, and opportunities for self-overcoming. Although love usually manifests as greediness and power struggles, Nietzsche's idea of great friendship sublimates the will to power, thus helping each other to be creative and find the way to the ideal of the *Übermensch*. If lovers were capable of friendship, then such love would involve striving together. Nietzsche proposed precisely this kind of great friendship will make a great marriage.

An indication that Nietzsche saw the same kind of possibilities for loving relationships appears in an early work: "for it is love alone that can bestow on the soul, not only a clear, discriminating and self-contemptuous view of itself, but also the desire to look beyond itself and to seek with all its might for a higher self as yet still concealed from it".[153] This suggests that Nietzsche saw the possibility of great love as compatible with striving for the ideal of the *Übermensch*, and a strong will is required for both. Nietzsche also supports such an idea in *The Will to Power* when he writes, "the greatest lovers are so from the strength of their ego".[154] Moreover, Nietzsche describes two types of love: a "slavish" and false love that is weak and decadent and a "divine" love that is based on the principles of friendship outlined above. It supports striving for the ideal of the *Übermensch* not only through loving, but also through being an enemy because at times the most loving thing to do is to provoke and challenge each other.[155]

Key considerations

While some of the contradictions within Nietzsche's views of romantic loving have been highlighted above, this section addresses more general criticisms with respect to Nietzsche's comments on romantic loving.

First, Nietzsche tends to overgeneralize about what men and women want, such as when he said that women like comfort and submitting to their lovers, but men want challenges and to dominate their lovers. However, Nietzsche was highly cognizant of the issues between the sexes and the dynamics that can destroy relationships and distract lovers from achieving their own goals. There is certainly merit in reinforcing such potential problems in romantic relationships: it is often more difficult for women than for men to be authentic; romantic loving is often egoistic even when it appears superficially to be self-sacrificial; concern for the beloved's welfare can easily be misdirected and can frustrate relations; and succumbing to one's impulsive loving urges is hedonistic and weak.

Second, Nietzsche's views on women's roles are contradictory. On the one hand, he did not explicitly exclude women from striving toward the ideal of the *Übermensch* or being a "star friend", but he did not specifically include them either. On the other hand, he worried that this striving would mean that women would lose their femininity. For example, he accused scholarly women of being stunted sexually. Education and femininity are, however, not mutually exclusive, and Nietzsche's concerns are unfounded.

Third, Nietzsche provided no concrete details or examples of the *Übermensch* and the ideal friendships that might develop. Nietzsche's omission or elusiveness at best was intentional: to provoke the reader to find one's own unique solution to becoming a creative individual rather than being distracted with trying to follow in the footsteps of someone else.[156]

Fourth, in terms of Nietzsche's vision of creating baby *Übermenschen* as well as his support for an aristocratic moral code, elitist self-development, and individualism, it is possible to see how this attitude was distorted by his anti-Semitic sister Elisabeth and used – albeit highly selectively and misleadingly – for fascist purposes. Nietzsche knew his writing was "dynamite" and even tried to recall *Thus Spoke Zarathustra*, "to protect it from mishaps (I read it in the last few days and almost died of emotion). It won't be ripe for publishing until after several decades of world historical crises–wars!"[157] With uncanny foresight, these statements suggest that, one, Nietzsche was quite confident of his pending fame, even if it was not to be fully realized during his lifetime, and that, two, he knew exactly how dangerous his books could be. Nevertheless, he also seemed aware of his limited appeal during his lifetime: "I've thrown my hook out to 'the few' instead, and even with them I'm prepared to be patient".[158]

Fifth, Nietzsche has been accused of pessimism, especially with respect to loving relationships.[159] Notwithstanding the many cynical things Nietzsche did say about romantic loving, there are indications that Nietzsche also thought very highly of it. Nietzsche respects romantic loving for its role in reinvigorating the passions after Christianity's attempt to extinguish them. Nevertheless, he is also highly skeptical of romantic loving because such relationships all too often descend into petty power struggles. Furthermore, frivolously indulging in one's passions is ephemeral and does not contribute to *Übermensch* striving. There are few details as to how romantic loving relationships might be reconciled with marriage and friendship; however, he has paved the way through his ideal of the *Übermensch* and friendship to find a way of being with lovers that is not doomed to pettiness and descending power games and that sublimates the will to power and one's sexual instincts into a romantic relationship. At least in this respect there is more than a glimmer of optimism.

Sixth, while Nietzsche's remarks about romantic loving are fragmented, he did provide valuable perspectives and practical suggestions for reinvigorating and strengthening romantic relationships. While initially some advice may appear frivolous,[160] for example, giving a woman a baby and taking a whip to her, I have shown through a number of alternative interpretations that Nietzsche's ideas are insightful. He saw it as natural that people fall in love and like to get married, but when relationships fall apart, they can be painful and despicable. He thought everyone would be better off if lovers would actively decide on, not dreamily slide into, marriage. Romantic relationships, he thought, can be great when they are between strong individuals. Yet, such relationships are rare, difficult, and conflicted. At times, the lovers will have to be enemies. Yet, Nietzsche would chuckle because he welcomed conflict and obstacles in life.

Although Nietzsche did not specifically refer to loving as romantic, he did indeed grapple with the key elements of romantic loving. He acknowledged and admired the passionate nature of romantic loving, but he warned that not to master one's lust and loving feelings is decadent and weak. There are indications that he thought great love to be possible for only those strong enough to master their passions – that is, to overcome the desire to possess or sacrifice themselves to their lovers and to master their lust and egoistic desires. He acknowledged that love is personal, but he was wary of the delusions that love evokes, not only enhancing and fabricating the beloved's merits but also boosting one's estimation of oneself. Nevertheless, he also admired the power of love's delusions and intoxications as valuable for creativity and providing relief from the anxiety of living in a nihilistic world. Nietzsche considered the ideal of romantic loving as everlasting to be one of its most damaging features. For those who do not master their passions, romantic loving is bound to be fleeting. Not only is this indicative of a weak will, but also it becomes particularly problematic when lovers frivolously seek to secure their love through marriage, which is rendered absurd when the basis for it, romantic loving, is exhausted. Nietzsche was also critical of the idea that romantic loving is a merger between two individuals. Problems with such an ideal manifest themselves when lovers seek to renounce themselves to the other in the name of love. Since individuals are will to power, all relationships are power struggles. However, great lovers sublimate the power struggle into striving for the ideal of the *Übermensch*. Weak lovers flounder in futile games of appropriation. This is problematic because they thwart each other's striving, for example, by locking each other up like exotic birds or by making their own life more peaceful by spoiling the other's adventures. If lovers are truly concerned about each other's welfare, then, according to Nietzsche, they ought to be constructively challenging. Ultimately, a great friendship is the basis for lovers to become great.

Nietzsche's revaluation of values contributes much to the discussion of romantic loving. He advocated that lovers free themselves from: the shackles of romantic mythology; sexual conventions; agapaic self-renunciation; suppression and ignorance of sexuality; decadent, instinctive, romantic, and sexual delusions; and the ideals of merging and everlasting love flippantly secured through marriage. To be free from such chains allows the lovers to be free to use their power to create their own values, to be secure in themselves rather than using the beloved to compensate for their own weaknesses, and to create strong relationships that allow individuals to strive toward the ideal of the *Übermensch*.

5
Jean-Paul Sartre and Loving Sadomasochistically

This study of loving existentially culminates with Jean-Paul Sartre and Simone de Beauvoir's philosophies. Beauvoir and Sartre were two of the leading atheistic existential thinkers and were involved in a very public and long-standing loving relationship. They met as young philosophy students in 1929. Sartre won first prize in the *agrégation*, France's highly competitive teachers' exam, after failing the first time. Beauvoir drew second place in what was a controversial and heated decision process.[1] They fell in love with, inspired, and challenged each other for the rest of their lives. They became highly admired teachers, writing about their new philosophies in smoky Paris cafés. In 1964, Sartre was awarded (but refused) the Nobel Prize for his autobiographical narrative *The Words*, while Beauvoir won France's top literary award, the Prix Goncourt for her 1954 novel *The Mandarins*.

Despite saying in a 1959 interview that he was not interested in writing about love, he did actually have plenty to say on the topic.[2] First, this chapter addresses why, in *Being and Nothingness*, Sartre thought love to be so alluring but problematic. Second, I seek solutions within Sartre's works, but for this we need to look beyond *Being and Nothingness* to such works as *Notebooks for an Ethics* ("*Notebooks*") and his fictional works, as well as to how he tried to resolve the issues in practice. However, Sartre's solutions are fragmented and undeveloped, and the value of his analysis of romantic loving lies firmly in understanding its problems.

Much of Sartre's existential writing was published in the 1940s. While he accepted and used the term "existential" in his early writing, later in life he said he thought the word was ridiculous but begrudgingly accepted it.[3] Since this analysis is existential, it deliberately excludes Sartre's later writings that veer toward Marxism. Although Sartre spoke about integrating existentialism and Marxism, he was never able to reconcile them.[4]

Attracted to philosophy through Henri Bergson's ideas about consciousness, Sartre began *Being and Nothingness* by rejecting Immanuel Kant's idea of noumena, which is the notion that appearances conceal essences.[5] Instead, he bases his phenomenology on that of Edmund Husserl and Martin Heidegger, wherein the essence is as it appears.[6]

While Sartre denied reading much Hegel before *Being and Nothingness*,[7] there are three key points relevant to this analysis that Sartre derives from Hegel. First, they both split being into opposing elements: the in-itself and the for-itself. Second, the role of the "Other" is a fundamental aspect of self-consciousness. Sartre was attracted to Hegel's idea that being-for-others is necessary for being-for-myself because so much of my existence depends on being recognized by others.[8]

The third key element that Hegel and Sartre have in common is the source of conflict in relationships. They discuss a form of encounter between humans, a master and slave interaction, as a "dialect", which is an oppositional and oscillating relationship. Hegel described the dialectic as two consciousnesses who meet, and in their recognition of each other, they realize there is a part of their being lost in the other. Both think that the other holds the missing piece of their being that will bring them full knowledge, certainty, and truth about themselves. There is no simple and friendly way to recover this part of their being, and so a "life-and-death struggle" ensues.[9] However, killing the other consciousness would be self-defeating because one would not be able to access what one was seeking in the first place – that is, self-certainty and alterity. So, it is essential that both consciousnesses survive in order to recognize each other as opposed. The more powerful one seizes the independent essential position of "lord" or "master" existing for-itself. The one who is more afraid of dying surrenders and becomes the dependent and unessential "bondsman" or "slave". The relationship is not quite so simple, however, and the story takes an unexpected turn. The lord finds that he is not as independent as he initially thought, because he needs the slave in order to establish his self-certainty. Paradoxically the bondsman becomes the essential and more powerful force in the relationship. This provokes the master-slave dialectic that Sartre explored with regard to sexual and loving relationships in *Being and Nothingness*.[10]

Except in a passing comparison with the Marquis de Sade, Sartre did not discuss Max Stirner.[11] Yet there are a number of similarities in their approaches, especially the idea that humans are creative nothingnesses. Nevertheless, Stirner would have criticized Sartre for his obsession with the "spook" of freedom because it is another abstraction and ideal to which individuals subordinate themselves.

Sartre would have us believe that his exploration of Kierkegaard was delayed until around 1939–1940 because he did not like the double *a* in his name.[12] Yet, Sartre's existential writing bears comparison to Kierkegaard's in terms of his emphasis on subjective truth, individualism, primacy of choice, and anxiety. In *Being and Nothingness*, Sartre adopts Kierkegaard's ideas about irony and anguish, and in *Existentialism is a Humanism*, he analyzes Kierkegaard's interpretation of Abraham's anxiety.[13]

While Sartre said that he read a lot of Nietzsche and found him interesting, Sartre dismissed him as not particularly important and said, "I hated him. I think his crap about the elite, his übermensch [sic], radicalized us a lot" when Sartre was a student.[14] Sartre and his friends used to throw urine-filled condoms on the heads of pretentious students who loved Nietzsche and shout "Thus pissed Zarathustra!"[15] Yet, Sartre has more in common with Nietzsche than he may be willing to admit because they both portray romantic loving as a desire to possess the other.

Before proceeding to the problems of romantic loving, I shall outline why Sartre proposed that romantic loving is so alluring. For Sartre, love is an important way of understanding oneself. To understand why this is the case, it is necessary first briefly to address Sartre's view of consciousness. In *Being and Nothingness*, Sartre identified two primary modes of being: being-for-itself (*l'être-pour-soi*) and being-in-itself (*l'être-en-soi*). The key difference between the two is that a for-itself, such as a human, is conscious, whereas an in-itself, such as a table, is not. The implication of this is that possibilities are available to a for-itself and not an in-itself. In other words, humans can modify their being and situation through the choices they make: to exist is to choose. In contrast, an in-itself can have possibilities only by being modified by a for-itself or another in-itself. For example, a table cannot paint itself; only a for-itself (a human) can. The significance of this emphasis on modification is that a for-itself acts intentionally; an in-itself does not.[16]

Another aspect of being is that it is more than "the self" because it cannot be understood without taking into account one's intentions and projects. This is why being implies becoming and is incomplete. Sartre referred to this incompleteness as a "lack", a "not yet", or a gap called "nothingness". Being cannot be completed until death, at which point there are no more possibilities. Death is the moment when a for-itself turns into an in-itself.[17]

However, human reality is a striving toward completion, or in other words, a project of becoming an in-itself-for-itself. One wants to become complete and secure to overcome the anxiety of the meaninglessness of life. Sartre defines such a project as *ens causa sui*: the project to be one's own foundation, that is, God.[18]

Human consciousness, according to Sartre, thrusts itself forward in the world, surpassing itself toward that which it lacks, or in other words, totality. Sartre incorporates a very similar idea to that of Nietzsche's self-overcoming when he referred to perpetual surpassing and suggested striving toward an ideal. Unlike Nietzsche, the striving that Sartre refers to is not toward something like the ideal of the *Übermensch*. Sartre's ideal is not predetermined. His concept is actually more similar to Stirner's view that one is a creative nothingness. Even though Sartre referred to the goal as becoming "perfect", he meant a completed or total being, that is, whoever one is when one dies.[19]

Like Kierkegaard, Sartre was anxious about not knowing whether he was becoming who he wanted to be. Also like Kierkegaard, Sartre argued that the consequence of being as an inherent lack, of the absurdity of life, and of the absence of predetermined values and morals is that it creates anguish. Whereas fear is of something external, anguish is internal. For example, walking along a mountain precipice alone, I am not *afraid* of falling into the abyss, as there is no one around to push me. However, I may be *anguished* about throwing myself into it. If I do not want to die, I take control of the situation and exert all my strength in order to make my preferred possibility come to be, that is, to avoid placing my foot in a spot where I might slip and fall. Unlike Kierkegaard, who proposed that a leap to faith neutralizes anguish, Sartre saw it as a fact of life that we cannot deactivate. For Sartre, it is perfectly normal to be anxious about our possibilities, freedom, or future.[20]

Sartre defines consciousness as being able to question oneself. There are two key implications of this definition: first, being conscious means not only that humans are able to question, but also that one's being is never simply given and is always a challenge; and second, following Husserl, being conscious is to be conscious *of* something, meaning also that consciousness does not possess or hold contents within it.[21] Moreover, being is intentional, meaning that actions are deliberate and goal-oriented, even if one does not reflect on reasons or consequences at the time. Intentions shape our world, according to Sartre, because intentions guide our actions toward certain ends, even if those ends are not ultimately achieved.[22] For Sartre, neither an unconscious force nor a Nietzschean will to power drives humans.

The fundamental problem is that in order to question oneself, one has to be able to objectify oneself. This is impossible, according to Sartre, because just as the eye cannot see itself, one cannot split in two to be a subject and an object at the same time. We have a conflict of interest in our self-reflection, which means our answers are tainted. So we look to others, especially lovers, for answers.

Sartre outlines three types of self-knowledge: ordinary simple reflection, deep self-reflection, and reflection gained through others. At the basic level, individuals are pre-reflectively conscious. This is spontaneous perception. One sees or does something, but does not focus on it. This differs from reflective consciousness, in which one knows one is aware of something and can pass judgment on it.[23]

To discover the third type of self-knowledge, one needs other people. There are aspects of one's psychology that cannot be grasped alone, so much so that "One would not know oneself without the Other".[24] Lovers are in a prime position to provide that deeper level of self-knowledge. Although many people come and go from one's life daily, lovers form some of the deepest, most intimate, and most intense relationships. While other relationships such as family, friends, and work colleagues can be more time-consuming than romantic loving, the former do not normally engage on a sensual level. Sartre places much importance on sensual engagement because it opens up possibilities for deeper intimacy than platonic relationships. Beyond sex, intimacy provides a means of discovering new dimensions of oneself and creating more profound experiences with and through others.[25] This is why, in his view, lovers are among the best people to provide a comprehensive and valued reflection for each other. Notwithstanding the allure of romantic loving, there are also inherent problems in such relationships, and it is these problems that shall now be addressed.

Problems of romantic loving

For Sartre, there are two aspects of human relationships: being-for-others and being-with-others. Being-for-others shall be addressed first. An experience such as shame is the key to understanding being-for-others. If one makes an awkward or vulgar gesture when one is alone, one does not judge oneself. According to Sartre, one cannot be ashamed unless other people are involved. The presence of someone else forces one to pass judgment on oneself as an object and reveals completely new aspects of oneself.

For example, one is alone and spying on someone through a keyhole. Alone, one sees nothing wrong with this, but if one realizes that someone is or might be watching, one becomes ashamed pre-reflectively. In this way, the other "decentralizes" one's whole world.[26] Sartre assumed that one's pre-reflective response will be shame, but this is by no means given. One's pre-reflective response will relate back to one's original choice about the way one wants to live. One possible reaction could indeed be shame but only if one's assumption about the world is that looking through a keyhole is taboo, if one expects the other to disapprove, and if one considers the other's opinion to be of value, which is generally the case with lovers.

The above example shows how people complicate each other's lives because everyone imposes their own meanings on the world and, in doing so, modifies each other's possibilities and brings each other's existence to a new level. Nevertheless, Sartre points out that the extent to which others are limiting depends on one's perspective: does one accept the limits that others attempt to exert, ignore them, or actively disobey them? Even if one is being tortured or one's life is threatened, one can still choose one's response. Pain or death may be preferable to life under certain circumstances.[27]

Another important point in the above example is that other people are limits only insofar as one recognizes them as part of one's self-definition.[28] The implication of this is that the more highly one regards the other, the more important their interpretation of one's actions becomes, the more power the other gains in one's self-recognition, the more dependent one becomes on the other's view, and the more desperate one is to control that view, fueling the conflict that Sartre said characterizes relationships. Lovers tend to be more concerned about each other's respective opinions than anyone else's, which is why conflict is particularly intense in loving relationships.

Sartre acknowledged that there are people who refuse to take into account the way others see them or deny that the way others perceive them is valid, but he dismissed it quickly and insufficiently by saying that this person would not be human.[29] The reason he did so is linked to his attempt to avoid solipsism by establishing a fundamental connection to others.

Aware of the risk of reducing others to utility, since interactions with others aim at becoming an in-itself-for-itself through the self-knowledge that others can provide, Sartre argued that he is also an object for the other. Thus, reciprocity is an integral part of one's being. If both value recognition, then the more one values the other's recognition, the more the other is likely to reciprocate. Nevertheless, there is no guarantee of mutual recognition, which seems to be why Sartre thinks that recognition is highly risky. This attitude reveals elements of Hegel's master-slave dialectic in which relations with others are an appeal to be recognized in order to establish one's self-certainty. However, Sartre criticized Hegel for his abstract understanding of consciousness and for being too optimistic. While Hegel thought it possible to understand oneself through the other, Sartre disagreed because we have no foundation on which to build reciprocity.[30]

The root of the problem is Sartre's skepticism about the attitude of being-*with*-others and the difficulties in the term "we". Whereas being-*for*-others is ontological, Sartre claimed that "we" is a psychological concept. Even though people identify with each other in the sense of common actions or aims, everyone's experiences and goals are different, and this difference is alienating. The prerequisite for honestly exploring the idea of "we" is to know who the other is, and this one cannot know beyond doubt. I cannot grasp another's subjectivity, I cannot know anything about how others see me, and so I learn nothing from them.[31]

Thus, there are at least three reasons why others are disruptive, for Sartre. First, others decentralize one's world, as in the shame analogy. More broadly speaking, the other reveals aspects of one's being that one cannot recognize alone because one cannot look at oneself as an object. In an idea similar to Nietzsche's ideal of how great friends could push each other to achieve more than they could alone, Sartre thought that others are the catalysts for us to understand ourselves better. It is out of vanity that we want to get close to others: we want them to reveal secrets about ourselves. How does one find out this secret of one's being? Just ask! Nevertheless, language is unreliable because people lie. Second, others modify one's possibilities. Sartre likes to talk about this in a negative sense in *Being and Nothingness*, likening another's existence to a "drain hole" that steals the world from him.[32] Third, in the presence of others one recognizes that one is vulnerable because one could be an instrument of others' possibilities, and it is terrifying to be a means to ends of which one is ignorant.[33] Sartre famously summed up this paradox in *Huis Clos*: "There's no need for red-hot pokers. Hell is...other people!" because they are adversaries who are vital in the process of self-discovery.[34]

For Sartre, loving relationships are alluring because the intimate nature of them would seem to provide the means of deeper self-reflection through an other whose opinion is held in high regard. However, the question is: if language is an unreliable means of revealing such understandings, what other means are available? Sartre outlined a number of strategies that lovers employ in order to become one's own foundation. In *Being and Nothingness*, he reduced relationships to two fundamental attitudes: assimilation and appropriation. The next section highlights some of the key elements of these two attitudes at play in romantic loving relationships – namely possession, freedom, seduction, sadism, and masochism.

Possession

The natural state of human affairs, according to Sartre, is conflict.[35] One is torn between being indebted to the other for being the catalyst by which one realizes whole other dimensions of one's being but also not wanting the other to steal one's being entirely. The problem is as follows. The other realizes an aspect of oneself that cannot be understood without being told because one cannot become other to oneself. Because the other holds the secret of one's being, one tries to enslave the other in order to learn these secrets. Yet, the other is trying to do the same. At the same time, both are trying to free themselves from each other's hold. Therein lies the battleground of consciousnesses.

This dynamic also means that being is a project of possession. Reminiscent of Stirner, Sartre indicates that one is the sum of one's possessions. For example, one owns a bicycle and exercises that possession not only by using it but also by using it up. Possession, for Sartre, involves wanting to integrate it into one's being, which means destroying it.[36] Sartre's statements overlook the idea that if one values a possession, then it is not just a matter of using it up but also a matter of maintaining, preserving, or improving it in order to extend its usability.

Nevertheless, even using something does not quench the desire to possess it, because nothing can ever actually be assimilated into one's being. Complete possession is impossible because although one can lock up a body or an object, there is actually nothing concrete in possession. For example, Proust's Marcel possesses his lover Albertine physically, but he is anxious that he does not possess her consciousness. Furthermore, to possess is more than simply to use because there are plenty of things that are used but not possessed – for example, a plate in a cafe. Rather, possession involves a desire to unite. This would explain why lovers tend to be possessive: they want to unite.[37]

Hegel argued that consciousness aims at recognition, which amounts to the desire to assimilate and destroy the other, but both must survive in order to recognize each other. Similarly, Sartre proposed that lovers are torn between wanting to unite and not wanting to destroy each other. This is why a lover does not want complete control over the beloved: because then the beloved would be no more than a robot; alterity would collapse; there would be no way to recover the secrets lost in the other; and love would die. This would be "to kill the hen that lays the golden eggs".[38]

As Kierkegaard's Johannes the Seducer brought to our attention, love is the desire for the beloved's freedom. Similarly, Sartre argued that on the one hand, lovers want to be loved freely. Yet, on the other hand, lovers do not want each other to be completely free, because they do not want the other to love anyone else. Sartre might well have had Nietzsche's suggestion in mind when he challenges the irony of this situation and pointed out that no lover would be satisfied with being loved solely for the sake of a vow. This tension, Sartre explained, arises because lovers want each other to make special exceptions to their freedom. Lovers do not want each other automatically to limit their freedom since this would imply some kind of causal determinism. Rather, lovers want each other freely to choose to limit their freedom and to become the absolute ends for each other. For example, lovers want to believe that their relationship usurps all other values and morals. They want to know that they would do anything and everything for each other, even breaking the law. Lovers want to be the absolute top priority for each other. If lovers become the end and justification of each other's lives, there is no need to worry that they are instruments or means to other's ends. This, according to Sartre, explains the joy of love.[39]

In *Nausea*, Sartre was already sowing the seed for this idea. Anny says to Roquentin, "I could very well think of you only as an abstract virtue, a sort of limit".[40] Roquentin had hoped that Anny would save him by providing him with a reason to live. Without her, he finds himself "Alone and free. But this freedom is rather like death".[41] Both characters illustrate the point that during their relationship they had sought justification for their existence in each other. Yet founding one's existence on an unknowable and unpredictable person is hazardous because there is always the risk that the relationship will break down. Nevertheless, it also indicates the importance of loving since, even though not loving means one is free from the futility of possessive dynamics, being free from a loving relationship is to withdraw from a vital part of existence – hence Roquentin's elegy about his deathly loneliness.

Seduction

Sartre concludes that lovers can neither ever truly find security nor know whether they are being used as instruments or are the absolute ends for each other. After all, a lover's real goal is a project of the self, that is, to discover secrets about oneself through the beloved. Love becomes an act of seduction in order to try to appropriate the beloved without the threat of being objectified. This is a matter of flaunting oneself like a peacock in an attempt to impress on the other that one is profoundly wise, worldly, and eminently powerful.[42]

Sartre was practiced in such activities. As a teenager, he realized he was unattractive. He told an early lover, Simone Jollivet, "Until last year I was very melancholy because I was ugly and that made me suffer. I have absolutely rid myself of that, because it's a weakness. Whoever knows his own strength must be joyful".[43] Sartre decided to seduce women with his power of language. In *War Diaries*, he said that he dreamed of being "a scholarly Don Juan, slaying women through the power of his golden tongue".[44] His ardent language and passionate love letters were highly successful tactics in seducing many young women. One of Sartre's lovers, Bianca Bienenfeld, wrote that he was "a master of the language of love" and that "just as a waiter plays the role of a waiter, Sartre played to perfection the role of a man in love".[45] She was satirizing one of Sartre's famous examples in which he illustrates how a waiter is in bad faith by playing a role.

Sartre understood that language plays an important role in establishing and amplifying love by making the world more beautiful through his words. He also loved the game. Not unlike Kierkegaard's Johannes, Sartre said that the possibility of winning over a woman and the opportunity to charm excited him most. He found the conquests easy, but the process draining: "I'd come back from a rendezvous, mouth dry, facial muscles tired from too much smiling, voice still dripping with honey and heart full of a disgust to which I was unwilling to pay any attention, and which was masked by satisfaction at having 'advanced my affairs'".[46]

However, in *Being and Nothingness*, Sartre argued that seduction and fascination are not enough. For love to come to fruition, one still needs the beloved's participation, which Sartre assumed would happen when he enchants the other's freedom. The frustration is that one cannot force another to reciprocate love, and no one wants to demand to be loved. Lovers want the other to freely choose to love them. Nevertheless, loving is ultimately a "project of making oneself be loved".[47]

Sartre concludes that love is destructible in three ways: dissatisfaction, insecurity, and interference by others. First, lovers will never be satisfied, because love is deceptive in that it involves a desire for reciprocation, but games of seduction and fascination mask it. However, it is debatable whether this is something to frown upon. It is wholly conceivable that two lovers know and accept that seduction and fascination are part of the game of loving relationships and embrace it, but Sartre neglects this line of thought. Second, love is insecure because at any time the beloved can break the spell of reciprocity and look at the lover as an object, that is, as a means to an end. Lovers can never fully trust each other: they can never truly know that they are not instruments for each other because they can never merge and thus never fully comprehend each other's consciousness, nor how they truly see each other. Third, there will always be other people who look at the lovers and disrupt the harmony and illusion they had with making each other the foundation of their existence and to transcend the lovers when they are trying so hard to be untranscendable. Sartre says this is why lovers like privacy: because other people are always looking, thereby revealing other possibilities for divulging lovers' secrets.[48]

Masochism

It is impossible to grasp the beloved's freedom through seduction while maintaining the objectivity that is necessary to understand how one is perceived. One does not want to end up with a puppet, because not only does that spell the end of the loving relationship, but also there is no possibility for self-discovery in a relationship with a puppet. Both lovers try to seduce and fascinate each other and are each other's projects. The failure of seduction turns to masochism. One lets oneself be used as an instrument in an attempt to reveal how one appears as an object. Nevertheless, one is still using the other as an instrument to achieve this goal and so masochism is also unsuccessful. And yet, Sartre supposes that failure is actually the goal anyway.[49] So, ironically, one succeeds in and enjoys failing. With the failure of masochism – a strategy of assimilating oneself into the beloved – one throws oneself back into trying to appropriate the beloved, and this is sadism.

Sadism

Before exposing Sartre's interest in sadism, it is important to note that there is something very unique about sexual desire for him. Unlike other forms of desire, such as hunger, fulfillment does not extinguish sexual desire. No matter how much sex one has, one always wants more. Sartre concludes that this means that there must be another goal besides satisfaction, and he proposes that it is incarnating the other's freedom.[50]

Incarnation in this context is the process of fascinating each other's freedom with caresses and to make it materialize through their flesh. Stripped of possibilities, freedom ought to be transfixed. Sartre likens it to skimming cream from milk, where the beloved's freedom is the cream, and body is the milk.[51] The idea is that unhomogenizing (i.e., incarnating) freedom from the body should give lovers more tangible insights into each other. This would go some way toward explaining why two people in love like to touch each other so much.

This would be an ideal strategy to capture glimpses of each other's secrets, except for three key problems, according to Sartre. One, this is only a temporary situation lasting as long as caresses can be enchanting.

Two, if one of the lovers stops transcending, that lover is effectively initiating a masochistic encounter. Three, in using bodies, each person becomes an instrument. As soon as one attempts to grasp the other's freedom, reciprocity breaks, and the affair turns sadistic.[52]

Whereas desire is about caressing and using one's own flesh to incarnate the other's freedom, sadism attempts to force it without reciprocity. Sadism treats the other as an instrument and uses violence to force the other into ungraceful positions and acts, which creates the illusion that one holds the other's freedom. The sadist's favorite moment is when a victim shows pain or humiliation because it looks as if the victim's consciousness is revealed through the body. Nevertheless, sadism also fails because the victim exercises freedom in two key respects: the victim freely chooses when to surrender, and the sadist cannot control the victim's gaze or thinking.[53]

The most pressing question regarding the above sadomasochistic strategies is why Sartre thought lovers' consciousnesses are better revealed during sex. Practically speaking, it makes sense that without clothes, where skin touches skin, it seems as if there is nothing physical coming between two bodies intertwined. People feel intensely intimate, as though they are present in the moment, forgetting everything except each other's touch. At this time, they tend to have a very narrow focus and purpose. Nevertheless, it is a stretch to propose that caressing is a reliable way to reveal thinking. Certainly, one might be able to see the other's body react to pleasure or pain, but whether and to what extent that contributes to deeper knowledge is questionable. Moreover, as Sartre recognized, it is easy to lie. In this case, it is not difficult to act as if one is swept away by the beloved's touch, while at the same time thinking about something completely different, such as plans for the weekend.

Sartre concludes that the goal of love, to merge, is impossible because people are fundamentally disconnected.[54] In his fictional works, he also illuminates the abyss between lovers. For example, in *The Room*, the sick husband Pierre asks his wife Eve about their eternal separation and voices the impossibility of love: "There is a wall between you and me. I see you, I speak to you, but you're on the other side. What keeps us from loving?"[55] Also, in *Lucifer and the Lord*, the warlord, Goetz, illustrates the frustration that lovers want what they cannot have. Goetz's unrealizable desire to merge with his lover Hilda perplexes him: "you *are not myself*. It's intolerable. I cannot understand why we are still two people. I should like to become you, and still remain myself".[56]

In sum, Sartre saw romantic loving as inherently problematic. The source of the problem is that lovers attempt to merge in order to discover aspects of themselves that they cannot alone because they think that this will help them to become complete. Nevertheless, there is an insurmountable abyss between people, which means that lovers can never completely know what each other thinks, and thus they can never definitively capture the secrets of their being lost to the other. The upshot is that people cannot truly apprehend one another, and lovers are forever caught in a vicious circle of assimilation and appropriation and are doomed to conflict.

Sartre's solutions

Now that we have seen why Sartre thought romantic loving to be so alluring but problematic, some possible solutions to be found within Sartre's writing and personal life are explored. These include: choosing to love, embracing the anxiety of love, respecting each other's freedom, being transparent to one another, and prioritizing each other.

Choosing to love

The allure of loving, according to Sartre, is the blissful feeling of having found one's *raison d'être*. This is the source of sentimental expressions such as being made for each other or soul mates.[57] Nevertheless, such phrases are fallacious because lovers are not destined for one another. Unlike Plato's character Aristophanes, who described love as looking for one's other half, Sartre said it would actually be humiliating to be made for one another because it would cheapen the relationship. Freely choosing to love is much more interesting.

The basis of such a choice is that "existence precedes essence", which means that one exists first and defines oneself through one's choice of action.[58] Such freedom renders existence absurd because with no foundations or a god we are abandoned without predetermined morals, values, reasons for existence, or natural affinities with others. Presumably even sharing a gene pool does not guarantee understanding. Nevertheless, Sartre's attitude is also positive and liberating because it gives us a blank slate to choose our own values and meaning. One of Dostoyevsky's characters famously claims that without God, everything is permitted. Sartre's existential thinking starts here. If God is dead, then what?[59]

Existence preceding essence also means that although one is nothing to begin with, one gives one's life meaning by purposefully launching oneself into life and striving for goals.[60] For Sartre, there is no such thing as an essence consisting of latent motives that cause one to act in a certain way. Although the past is like a ball and chain because one is the sum of one's actions, one can always choose to change one's behavior. Psychological determinism is alluring because it seems to provide a means of escape from the anxiety of having to choose and take responsibility for one's actions, but it is what Sartre called bad faith. Bad faith is hiding the truth from oneself. Nevertheless, since Sartre rejected the Freudian idea of unconscious phenomena, he considered it impossible to hide the truth from oneself. Either one knows the truth, is ignorant of it, or is mistaken.[61]

Action incorporates intention and choosing; otherwise, it would be simply motion. Only by throwing oneself into living and loving does one discover one's intentions. Sartre's emphasis on action suggests that just as the hammering exposes that something is a hammer, so too does loving reveal love.[62] In *Existentialism is a Humanism*, Sartre reiterates that we are what we do, and a romantic loving relationship is the sum of the loving actions.[63] This also means that loving is not an abstraction or a mystical force. Loving is intentional: it is love *of* and sparked *by* someone.[64] Lovers choose to love and choose to do loving things, and those loving actions are directed toward a particular lover. While it might feel like we have been hit by cupid's arrow when we fall in love, it is up to us to decide whether to act on the feelings, to take charge of creating loving relationships, and to write our own love narratives.

However, Sartre also suggested that loving is more than an action because no matter how commonplace the relationship appears, no one experiences it in exactly the same way. From a functional point of view, almost anyone could perform those actions usually associated with love, such as dating and starting a family. However, if love is reduced to utility or outcome, then it is impersonal.[65] Every person's experiences, choices, emotions, and ends are unique. Actions always occur within a situation and so derive meaning from the context. Hence, for Sartre, loving is also to choose oneself as one who does loving things.[66]

For example, in *Huis Clos*, one man, Garcin, and two women, Estelle and Inez, find themselves in hell, which consists of an eternity together in a small sparse room without mirrors. Unconvincingly, Garcin suggests to the glamorous Estelle that love is a choice: "But if you'll make the effort, if you'll only *will* it hard enough, I dare say we can really love each other".[67] His pathetic plea raises the question as to whether love conceived as purely choice is sufficient.

Yet, classifying loving as purely a feeling is also insufficient. In an attempt to reconcile loving as a choice and a feeling, Sartre introduces the idea of a state. A state is a synthesis of activities directed toward an overarching project.[68] In this sense, loving is not simply a collection of discrete loving actions but an enterprise that ventures toward creating a relationship. Loving actions contribute toward and reaffirm one's original choice to engage in the loving relationship.

The key difference between a state and a feeling can be painted through an example: when lovers argue, both are angry; neither feels loving at that point, yet both still conceivably claim to love each other overall. This understanding of loving as a state means that one can behave unlovingly and yet still claim to live the state of loving. However, this contradicts Sartre's idea that only loving actions reveal love.

A loving relationship, in Sartre's view, is a synthesis of past loving actions, presently choosing oneself as a loving person doing loving things, and projecting oneself into the future as one who will love a particular person. Sartre emphasized the personal nature of loving and the important role of choice. The problem is that lovers can always choose differently. This appears to be one of the reasons that Sartre places so much emphasis on the future and becoming, so much so that he claimed that "love is given its meaning as love by its being in the future".[69] Here he highlights a central feature of romantic loving that is the hope that it lasts beyond the passion of the moment.

In *Notebooks*, Sartre further explored loving as a choice, and his portrayal appears to be related to Kierkegaard's leap when he said love involves "undertakings" and "oaths".[70] As a conscious choice, it is neither a given nor a "reality underlying my being".[71] Nor is love simply an experience, because to treat it so is "to decide to decide at every instant whether one loves, which is already not to love, not to see that to love and to will to love are one and the same".[72] The problem is that, on the one hand, if it were just a matter of willing to love, it would be an "abstract decision"; and on the other hand, if it were just a matter of loving without willing it or without choosing it, it would be a "purely passive experience".[73] So, it is a matter of both choosing to love and allowing "oneself to be overcome by one's love".[74] This makes sense if love is understood as being aroused by someone and emphasizes that reciprocity is required for a loving relationship.

In *Being and Nothingness*, we saw that Sartre qualified the idea that loving is an action by arguing that it is not a matter of fulfilling a function but rather a state. Later, in *Notebooks*, he suggests that loving is a choice as well as a feeling. Nevertheless, Sartre's explanation is ambiguous because he did not identify which elements of a loving relationship are chosen. Moreover, it is confusing when he said that to choose to love is not to love, and to love and to will to love are the same thing. Although he said that choice supports loving feelings, in an earlier work he had argued that feelings *are* choices: emotions are free because they are responses to given situations, ways of relating to the world, strategies, and means to ends.[75] Similarly in *Being and Nothingness*, he classifies love as a series of actions directed toward an original choice. All these instances do point to loving as a choice. However, later, in *Notebooks*, Sartre indicates that there is something about loving that choosing and willing cannot fully explain. It is as if instead of addressing it, he sidesteps around it, and his failure to resolve and clarify this issue would go some way to explaining why he never wrote a cohesive piece on loving.

Embracing the anxiety of loving

There are some indications that Sartre was looking to expand his views about romantic loving beyond the fundamental attitudes in *Being and Nothingness* of assimilating and appropriating. One hint appears in a cryptic footnote, where he refers to a possibility of "deliverance and salvation" via "a radical conversion" but did not expand on it.[76] Another clue appears in a later interview where he said that although sadism and masochism normally taint love, there are possibilities for moving beyond that dynamic.[77] Sartre's other existential works provide more cues about what such a radical conversion could be.

Notwithstanding Sartre's defense in *Being and Nothingness* of the radical separation between freedoms and associated frustration and anxiety, elsewhere Sartre suggests leaping into relationships in spite of the issues. In *Notebooks*, Sartre said that a fundamental anxiety exists in the structure of love because lovers hate to think the relationship will end, but there is every possibility it will because love given freely can also be withdrawn freely. The only way to deal with the anxiety is to embrace it.[78] Like Kierkegaard's leap, being in a romantic loving relationship is a difficult and life-changing decision. It is filled with anxiety because it is unknown where one will land and what one will find there. There are no guarantees that the beloved will reciprocate or that one will find any kind of safety in the other.

For example, in *Nausea*, although Anny has a new lover, she says that she does not think she will ever feel as passionate about anyone as much as her ex-boyfriend Roquentin and does not want to become as deeply engaged ever again, because it requires such a massive effort. She says to Roquentin about loving someone: "You have to have energy, generosity, blindness. There is even a moment, in the very beginning, when you have to jump across a precipice: if you think about it you don't do it. I know I'll never jump again".[79]

Orestes in Sartre's play *The Flies* explores a similar theme. He comes to realize that he is incapable of loving because he does not leap. Without ties, commitments, and responsibilities, he is "gloriously aloof", "light as gossamer", "like strands torn by the wind from spiders' webs that one sees floating ten feet above the ground".[80] However, this sort of freedom is meaningless because he is not engaging concretely in life, and on reflection he describes himself as "a mere shadow of a man".[81] His loving relationships are also vacuous: "The only loves I've known were phantom loves, rare and vacillating as will-o'-the-wisps. The solid passions of the living were never mine".[82] He is free from many things but realizes he is not using his freedom to do anything meaningful. Another point that Orestes raises is that love requires self-surrender, but he has never had anything concrete in his life to surrender. He alludes to the idea that self-surrender in this case is not self-denial, but rather risking oneself by leaping into life.

Sartre's film *The Chips are Down* also provides a variation on this theme. It is a story about Pierre and Eve who meet in the afterlife, fall in love, discover they were destined for one another, and are given another chance to live. If they succeed in loving each other "with perfect confidence" for 24 hours, they will be granted a second life on earth together.[83] If they fail, they will return to the afterlife and go their separate ways because love has a future only in living. Pierre and Eve do fail, but do not try to stop another couple:

> Pierre and Eve look at each other, hesitating.
> They smile gently at the young couple.
> "Try," Pierre advises.
> "Try it anyway," murmurs Eve.[84]

Pierre and Eve are not suggesting that such a goal is achievable but rather that loving requires a leap, since it entails engaging with others regardless of its potential for success. Leaping is unlikely to be a portal out of the circle of bad faith relations mentioned in *Being and Nothingness* because it will ultimately be unsuccessful, reiterating Sartre's conclusion that romantic relationships begin and end in failure. In Sartre's writing, there is no happily ever after.

Respecting each other's freedom

In *Notebooks*, Sartre realized a new possibility for loving: a kind of authentic love that respects the others' freedom and goals.[85] Although he still maintained that sadism and masochism are lovers' *modi operandi*, this development in his thinking is much more similar to Simone de Beauvoir's understanding of authentic loving. This portrayal emphasizes freedom as the dominant dynamic rather than power because it appreciates the other as a subject, acknowledges that total possession is neither possible nor desirable, indicates that mutually respecting other freedoms is the basis for connecting with others and overcoming the great divide, and is also more reminiscent of friendship. In an interview, he also said that true relationships would be based on "love and esteem", but he suggests that people tend not to be enlightened enough to transcend sadomasochistic distractions.[86]

Herewith Sartre offered a competing view of the theme in *Being and Nothingness* – conflict in romantic relationships means that they contain the seed of their own destruction. Sparks of such an attitude do exist with the idea that recognition depends on how two people value each other. Nevertheless, Sartre did not explore this in depth and was quick to conclude that conflict ensues.

Notebooks opens up the possibility of a loving relationship that is more palatable to those looking for more positivity in love: the joy and safety one gets from being in a relationship where one does not feel as though one is a possession or wants to possess the beloved and respects the other person's goals. Nevertheless, it remains ambiguous as to how such a loving relationship can be constructed. Moreover, he said that the attempt to overcome sadomasochism destroys loving because it skips over the "unveiling" that occurs on the sexual playfield.[87] While it is a bleak attitude because sadomasochism is part and parcel of love, it also suggests that sexual games are still worth playing because it is a way of learning about oneself and each other.

Being transparent

Looking to the way Sartre lived his philosophy reveals further possibilities. First, there is the practice of transparency. In *War Diaries*, Sartre explained that he thought that a great man had to keep himself free. So, after seducing a woman, Sartre would insist that she not infringe on his freedom, which meant that she must permit him to pursue relationships with other women. Not wanting to be a hypocrite, Sartre grandly offered the same precious gift of freedom to his girlfriends. Initially the women accepted. Yet after a while, they would give up on him and happily he would return to his bachelor status before seeking another girlfriend with whom he would demonstrate his freedom. As usual, after falling in love with Beauvoir, he offered her this gift of her freedom (as if he owned it to give). Initially, Sartre was shocked and disappointed that Beauvoir accepted his terms, but later realized how lucky he was.[88]

Although Beauvoir and Sartre were devoted, intellectual, loving companions for life, they did not marry or have children and were not monogamous. They considered their relationship to be essential and primary, meaning that they were the most important person for one another but free to have other love affairs, which they saw as contingent or secondary loves.[89] In practice, this meant that although they allowed each other to fall in love with other people, they would never allow their love for, or commitment to, each other to be usurped by one of the contingent lovers. Their relationship was based on trust rather than sexual monogamy.[90]

In an arrangement of which Nietzsche would have approved, Beauvoir and Sartre agreed to a two-year relationship and thought that being completely honest and open with each other would avoid jealousy.[91] They entered a transparency pact to tell each other every sordid detail of other relationships. However, they found they could not be completely open to everyone. They lied profusely to their secondary lovers to spare their feelings. For example, they often lied about with whom Sartre was spending his time. As much as possible, he kept his lovers in total ignorance of each other because they were notoriously possessive and demanding.[92]

Another issue is how transparent one can be with another. In an interview, and to another girlfriend, Sartre admitted that he often lied to Beauvoir.[93] While in *Being and Nothingness* Sartre saw lying to oneself as a form of bad faith, there is no philosophical issue with lying to others. Sartre's comments reiterate the problem of complete disclosure and futility of the romantic ideal. Moreover, if it is true, it is a confession that he could not maintain both transparency and freedom in his loving relationships.

Treating each other as the most important person

Another solution that Sartre and Beauvoir practiced, and that Sartre discussed philosophically, was establishing the beloved as the most important relationship in one's life. Despite having many significant relationships, Sartre and Beauvoir did forever treat each other as primary, that is, more important than any other. This is a manifestation of Sartre's discussion in *Being and Nothingness* about lovers seeking to become the limit of each other's freedom.

However, this creates a problem that was addressed in *The Chips are Down*. Both Pierre and Eve have personal ends that were left incomplete at the time of their deaths. During the 24-hour trial period, they each attempt to pursue their unfinished business. Specifically, Pierre finds out that his comrades will be massacred the following day and on returning to earth tries to warn them. In the meantime, Eve pursues her goal, which is trying to save her sister who is in love with Eve's gold-digging and murderous husband. Pierre chooses to die fighting for his friends rather than to live on earth to love Eve. If love is placing the beloved above all else and making them the source of all values, then Pierre fails in this respect. It is ambiguous whether Eve pursues her goals in response to Pierre's leaving or whether she would have done so anyway. However, there is every indication that she was waiting for Pierre, and her relationship with him was more important than the one with her sister. When Pierre tells Eve that he will not be back in time for the deadline, Eve is devastated, and her husband murders her – again. It must also be noted, however, that she does not give up her own ends to help Pierre achieve his. Neither makes the other's ends their own, which as per *Notebooks* is part of authentic loving. Thus, it is understandable that once they meet up again in the afterlife, Eve considers Pierre's claim to love her as inane.

This example highlights the magnitude of the decisions that lovers make: Pierre was torn between loving Eve and saving the lives of his comrades. They were neither the most important people nor the main project in each other's lives. An important condition Sartre raises in *Being and Nothingness* with respect to freedom is: *at what price* can one choose otherwise? The issue is that while other choices are possible, they would be inconsistent with the way one chooses oneself and gives one's world meaning. One's possibilities depend on how one chooses to live. While insisting on radical freedom, it can be seen here that one's being can be understood in terms of an overarching project in life, that of creating oneself. Sartre's existential psychoanalysis aims to uncover this project by exploring the meaning one gives to one's actions.

One's subjective interpretation of things as threats or opportunities limits one's world, not the objective presence of such things. In this way, one is entirely responsible for one's situation. For example, one looks upon a mountain crag and decides it is unclimbable. Yet, it has become an obstacle only because one recognizes the possibility of climbing it. Others may have never even contemplated the idea of climbing it, and so it could never be a limit to them. This is similar to Kierkegaard's and Nietzsche's ideas that some people do not look into the abyss. Thus, Sartre proposed, we create our own obstacles because they reveal themselves through the ends that we choose. Similarly, commitments such as marriage are not limitations but rather freely chosen priorities that one maintains if one's intention is to honor one's wedding vows.[94]

While Sartre's later writings feature the element of authenticity, he avoids it as much as possible in *Being and Nothingness* because, he said, it implies morality.[95] It implies morality because it could be taken to mean that someone *should* strive to achieve authenticity; or in other words, it implies a prescribed set of values and thus risks becoming a project of bad faith. This is something Sartre wanted to avoid – or at least to defer – since he emphasized choosing one's own values. In an ambiguous footnote, Sartre suggested that authenticity is the key to escaping bad faith, but he dismissed it as a digression.[96] Yet in a statement that sounds like authenticity, Sartre said that if an act is consistent with how one wants to be, or in other words, if it is in accordance with one's chosen project or essence, then it is free.[97] Sartre alludes to a view similar to Stirner: that one imagines oneself as the center and author of one's own universe.

In *War Diaries*, Sartre discussed a man who is called to war. The experience shocked him into realizing that his pre-war life was inauthentic and bourgeois. He wonders how to behave when his wife visits him at the front. Does he reveal his new authentic attitude or comply with his wife's expectations and play the role of a loving committed husband?[98] The old project was inauthentic, the new project is authentic, and so the answer seems clear: he ought to break his previous inauthentic commitments. But what if the man had authentically committed himself to the project of being a loving husband? Sartre assumed being a soldier and a loving husband are mutually exclusive for this man, and he did not address what happens when authentic projects change and clash.

Being responsible for one's interpretation, and by extension one's actions, means that individuals are "condemned to be free".[99] In light of this, the loving relationship between Pierre and Eve can be viewed either deterministically, as though it were destined to fail, or existentially, as though Pierre and Eve made their choices with full awareness of the consequences and embraced the responsibility for their actions and choice of being. They had every intention of placing each other as their top priorities during their second chance on earth, but they did not know until they threw themselves into life. As Sartre pointed out in *Being and Nothingness*, at what cost can one do such a thing? Only with a radical modification of his very being could Pierre have left his friends to the ambush. The cost, it seems, was too great for Pierre. Their loving relationship fails because it does not fit within their fundamental projects in life and confirms the fragility of romantic loving. Yet Pierre and Eve's response to the young couple, to try anyway, shows that Sartre acknowledged the importance of leaping in the face of absurdity.

Key considerations

Narcissistic view of romantic loving

Sartre suggested that our vanity drives us to find out how others perceive us.[100] Such statements as this open Sartre to the accusation that his philosophy of love is narcissistic or egoistic.[101] Sartre's overemphasis on love as the desire to be loved partially justifies such criticism. Indeed, Sartre admitted that individuals can be construed as self-interested or egoistic because life is a project of one's self. However, Sartre's philosophy is more nuanced. Self-interest is only one possible way of being.[102] In an interview, he explained that narcissism is the fixation with an idea or image that one has of oneself, which he would not advocate.[103] Rather, he promoted actively to engage in the world and with others to deepen self-knowledge.

In Sartre's view, loving others is just as important as loving oneself because they are vital in self-discovery. One loves in order to become oneself, and the other is a condition for becoming. Understanding oneself is not necessarily detrimental to others. It does not mean that one disregards the other's rights and welfare. Nevertheless, one does so because one values the other's opinion. Thus, being-for-others is an important and necessary aspect of being human.

At times, Sartre was ashamed about how he treated women and told Beauvoir that he felt "like a grubby bastard. A really small-time bastard at that, a sort of sadistic university type and civil-service Don Juan–disgusting", and he vowed to change his vulgar ways.[104] Nevertheless, he seemed to care for the welfare of his lovers and ex-lovers. He was extremely generous, writing plays in which they would act, and he enjoyed supporting them financially.

He had so many mistresses that he had to keep a strict schedule to fit them in with time for his writing. He referred to himself as "the district nurse" who went on rounds to visit his insecure and devoted lovers.[105] Sylvie Le Bon, who became Beauvoir's executrix, accused Sartre of having a "god complex", driving his lovers into dependency and creating for himself a twisted pseudo-family that he had tried so hard to avoid. Sartre said he did not want to be a "jerk" and abandon them and felt obliged and grateful to them.[106] Beauvoir said that he just felt guilty.[107]

The fact that Sartre condemned the way he treated women suggests that if he lived consistently with his philosophy, then he was judging it to be ignoble. On the one hand, he seemed to be living inconsistently with his philosophy in *Being and Nothingness* since despite his philosophical emphasis on freedom, he did not seem to think himself free from obligations to secondary lovers after the affairs ended. However, there are elements that are consistent with his philosophy, such as the desire to be everything to a lover and to remain free from constraints of money and possessions.

Romantic loving is not a good basis for self-discovery

Sartre presents contradictory portrayals of lovers' abilities to provide sufficiently deep reflections and understanding. In *Being and Nothingness*, Sartre argued that because another holds the secret to what one is, one tries to be as close as possible to the other to discover those secrets. This is why he proposed that intimacy and sensuality are important ways of exploring oneself through and with lovers and unleashing deeper levels of understanding.[108] The implication is that the person with whom one can achieve maximum intimacy ought to be able to provide the best reflection. Indeed, lovers often do value each other's opinions more highly than anyone else's.

Yet, it is conceivable that intimate relations close down certain possibilities for knowledge about oneself, especially when awkwardness, discomfort, or regret ensues. Furthermore, some lovers do not want a partner to unleash self-discovery, especially if it brings to light unpleasant aspects of oneself. Alternatively, lovers become agreeable and accepting of each other to such an extent that they fail to provide any reflection or insight into each other. Further to this, it is also conceivable that other people with whom one is not intimately involved could better fill this role, such as friends and family or, as Nietzsche also acknowledged, enemies.

Sartre broaches this latter view – that enemies provide better reflections than lovers – in some of his fictional works. For example, in *Huis Clos*, when there are only two people whom Garcin can talk to in order to explore that deeper aspect of his being, he says the acquiescent Estelle does not matter, but Inez does because she hates and challenges him.[109] Goetz, the ruthless general in *Lucifer and the Lord*, also demonstrates that lovers do not provide valuable reflections. Goetz has kept a woman, Catherine, by force and values her only to the extent that she hates him. Later in the story, he tells another lover, Hilda, "I cannot see my soul any longer, because it is under my nose; I need someone to lend me his eyes".[110] Hilda cannot see him because she loves him, Goetz grumbles, and so he sets out to find his most hated enemy.

In these plays Sartre suggested that the reason enemies are better for exploring one's being than lovers is because their distance enables them to provide a more critical perspective. In a passage reminiscent of Nietzsche's admiration for friends who can be enemies, Sartre warned against acquiescence in *Being and Nothingness*. Resistance is preferable because it provokes us to be brave and bold and to stand up for what we want and believe in.[111]

In the context of loving, this comment suggests that tolerance is highly undesirable. Sartre did not explore the possibility of romantic loving that would include constructive criticism, which is a connection that Nietzsche seemed also reluctant to make explicit. If the lovers in each of the examples above had been more challenging, then they would have provided a more helpful basis for self-discovery. If the purpose of a loving relationship is to discover as much as possible about oneself, then the more motivating that partners can be for one another, the better. Indeed, Sartre's relationship with Beauvoir suggests lovers can be good sparring partners.[112]

Narrow view of romantic loving

Sartre's assumption in *Being and Nothingness* is that wanting to discover one's being through the eyes of the beloved means one desires to merge with the beloved, but he proposed that this is impossible. Nevertheless, Goetz in *Lucifer and the Lord* tells Hilda toward the end of the play that "You are myself", suggesting that lovers come to feel *as if* they are merged.[113] Sartre's philosophy does not account for such feelings of bonding.

Sartre might respond that the problem with connections to others is that they are ambiguous and tenuous. It is certainly possible to find commonalities with others – for example, with those with the same types of chromosomes – but this is not a ready-made platform for full disclosure of each other's consciousnesses. For example, it would be mistaken to assume that every woman apprehends femininity or every man apprehends masculinity in exactly the same way, especially as there is no universal understanding of gender. Similarly, how people use language and form opinions is individual. Sartre was right in acknowledging that while another person can tell us what they think, we will never know with perfect confidence if they are telling the truth. One can approximate another's consciousness or make assumptions about what it must be like but can never know it.

Although Sartre took a broader view of romantic loving in *Notebooks*, his conclusions remain ambiguous and underdeveloped. Taking his ideas further would require him to dispute the assumption that lovers aim to merge, and this would require either a reassessment of the two fundamental attitudes in *Being and Nothingness* – that is, assimilation and appropriation – or the creation of another attitude. Limiting himself to only two attitudes leaves romantic loving relationships inside the vicious circle, and lovers keep flipping from one attitude to the other with no escape.

Sartre's contributions to our understanding of romantic loving are as follows. First, Sartre places great importance on the sexual aspects of relationships since the intimacy developed through such interactions opens up a new means of communication and understanding between people. Nevertheless, it is an unreliable means of doing so.

Second, Sartre pointed out that loving understood as an action risks reducing loving to a function. However, he avoids such a conclusion by emphasizing the uniqueness of every loving experience. Because one is an individual, one's loving experiences, choices, and projects are unique.

Third, Sartre and Beauvoir established a life-long loving relationship. Although some of the romantic elements faded, such as sexual passion, they sought romantic involvements elsewhere. One of the underlying issues for them in practice was that although they had established their own relationship as primary, the secondary lovers were disappointed to discover that they were not in an exclusive relationship and that they were not the most important person in the other's life. This made the secondary relationships unromantic and unsustainable. Some of Sartre's plays emphasized the effort and bravery that leaping into loving requires and also the desire for lovers to justify their being in each other. However, as Sartre pointed out in *Being and Nothingness*, there will always be others with more opinions of us, meaning that even if merging with another for eternity were possible, it is inherently an unstable means of justifying one's existence.

Fourth, Sartre's understanding of romantic loving implies that through merging lovers hope to become complete because they can find lost aspects of their being through the other. The problem is that a lover is faced with two alternatives: either merge with the beloved, which destroys the other's objectivity and means one cannot discover anything (as per *Being and Nothingness*); or leave the beloved as they are and respect the beloved's freedom (as per *Notebooks*), in which case the lover also does not achieve any understanding through the other, since there is no reliable means of establishing a connection. Nevertheless, in Sartre's own experience, lovers do feel united. While Sartre said that he lived his loving relationship with Beauvoir as a "we", philosophically he identified such an idea as problematic, since to be able to say "we", one must understand the other. However, understanding the other is tenuous because of the insurmountable abyss between lovers.

Moreover, in some of his plays Sartre revealed skepticism about whether a beloved would be able to provide a rigorous enough reflection to assist with understanding oneself, and he instead suggested that enemies would be better candidates. While Nietzsche implied the possibility of lovers and married couples also being friends and enemies, Sartre did not take his philosophy in such a direction.

Finally, Sartre's philosophy in *Being and Nothingness* raises questions about how concerned for the beloved's welfare one is, since one is concerned with the other only insofar as one's existence is in question and values the other. Nevertheless, he also condemns the attitude of being indifferent to others. Moreover, Sartre argued that romantic loving is a manifestation of a master-slave dialectic, but romantic loving as he said he experienced it with Beauvoir was different.

Sartre emphasized the importance of freeing oneself from deterministic illusions, such as lovers being destined for one another, in order to be free to choose the loving relationships that one perceives will be most valuable for understanding oneself. Nevertheless, the implication of Sartre's discussion is that romantic loving relationships are inherently disappointing and frustrating. They are conflicted and begin and end in failure because in attempting to merge lovers aim at possessing each other and impinging on each other's freedom. While Sartre did mention the possibility of an attitude to others that breaks the vicious circle of bad faith relations in *Being and Nothingness*, he did not provide a comprehensive resolution to amicable being-with-others within his existential realm.

For Sartre, one loves the experience that lovers arouse. One chooses love by choosing loving behavior, which is an attempt to complete one's being by becoming one's own foundation. Others reveal new dimensions of one's being and expand one's possibilities. Others can also limit one's freedom but only insofar as one accepts their authority. Lovers tend to be so important to each other that they value each other's opinions above anyone else's. This gives lovers great power to define each other. Being desperate to control that view, lovers attempt to possess each other's freedom. However, possessing or merging is impossible because there is no reliable basis for connecting, and lovers are rendered vulnerable and frustrated. Anxiety is inevitable because romantic loving is insecure, but it must be accepted and lived. Authenticity is impossible unless lovers let go of the desire to merge, but since the desire to understand oneself and become complete is fundamentally human, this letting go is unlikely. This is one explanation as to why romantic loving relationships can be so frustrating and disappointing.

6
Simone de Beauvoir and Loving Authentically

Romantic loving is, for Simone de Beauvoir, existentially dangerous. The two most important points of departure from the treatment of loving that Stirner, Kierkegaard, Nietzsche, and Sartre identified are: Beauvoir's acknowledgment that situations modify freedom; her attempt to create an ethics; and the way she incorporates equality and economic independence as a way to navigate through the dangers of love. Less concerned with creating a system than Jean-Paul Sartre was, Beauvoir was more attentive to practical solutions.[1] I argue that while Beauvoir did not solve all the existential dilemmas (mainly because she appeals to non-existential solutions), she does enrich our understanding of the complexity of the problems of loving with her analysis of what constitutes inauthentic loving and the conditions under which authentic loving ought to be achievable.

Beauvoir argued in *The Second Sex* that one has to be free from oppression in order to be free to love authentically. The problem for women is that throughout all of history, they have been subordinate to men. Our patriarchal society has shaped women's situation, inhibited women's capacity for free choice, and so practically, women have had fewer possibilities available to them than men have had. Women's disadvantaged status explains why dependency became a ubiquitous condition for them. This is undesirable existentially because it is an escape from standing forth in the world as a self-governing subject. The existential rub lies in the fact that individuals are responsible for their actions, and therefore, women have been complicit in their subordinate situation. Beauvoir called for men to end the oppression and for women to stop accepting it. Only when women are free from oppression and dependence and are free to pursue the same opportunities as men will authentic loving be possible, according to Beauvoir.

Unlike the philosophy of Sartre, whose pre-Marxist existentialism can be quarantined to his early works, Beauvoir's writing is more integrated, making it difficult to isolate existential texts. For example, her magnum opus *The Second Sex* is a medley of existentialism in the premium it places on individual self-assertion and transcendence, Marxism in the emphasis she gives to work as the path to freedom and equality, and Marxist determinism in her thesis that economic changes will bring about social change. It also includes social and biological determinism in her pardoning of women's bad faith on account of their upbringing and reproductive organs. This breadth of ideas shall be discussed further in the context of her philosophy of loving.

The phrase "I am not myself today" is common enough, but *how* or *why* one is oneself is much less common. Beauvoir's philosophy begins here. She finds it astonishing that she should be in this particular life as opposed to thousands of other possibilities and starts questioning her existence.[2]

Like her existentially minded predecessors, Beauvoir agreed that one is what one does, existence precedes essence, individuals create their own values and reasons for living, and one's being is one's passion, which is one's choice.[3] To be an individual is to express oneself meaningfully by engaging in the world and striving toward concrete ends. Beauvoir replaced Nietzsche's ideal of the *Übermensch* with a more general view of striving toward whatever one chooses via concrete projects. Exciting and liberating, Beauvoir said existentialism provides the clarity to realize that one's destiny is in one's hands. The very antithesis of doom and gloom, existentialism aims at self-fulfillment through whatever project one chooses in life. The question of life is not whether it is useful or worthwhile but whether and how one wants to live.[4]

We are not, however, absolutely free, according to Beauvoir. To adjust one's possibilities in light of limitations, as Sartre argued in *Being and Nothingness*, is an abstract and passive notion of freedom. In Beauvoir's estimation, there are some things that cannot be controlled, such as being seasick or crying. Another example is a woman shut up in a harem. Beauvoir disagreed with Sartre's point that she is free (albeit within her confines) on the grounds that a harem girl cannot transcend her situation, and so her mental freedom is meaningless. Beauvoir realized that she needed to appeal to a collective struggle, and this is where she betrayed her existentialism: by trying to reconcile it with Marxism.[5]

Importance of others

Beauvoir was compelled to find a means of relating to others that overcomes Sartre's pessimism and is based on respect. She discounted egoism as naïve because its reaction to others stealing the world is hatred, and it neglects the positive side of others' existences. She acknowledged that beings are separate and opposed, and we cannot be united because we have different ends.[6] However, this is nothing to be depressed about because others also *give* the world by infusing our environment and endeavors with meaning and possibilities.[7] We learn about our existence, our freedom, and our individuality through relationships with the world and other people because, for better or worse, they influence our actions and situations.

Beauvoir agreed with Sartre that conflict is a fundamental part of life because we clash with other freedoms.[8] Nevertheless, embracing the conflict is a necessary part of life because transcending (*pour-soi*) is not easy, and giving it up means giving up existing.[9] Transcendence is necessary to being a sovereign subject, which Beauvoir defines as actively, assertively, ambitiously, creatively, and courageously pushing oneself forward in the world, overcoming oneself, going beyond the given in life to be an agent in one's life, and engaging in projects that one creates for oneself.

The opposite of transcendence is immanence (*en-soi*). Facticity is the given of one's existence, that is, the situation one finds oneself in, including one's body, anatomy, nationality, class, roles, or functions.[10] Passively to accept one's facticity is to live immanently. Traditionally, according to Beauvoir, women have been doomed to immanence because they passively maintained life instead of risking it like men. Their normal destiny was marriage and maternity, relegated to the monotonous chores of childbearing and housework that she said are the boring, repetitive, unproductive, and uncreative maintenance activities of life that are not future-oriented.[11] This was, however, generally the easiest option for women because of the unequal opportunities afforded to men and women, historically. For example, the workplace has been an unattractive option because women have been less respected, have suffered more mundane work, and have earned less than men for the same work.[12]

To resign oneself to the separation between people and disengaging from others means one is taking the easy road by turning away from possibilities and, hence, ceasing to transcend. For example, in *Who Shall Die?* the character Jean-Pierre adopts a nihilistic outlook because he assumes that there is no possible connection between people. He avoids telling Clarice he loves her because if people are forever separate, commitment and promises must be nonsense and love must be a lie. Yet, one is the sum of one's actions, and by doing nothing, Jean-Pierre is nothing. It is only by daring to vow that he loves Clarice, throwing himself into loving activities, and projecting a future with her that he is able to live and love authentically. Thus, Beauvoir concludes, we need other people to justify our existence.[13]

Nevertheless, Beauvoir did not mean that the need for others should be taken in the Machiavellian sense of using each other as means to ends. Rather, each individual acts in the context of society. For Beauvoir, people are not always hell, as Sartre's Garcin grumbles in *Huis Clos*, because they give us possibilities that would not exist without them. The important thing for Beauvoir is acknowledging that the world is shared with other people and that one way or another individuals depend on the community for survival, self-definition, and meaning.

The foundation of Beauvoir's philosophy regarding being with others is that they are there. From this, she derived an ethics that makes one accountable to others by virtue of their presence. The question is then: how to reconcile existential philosophy, which emphasizes individual freedom, with her desire for equality and freedom for all? If individuals are free to choose how to live, then is everything permitted, as per Dostoyevsky's character Ivan Karamazov? Beauvoir said that the problem with Nietzsche's will-to-power is that it turns existentialism into solipsism because imposing one's values on others only disbands people and cements their alienation from one another.[14] She wanted to veer away from this, and her attempt to create an existential ethics is a response to this conclusion toward which existential freedom leads.

In *Who Shall Die?* Beauvoir toyed with the hazards of living in a world in which power trumps freedom. It is fourteenth-century Flanders. The town of Vaucelles is under siege. Food supplies are running short. Louis the alderman and the council want to protect the city at all costs, so they decide to evict all the women, children, old, and sick people – "useless mouths" – from the town so that there is more food for the men to protect the city for longer. The decree gives way to an ethical void, paving the way for a new morality based on power. Georges demonstrates the implications of the new situation when he attempts to rape his sister Clarice. Georges argues that his father Louis is effectively murdering Clarice by ousting her useless mouth. George proposes that Louis has replaced laws of justice with power.[15]

It is not until Louis discovers Georges is plotting to kill him and take over the city that Louis finally comprehends his son's warning: once individual freedom is violated, right and wrong no longer matter, and the door is opened to a world in which power triumphs and "Might makes right".[16] Beauvoir's siren is that without ethics based on respect for freedom for all, a savage world emerges.

This means Beauvoir's answer in *The Ethics of Ambiguity* to whether everything is permitted is no. Reasons to get out of bed in the morning do not exist in an abstract Platonic sense, nor does a god give them. One is free to create one's own meaning and values, which are realized through concrete human action. While freedom could mean all-out anarchy, Beauvoir believed it is kept in check because without a god, there is no one at the pearly gates to forgive our sins, and so the responsibility for behavior lies squarely with individuals.[17]

Beauvoir appealed to a moral claim to support one's obligation to others in society. She takes a Kantian approach, by which there are moral capacities inherent in freedom and that people are aware of the difference between one's passion and what is right. One has a moral duty to others because if one values freedom for oneself, then one values it for others. Although an individual is unique and sovereign, so is everyone else. The human condition is universal and collective. Responsibility must exist, according to Beauvoir's ethics, by default of involvement in each other's lives, regardless of choice. Hence, her message in *The Blood of Others* is that coexistence is the bane of our existence.[18] For example, even though Blomart told Hélène he did not love her, he comes to realize that just by consequence of having met her, he is responsible for her. Perturbed, he asks: "what kind of choice had been given her? Could she choose that I love her? That I should not exist? That she should not have met me?...She was there, bound by my docile hands, imprisoned in a joyless love. In spite of herself and in spite of me".[19] The problem is that being responsible for another person negates the other's freedom because people are responsible for themselves.

To summarize Beauvoir's approach to being in the world with others, she maintained that we are abandoned on earth together, and although we are individual and separate, we share common ground, that is, the same world and human condition. Beauvoir appealed to a sort of empathy on these grounds to salvage an "ethics of ambiguity" in which struggles and conflicts are transcended in order to reach for that connection with others. In her sustained attempt to do so, she differentiates herself from Sartre. However, Beauvoir recognized that in practice one's freedom often comes at the expense of others and admits that violence is sometimes necessary to enforce freedom.[20] This suggests that a savage world can emerge even from an ethics based on respect for freedom for all.

Problems of romantic loving

Romantic relationships can be such intoxicating experiences that lovers get lost in euphoria. Like *Tristan and Isolde*, they passionately sink together into the muck and mire of couple-centered immanence, which Beauvoir dismissed as inauthentic or bad faith loving.[21] While anyone can be guilty of inauthentic loving, women have been more susceptible to it than men have because of their oppressive situation. Historically, the problem for women, according to Beauvoir, is that while men appropriated the role of subject, women were delegated to the inessential role of "the Other". Women did not originally choose to be wives and mothers; it was their duty and role in society and the happenstance of biology.

For the existential philosophers, freedom is implicit in one's consciousness. This is one of the meanings of "existence precedes essence": one is born free and creates one's being. Beauvoir suggested that while women have always been ontologically free, they have not been situationally free. However, Beauvoir might better have spoken of restrictions on women's psychosocial freedom, that is, women's social situation limited their perceived freedom, which through their actions (or lack thereof) perpetuated their predicament and influenced their attitude. Society's concept of woman defined her actions instead of a woman's existentially choosing her passion and defining herself.

Beauvoir granted that while there have been many factors influencing women's position as the second sex, the key issue is that women have been complicit in their subordination. Beauvoir built on Hegel's masterslave dialectic but explained that while the slave's oppression is not voluntary, women's is, taking the form of a problem-solving strategy.[22] Women accepted the externally imposed limitations on their social freedom, allowed men to dominate, and have not stood up for their rights – until fairly recently. To voluntarily renounce one's freedom, however, is what Beauvoir called a moral fault or bad faith. Beauvoir mitigates women's complicity when she acknowledges that such renunciation is understandable given that their whole world is constructed in a way that lures them into oppression.[23] So, Beauvoir implied, women's bad faith was a rational decision given that the alternatives and consequences were too costly or unsavory, such as being ostracized from social circles.

It is difficult to see from the existential perspective how Beauvoir can blame women for choosing to accept and perpetuate their condition and yet exonerate them from responsibility for their choice. Beauvoir wanted it both contradictory ways. It is perplexing that she accused women of being complicit in their subservience: "she cheerfully accepts" male propaganda because it is the easiest path; she allows herself to surrender to dependency; and temptations are not totally but "nearly irresistible".[24] Beauvoir did not go so far as to say that women have been ignorant, but rather they have accepted that it is in their best interest to be the second sex.

Then in the next breath Beauvoir seemed to release women from the responsibility of these choices by introducing situation as a limitation on their freedom. For example, Beauvoir said that women have been forced into immanence and otherness, traditions imprison women, and others determine and limit them.[25] Here Beauvoir did not acknowledge women's existential responsibility to be the sum of their actions and their responsibility for creating themselves.

The core problem with Beauvoir's argument is that she equates unpleasant choices with having no choice, which is clearly false. Because we are free, choice is ontological, cannot be denied, and thus one is condemned to choose irrespective of sex and situation. Women always had choices but usually chose to conform because, according to Beauvoir, it was the least strenuous choice. Women may have been making pragmatic decisions, but that does not make them existential choices made in fear and trembling with the anxiety of associated consequences. For example, a harem girl can choose to accept her situation or choose to attempt to leave. The consequences are a separate matter. By daring to escape, it is possible that she finds herself in an even worse situation; yet, it is feasible that in some cases punishment, death, or poverty is preferable. Beauvoir has forgotten the question that she asked in *The Ethics of Ambiguity*: how does one want to live? Nevertheless, let us continue to explore why Beauvoir affirmed that voluntary servitude has been so convenient for women in love, by outlining seven deadly sins of inauthentic loving.

Beauvoir was an atheist, so it was not actually sins that she expounded but rather the existential equivalent of a sin: bad faith. They are not physically deadly, but according to Beauvoir, indulging in such moral faults as these is parallel to metaphysical suicide: the realm of non-being where transcendence decays into immanence and freedom fades into facticity.[26]

Idolizing and subordinating to a lover

One issue with romantic loving, according to Beauvoir, is the temptation to idolize a lover because it means voluntarily subordinating oneself. Paula in *The Mandarins* is a prime example of a woman loving idolatrously. She uses love as an excuse to evade responsibility for establishing her own independent existence. She sacrifices her singing career and flees from any possibility of taking up her own projects on the pretext that loving Henri is a full-time vocation. Henri, on the other hand, sees it as "vegetating".[27] Paula's reward for her dependence is a false sense of security and a feeble *raison d'être* because she erroneously feels necessary to her lover. Paula asks Henri:

> "Could you get along without me?"
>
> "You know very well I couldn't."
>
> "Yes, I know," she said happily. "Even if you said you could, I wouldn't believe you."
>
> She walked towards the bathroom. It was impossible not to weaken from time to time and speak a few kind words to her, smile gently at her.[28]

While men do not need women and often find them a burden, according to Beauvoir, Paula's desire to be necessary to her lover is a typical characteristic of a woman in love. In *The Second Sex*, Beauvoir said that women are happiest when they love and are loved by a man whom they revere as a god-like being because they derive a sense of prestige and justification from him.[29] Such women are like romantic rent-seekers; that is, they parasitically gain value and identity in their lives from their lover without reciprocating any meaningful benefits. In becoming dependent on a male lover, women piggyback on his life so as to avoid the hassles of taking on their own projects, defining themselves, asserting themselves, and undertaking their own independent authentic existence. To deny one's freedom and to live in immanence, as Paula does, is bad faith and characteristic of inauthentic loving. Such idolatrous lovers as Paula think that love will save them, but they only sabotage themselves.[30]

If we accept Beauvoir's argument, that idolization was a rational choice given the alternatives, what can be said about this dynamic today? After all, much has changed since Beauvoir's time. In the Western world we have had many years of anti-discrimination and equal opportunity legislation; many women are virtually in control of reproduction through birth control and abortion; the majority of women now work and expect to work; women's chances for success in the workplace has increased; and the pay gap between men and women has narrowed, although there is still a gap.

Certainly, Beauvoir argued, women will still be tempted to idolize and serve their lover because it is easy. However, there is also a second reason Beauvoir saw perpetuating this dynamic. A view that she has in common with Nietzsche is that transcendence is unfeminine, and women can do little to change this. Beauvoir surreptitiously assumed that man is the standard by which the idea of the feminine is constructed and not conforming to the ideal is social suicide.

For example, according to Beauvoir, a woman trying to charm a man will need to suppress her transcendental qualities – that is, intelligence and independence – and present herself as "a subtle carnal throb".[31] Some women do overtly debase their freedom and use their power of beauty and charm to seduce men. This poses a problem to an independent woman who, according to Beauvoir, is too busy for slavery and grooming and refuses to fall into bad faith by playing the adoring chattel.

Beauvoir did not mention that sex object status is not a long-term sustainable situation because although lust, passion, and the adrenaline rush are part of the experience, relationships that depend entirely on these elements tend to be short-lived. Moreover, it is an overgeneralization to suggest that all men want what Beauvoir called "a statue animated by hidden vibrations".[32] Brains and feminine charm are not mutually exclusive.

Additionally, for women to allow externally socially imposed ideals of beauty to guide their choices is bad faith. A woman acting existentially would not let others choose what is beautiful or what defines her. Some women claim that it is an authentic choice and being more beautiful makes them feel better about themselves. But perhaps they feel better about themselves only because they think they look better through the gaze of others.

Merging with a lover

Lovers commonly refer to each other as their "other half", implying that in finding each other, they become complete. Beauvoir said that a woman who idolizes her lover imagines that by integrating with him, she can obliterate the "I" and become a delectable "we".[33]

The dream of unity is a phenomenon that Beauvoir said that she experienced in her relationship with Sartre (and that Sartre said he experienced in his relationship with Beauvoir). For example, in Beauvoir's memoirs and letters, she said she feels that she and Sartre are one, and she often referred to him as her life, happiness, and self.[34]

Notwithstanding these declarations of unity, Beauvoir maintained in her philosophy that one of the main pitfalls in inauthentic loving is the dream of merging because, as we have seen, Beauvoir maintained that we are separate beings. Dreaming of unity is bad faith if one knows it is impossible to achieve. In *The Prime of Life*, Beauvoir said that when she and Sartre disagreed twice, her world was shaken to the core.[35]

The surprise and disappointment of the shattered dream of merging is a recurring theme in Beauvoir's work. For example, it comes as an awkward surprise to Françoise in *She Came to Stay* to discover that she and Pierre are not one. The arrival of the young, beautiful, and impulsive Xavière disrupts their perfect union. When they create a feisty *ménage-à-trois*, Françoise's dream of unity melts into alienation because her opinion of Xavière is poles apart from Pierre's: Françoise sees her as immature, and Pierre finds her to be enchanting.[36]

Likewise, Laurence in *Les Belles Images* is astounded when she discovers that she and her husband Jean-Charles disagree. Laurence swerves to avoid hitting a cyclist and their car rolls into a ditch. While Laurence is relieved that no one is injured, Jean-Charles would have preferred to hit the cyclist instead of writing off the car. Stupefied, Laurence reflects on the cognitive dissonance between her assumption that they were one entity and her independent reaction to the accident.[37]

In Beauvoir's writing, the dream of unity is exclusively a woman's delusion. Her male characters are not sidetracked by the desire to merge with lovers because they are focused on independent projects and do not want to be weighed down with another person. Nevertheless, there is no reason why a man would not also dream of this. There are men who are distraught to discover their lovers have opposing or disagreeable views, but Beauvoir did not write about these.

Furthermore, Beauvoir defines this sense of oneness as having the same views and opinions, and differences in thinking reveal the rift. Yet the existential problem with this view is clear. Differences should come as no surprise. Sameness and acquiescence are not admirable qualities, because they overlook the individuals' unique characteristics, their independence of thinking, and the benefits of otherness. Later, Beauvoir realized her mistake: "There were some experiences that each individual lived through alone ... Harmony between individuals is never a *donnée*; it must be worked for continually".[38]

Possessing and dominating a lover

Possessiveness is implied in the metaphysical dream of loving unity because when lovers imagine themselves as one, there is no room for a third person. This is most poignantly portrayed in *She Came to Stay*, when Françoise and Pierre bring Xavière into their inner circle. Not only does Pierre want to be the most important thing in Xavière's world, but he covets the moments when he is the only thing that matters to her.[39] Yet it was not a reciprocal arrangement. Xavière hated the open relationship and takes comfort in the arms of another man who offered exclusivity.

This example demonstrates that both men and women succumb to the desire to dominate and possess. Pierre and Françoise's obsession over Xavière raises questions about who really holds the advantage in the *ménage-à-trois*. This is a prime example of Hegel's master-slave dialectic where the slave ends up with the power to define the master, which Sartre came to discuss in *Being and Nothingness*. Xavière was initially perceived as being in a subservient position, but she ended up with such power that Pierre's sense of self-assurance depends on her, and Françoise attempts to murder her. Pierre reinforces that we need others to define ourselves, but concomitant with the need for others is their power to define us in a disagreeable manner. Thus, lovers want to control each other so that they can control that aspect of themselves. Françoise wants Xavière dead because she did not like the way Xavière's saw her.[40]

Beauvoir's problem with possessiveness in loving is that the other is treated as an object rather than being accepted and respected as a free subject. Françoise initially treats Xavière as an object, especially when she talks about "handing her over" to Pierre like a prized Barbie doll: "Henceforth, Xavière belonged to Pierre".[41] Possessiveness is bad faith because, for Beauvoir as for Sartre, humans are not objects that can be annexed. Moreover, possessive games encourage inauthenticity because of the strategies that lovers use in order to try to charm, merge, and justify their lives. Nevertheless, people do fool themselves into thinking if they possessed their lover, they would be able to control them.

Devoting oneself to a lover

One of the key misconceptions about love is that devotion is good, selfless, generous, and virtuous. However, Beauvoir suggested that devotion is rarely any of these things because it demands something in return. Reminiscent of Nietzsche, she said that a woman in love desperately wants her love to be requited, and thus devotion, which she equates with loving generosity, often becomes a coercion strategy. As already seen with Paula and Henri in *The Mandarins*, the woman who generously becomes a slave to her lover is presenting an emotional Trojan horse: he is obliged to accept her so-called benevolent gift, which is actually tyranny cloaked in altruism.

Superficially, devotion implies that one wants the best for the beloved. Beauvoir casts a stormy shadow over this assumption. The problem, as she outlined in *Pyrrhus and Cineas*, is threefold.[42] First, the devoted person chooses the goal. For example, in devoting herself to Henri, Paula made him her project. She wanted to be the mastermind of his career decisions. This is an existential misdemeanor because it is the responsibility of all individuals to create themselves and define their own unique essence. No one else can do that for them. Paula's existential problem is as follows. Paula defines herself through Henri's actions. Yet Paula cannot control Henri's actions. So when Henri acts in ways that Paula does not approve of, she becomes distraught because she does not like how he defines himself and, by association, herself. Her attempt to define his project for him undermines his sovereign right to define himself.

A second problem with devotion is that a devoted person aims to do what is in the other's best interest. The devoted person presumes to know what the other is lacking as well as how to fix it. The problem is that nothingness is part of every being, so one cannot complete another or truly know what is in the other's best interest. The third problem that Beauvoir highlights is that devotion means adopting the same end as the lover. But no one can truly know another's end. It is arrogant to assume that one has such intimate knowledge of an other. Even the other may not be aware of it.

Beauvoir frequently portrayed devotion as selfishness and tyranny in disguise. This should come as no surprise, however, considering loving includes love of loving. For example, in *The Woman Destroyed* Maurice and Monique recognize the selfish aspects of their love: Maurice loves loving, and Monique loves to please others.[43] Elisabeth in *She Came to Stay* also becomes aware of the selfishness of love when she admits to Claude that her generosity is a form of demandingness.[44] A generous love would be more pleasant, yet it risks becoming a tyranny if the recipient does not want it or if the giver seeks *quid pro quo*.

Justifying oneself in a lover

One of the reasons that women in love are so willing to devote themselves to their lover, according to Beauvoir, is to attempt to find their *raison d'être* by making the lover their project. Part of our being is nothingness, and latching on like a leech to a lover who appears to be a sovereign subject might seem like an easy option, but it is naïve and futile because no one is perfect or complete. We are creative nothingnesses and are constantly changing until death.

For example, Blomart in *The Blood of Others* points out the absurdity of Hélène's attempt to justify her life through him since he was clueless about it himself.[45] The trouble with justifying one's existence in another's is that others have their own justifications – or not, as in Blomart's case – making Hélène's justification completely hollow.

Similarly, in *The Mandarins* Paula uses Henri as the justification of her life. As her one and only project, Paula sees herself as having created Henri and takes credit for his life. When he strays from his original mission, Paula thinks it is her job to bring him back on track. Yet for Henri to act authentically, he must create his own track. Paula's choosing for him is tantamount to hijacking his freedom. This is characteristic of inauthentic loving because it does not respect the other as a free subject. Beauvoir argued similarly in *Pyrrhus and Cineas* that one must neither thrust one's justification onto another nor usurp another's project, because individuals cannot be relieved of the responsibility of their own life or escape the associated risk and anguish.

Not diversifying

Beauvoir agrees with Nietzsche that the differences in the way men and women love each other is a source of conflict and misunderstanding. While women in love make the relationship not just the most important thing in their whole lives, but also often the *only* thing in their lives, men see it as only one element.[46]

For example, this is the case with Paula and Henri in *The Mandarins*. Henri's freedom, work, and travel matter more than his atrophying love for Paula. Paula lives for only the relationship, and she emotionally blackmails Henri into feeling temporarily guilty about having other interests.[47] Frustration and disappointment set in when Paula finally realizes she is a burden to Henri, he gets sick of her, and he leaves her.

Similarly, Hélène in *The Blood of Others* understands love as total absorption into each other. She cannot fathom that her first boyfriend's work is more important to him than she is and that he would not kill himself if she died. Hélène runs into the same problem with her next boyfriend, Blomart. She sees love as being each other's whole life and cannot accept that love involves friendship, which means accepting that the other has interests outside the relationship. Blomart does not respect her until she leaves him. He loves her only as she walks out the door.

An understanding of love that includes friendship is a recurring theme in Beauvoir's work and personal life. In a letter to the American novelist Nelson Algren, with whom Beauvoir had an intense romantic affair, she suggested that one of the things she loved most about the relationship was that they were both lovers and friends, by which she meant that they could have open and intimate conversations.[48] Two individuals having the same understanding of what it means to love is imperative for successful relationships. According to Beauvoir, the right way to love is the way men in her novels love. She supported the idea that love is about sharing individual lives, not making the other person all-consuming, because lives with nothing else are hollow.

Yet what, might one ask, is the risk of loving the way Beauvoir says women do? Her concern was with being dependent on a single source of meaning in one's life, which contrasts with Kierkegaard's extolling the virtues of willing one thing. Beauvoir demonstrated repeatedly the devastation that dependency has on a woman when the relationship fails. Life is impermanent and everlasting love tends to be the exception not the rule. If the lovers make the relationship their only project in life, the entire meaning in their life, or the only source of their happiness, then they are left empty handed when the relationship ceases. For example, in *The Woman Destroyed* when Monique's husband leaves, she feels that her life is empty and pointless. Also, sisters Marcelle and Marguerite in *When Things of the Spirit Come First* each in turn fall in love with the fickle and avaricious Denis and dream of being his savior. Denis treats both women like doormats, and when he leaves them, they are paralyzed with despair about how they will live without him.[49]

Beauvoir's legacy is to have a back-up strategy through diverse projects in case things go wrong. A man is not a retirement plan. Beauvoir's premise appears to rest on the assumption that older women will find it harder to support themselves once a relationship ends. So, breaking up often means poverty and situations that afford fewer possibilities. While being left without meaning and justification in life is initially a shock, there is no reason why one cannot find a new justification. All Beauvoir's women survive, and some even show hope of discovering themselves. For example, in *The Blood of Others*, after breaking with Blomart, Hélène eagerly joins the resistance. When Denis leaves Marguerite in *When Things of the Spirit Come First* she discovers her own possibilities in the void that Denis left. The women began bravely to think about what they wanted in life rather than trying to please their lovers, if only fleetingly.

Beauvoir shows in her novels that a woman who loves inauthentically may have further to recover, but all is not lost. While her intention is to warn against throwing caution to the wind by delving passionately into a loving relationship, she is not completely convincing when she suggests that such a strategy is existentially dangerous. Nevertheless, her message is prudent: it is risky and reckless to make a lover one's primary project. The women in the above examples would have been better off had they had diverse and independent interests. The more committed to a single project one is, the harder it is to change if it fails. It is thus prudent to maintain and actively follow multiple projects.

Believing in destiny

According to Beauvoir's existential principles, to be human is to strive toward freely chosen ends, so believing in destiny is defective. Beauvoir claimed that one of the problems women face in romantic loving is that they have been culturally conditioned to want the traditional feminine destiny of being a wife and mother. A young girl's upbringing, coupled with pressure to marry and have babies, glorifies and tempts women toward these roles. The Prince Charming fantasy of a man to love and be loved by, the romance of an expensive ring to value her worth, the glory of a wedding day dedicated entirely to the woman where she is the center of attention, and the production of children to dote upon are all ideas instilled in girls from a very early age. From an existential point of view, Beauvoir should dismiss this social conditioning as bad faith on the basis that it is deterministic, but she did not.

Beauvoir plummets even further down the slippery slope of determinism when she said that men do not experience nearly as much conflict with masculine destiny as do women with feminine destiny. Such female biological functions as childbirth and breastfeeding are crippling and are to blame for rendering women subordinate and dependent. Men, on the other hand, have a ready-made tool for asserting themselves in the world: "the phallus is the fleshy incarnation of transcendence".[50]

Beauvoir's aim is to dispute determinism since "One is not born, but rather becomes, woman".[51] Also, Beauvoir refused to accept "a fixed destiny" for women and argued, "anatomy and hormones never define anything but a situation".[52] Nevertheless, it is a form of biological determinism to assert that transcendence is natural for men and unnatural for women. Not only is determinism an example of existential bad faith, but her stance, that men's transcendence is not a choice, undermines her existential argument that we are free to choose our passion. Rather, it is up to women to realize that while such factors as society and biology can influence thinking, authentic behavior is not determined by it.

This section has outlined the traps that women usually fall into when loving or seeking love. There is one final point in reference to her description of the problem of inauthentic loving: what men want. Her novels tend to polarize men into happy if they are in an open relationship (e.g., Pierre in *She Came to Stay* and Robert in *The Mandarins*) and miserable and trapped if they are not (e.g., Henri in *She Came to Stay*, Maurice in *The Woman Destroyed*, and Denis in *When Things of the Spirit Come First*). This seems to be a rather bland portrayal of men. To assume that men are bored by monogamy is an overgeneralization.

Moreover, Beauvoir argued that it is difficult for both partners to give up playing power games because men want to dominate women and women know this. As a consequence, women behave submissively because either they believe they are not as good as men or they are afraid that appearing to be intelligent and independent is unattractive, hindering their chances of finding a lover. While a love slave is appealing to some men, it is far from being the rule and is an unreliable stratagem. The point that Beauvoir did not sufficiently explore is that men are individuals and are attracted to different types of women. Indeed, Beauvoir often portrayed men who have female love-slaves as losing interest quickly, especially when they realize that they are not the dominant one in the relationship. Plenty of men want someone to enrich their life rather than just do their laundry. There are easier ways to find housekeepers.

Much of what Beauvoir said about women can be applied to men too. There is no reason why anxieties about loving relationships apply to only women. It is equally possible for a man to be anxious about the security of a relationship, living up to the masculine ideal, how he should present himself to a girlfriend, idolizing and being subservient to his lover, or running into issues with devotion. It could also be argued that masculinity is imposed from the outside and defined by customs and fashion. For example, those who show vulnerability, do not behave aggressively, or do not go out to work every day can be cast as lazy or weak. Beauvoir's focus was on the female sex, but it would be a more rounded and comprehensive analysis had she addressed the anxiety and psychodynamics of relationships between the sexes. As it stands, it leaves much unsaid and paints an unbalanced picture.

Nevertheless, Beauvoir's key message still stands: women should stop trying so hard to please their lovers at the expense of pursuing a rich and diversified life. For Beauvoir, more often than not, the goal of love is to find the justification of one's existence and self-worth through another. This strategy is fraught with danger because the other's justification for their existence is unreliable. The desperate attempt to merge with and justify one's life in the lover is why lovers tend to forget all else and play games of idolization, devotion, submission, domination, and possession. These are all examples of bad faith and are characteristic of inauthentic loving. Now that we have canvassed the problems Beauvoir saw in romantic loving relationships, we shall turn to her solution: to reconcile romantic loving and authenticity.

Beauvoir's solutions

In *The Second Sex*, Beauvoir outlines a definition of authentic loving and four key elements characterize it: respecting each other's freedom, appreciating oneself as both subject and other, transcending together, and mutually creating meaning.[53] This proposition is analyzed in terms of the four key components below.

Respecting each other's freedom

Beauvoir argued that in a trusting relationship, authenticity is achievable if lovers believe and recognize each other as free and equal – and act accordingly. This means both partners are economically independent sovereign subjects. To lift themselves above patriarchal power games, lovers need to cooperate, be generous, trust each other, and appreciate each other as autonomous individuals.[54]

In *Who Shall Die?* Beauvoir demonstrated this point through a relationship that violates reciprocal recognition. Louis, the alderman of Vaucelles, and his wise wife Catherine initially consider themselves a partnership of equals because they discuss and agree together on important decisions. When Catherine learns that Louis has cast her as a useless mouth and sentenced her to certain death, he introduces a power relationship. Reminiscent of Hegel's master-slave dialectic, Louis asserts himself as the master and relegates Catherine to the status of a slave. Catherine accuses him of treating her not as a wife but rather as a disposable object.[55]

Catherine takes her dagger and tries to stab Louis. While the reason for her attack is not made explicit, feelings of anger, vengeance, and betrayal are all perfectly understandable possibilities. What is obvious is that in her attempt to murder Louis, Catherine refuses to be an object or a victim and asserts her independence. Authentic loving is, for Beauvoir, impossible when there is oppression, and Catherine's retaliation illustrates her defiance and establishes her as a woman striving for authenticity. Louis takes a surprisingly enlightened stance. Instead of being angry, he perceives the attempted murder to be evidence that Catherine loves him. In spite of the knifing – or perhaps because of it – their relationship is portrayed as both authentic and loving.

Turning to women's situation 700 years after Catherine, the question of what a woman is to do with her future has become complicated by her newly recognized psychosocial freedom. Should she choose a career or marry and procreate? Beauvoir noted that it is much more difficult for a woman to juggle such possibilities.[56]

Although women have always been ontologically free, there are now fewer obstacles than ever to women's choosing their passion. Although growing and delivering a baby is still a female act, it is about the only thing, apart from breastfeeding, related to children that still is. With access to birth control, Cesarean deliveries to avoid difficulties, the proliferation of mobile communication, widespread availability of baby milk formula, government-subsidized childcare, paid parental leave, and the possibility of a male being the primary carer, a woman need take little time away from work in many Western societies. These changes in the structure of Western society have made it easier for women to choose both family and career; they are no longer mutually exclusive.

Women seem to have discovered that with higher education and economic independence, it is relatively easy to refuse to give up transcending for the sake of support. Women are no longer doomed to immanence, because they have established their psychosocial freedom to pursue economic independence, are transcending *en masse*, and are no longer required to marry and procreate in order to survive as members of a social community and be successful in life.

However, even though more women are working, they tend still to do more housework and childcare than men. Beauvoir proposed that this dynamic exists because women want both a career and to please their husbands by not allowing their job to interfere with historically standard wifely duties.[57] While imaginably such duties were historically a relevant criterion for mate selection, in the twenty-first century one would hope that Western society has moved beyond classifying housekeeping as a primary wifely virtue. Nevertheless, other possible reasons why women choose to do such tasks include wanting to control what is done, how duties are done, and how well they are done.

The obvious advantage that men derive from outsourcing such immanent activities as housework is that they have more time for creative and transcending endeavors. Indeed, Beauvoir said historically this is why women have placed so much importance on love: since their time was spent finding and keeping a husband and having children, these enterprises became the most significant aspects of their lives. The risk for lovers these days, however, is resentment and potentially destructive conflict stemming from unequal effort put into the maintenance activities of life. Maintenance activities in life are essentially mundane, but they have to be done. Beauvoir's aim is for lovers to be, and treat each other as, equal. Nevertheless, equality can negate freedom since individual freedom also means freedom to treat others unequally and to exploit them. Moreover, if one cannot pursue one's projects because there are restrictions in place ensuring equality, then authenticity is also compromised.

There will be times when lovers are dominant and submissive for the purposes of efficiency and getting things done – for example, cooking a meal or doing the washing – and such tasks do not necessarily constitute a master-slave dynamic. Even so, some women, such as Paula in *The Mandarins*, do give up their careers in order to support their partner. If she is choosing subservience, this is existentially problematic because choosing not to choose, choosing to hand one's future over to another, and choosing to avoid responsibility for one's life are all examples of bad faith.

Beauvoir did not seem to appreciate just how free women could be from the burdens of childcare; nor did she consider a man as the primary caregiver for a child. She did, however, emphasize that the advantage of ending women's oppression is not only the social benefit of contributing toward a stronger workforce, but also the existential argument that women will become sovereign subjects, and, as a side-effect, relationships will be enriched. Beauvoir hypothesizes that a woman who flourishes outside her domestic role would be best able to enrich her child's life.[58] While such a controversial statement might provoke the ire of stay-at-home mothers, such a principle could appropriately be applied to romantic relationships. The idea is that less dependency and less need for one another makes for more interesting partners.

Appreciating oneself as both subject and other

A second element in Beauvoir's formulation of authentic love is that both lovers maintain themselves simultaneously as self and other. As if creating a third attitude to escape Sartre's vicious cycle of sadomasochism, Beauvoir proposed that lovers would do well to appreciate each other's differences.[59] In this way, both lovers maintain their subjectivity and transcendence while opening themselves up to the benefits of otherness.

Nevertheless, Beauvoir's language is confusing, given that elsewhere in *The Second Sex* she criticizes women who assume themselves as both self and other because in being both passive and active they are being duplicitous.[60] Despite this contradiction, what she wants is to discourage women from adopting the position of "other" in the traditional sense of being weak and instead realize strength that is derived from being both a subject and an other.

In *She Came to Stay*, Beauvoir had already explored this point. In practice, authentic loving means that lovers are sensual, affectionate, and most importantly friends, which incorporates being respectful of each other and their projects.[61] This is the problem with selfishness: Beauvoir suggested that it is inconsistent with friendship because it treats the other as an object to be possessed or dominated. Love can exist without friendship, but Françoise complains that it is impersonal because it makes her feel like she is an object, and thus she dismisses it as despicable.[62] Nevertheless, Beauvoir did not elaborate on the other aspects of the effect of friendship: does the relationship then involve less commitment, passion, intimacy, emotional attachment, or continuity, as friendship implies? Moreover, she did not seem to consider that friends could also be possessive and dominating.

In addition to friendship, the key to rising above the hell of each other, according to Beauvoir, is tender lovemaking because in this activity, lovers experience a higher connectedness or what she referred to as an "intersubjective experience".[63] Sharing Sartre's idea that sexual love is a strategy to incarnate the other's consciousness through the flesh, Beauvoir concurred that it is doomed because the other's subjectivity can never be comprehensively understood. However, she stands apart from Sartre on two points. One, sexual love need not be hostile if based on friendship, caring, equality, and affection.[64] Two, Beauvoir separates consciousness into thinking and feeling (which is not an existential way of thinking). In the state of emotional intoxication of sexual loving, Beauvoir argued in *Must We Burn Sade?* that lovers forget themselves and become more aware of each other's reality. Lovers simultaneously experience themselves as "subjectivity and passivity", dissolving their personal boundaries, feeling as though they become one merged consciousness, and finding a bridge between them – that is, "immediate communication".[65] In *The Second Sex*, she is more explicit when she suggests that the key to achieving this connection is orgasm.[66]

Pitying the Marquis de Sade, Beauvoir said that despite his passionate desires, he could never be truly satisfied because he was always overthinking everything. He never allowed himself to indulge in emotional intoxication. He was caught forever in a battle with the other because while he mastered sensuality, the other elements of authentic loving – friendship and affection – were seriously lacking.

Let us note here that in the state of emotional intoxication, Beauvoir threw out her rulebook about inauthentic loving: unity is possible and desirable, passivity is appropriate, and abandoning oneself is necessary. It is unclear why these are acceptable in sexual loving and nowhere else. The difference, Beauvoir suggested unconvincingly, is that she surrenders without forfeiting her freedom.[67]

Beauvoir proposed that this is possible because the elements of respect and sharing enable lovers to experience pleasure simultaneously and become aware that the source of their pleasure is in the other. Elevated above the battlefield, they transcend themselves, generously giving but not surrendering themselves, and enjoying the experience of unity.[68] One would not be blamed for being confused here that Beauvoir said lovers must not lose themselves; and yet, as discussed above, intoxication is essential, and her evaluation of Sade's problem was his inability to lose himself. However, just as one cannot know what the other thinks, there is no reason why one should assume that it is possible to tell what another person is feeling.

Transcending together

For Beauvoir, transcending is the most important activity in living existentially. This is why voluntary subordination and renouncing transcendence is tantamount to annihilating oneself. Traditionally, men live transcendentally because, Beauvoir asserts, their work contributes more to society than caring for the family.[69] For Beauvoir, transcendence would be more available to women with access to rewarding employment and birth control.

Beauvoir admitted that in the beginning of her relationship with Sartre, she did what she would later warn against: justifying herself through her lover.[70] Upon realizing this, she set out to rectify the situation by doing something that only she could be responsible for: writing. In her first novel, *She Came to Stay*, the protagonist, Françoise, finds a similar need to break her dependence on her lover Pierre and does so through setting out to murder Xavière, the third wheel in their *ménage-à-trois*. Beauvoir said that through this story, she was resolving her animosity toward Olga Kosakiewicz, her student and lover, on whom she based the character Xavière and to whom she dedicated the novel.[71] Later, Beauvoir conceded that it was a mistake to propose murder as a viable means of resolving issues with others, lest we all become serial killers.[72]

Beauvoir suggested that many men are reluctant to support social change toward women's transcendence. Possible reasons include that men enjoy having a dependent partner because they find autonomous women draining; they fear having to play the slave themselves; or they derive a sense of self-worth, security, superiority, and power from having a socially acceptable form of domestic slavery.

However, Beauvoir was implicitly criticizing such men and gives numerous reasons why women's transcendence is of benefit to everyone. First, partners will be able to understand each other better.[73] Second, presumably because the relationship is between two more interesting individuals, love enriches their lives.[74] Third, men are more liberated because they do not have a dependant. More women are working in the twenty-first century than in Beauvoir's era, and they assist in providing for the family, thereby relieving men of the full responsibility of being the chief breadwinner. There is also increased security for each person's independence in the occupation of the other. Yet, arguably, the most profound benefit of all is that the understanding one gains through the gaze of an independent other is much deeper than that of a slave. As Nietzsche and Sartre also pointed out, one learns nothing through a passive, tolerant, and opaque reflection.

It is not enough, however, for lovers to transcend themselves independently. Transcending *together* gives relationships strength and depth. Otherwise, it is the difference between Mr or Mrs Right and Mr or Mrs Right-Now. Beauvoir would have agreed with Kierkegaard's critique of Don Giovanni and Johannes the Seducer: the value of relationships is not in enjoying the moment, but rather in projecting a future together.[75] This appears to be part of the problem in Beauvoir's relationship with Nelson Algren. They were both transcending, but not together. Algren knew Beauvoir would always leave, and so they were not building a future or creating meaning together. Algren wanted all of her, but Beauvoir would agree to an annual vacation only, to which Algren responded with emotional detachment.[76]

Mutually creating meaning

In *The Second Sex* and *Must We Burn Sade?* Beauvoir focused on how lovers forge connections in the bedroom, but she did open up other doors elsewhere. Beauvoir indicates that adopting a common goal also seals lovers' understanding. It is up to each couple to agree what that trajectory will be. It could include work, children, hopes, or simply their attachment.[77] Beauvoir admits so many degrees of commonality that it could conceivably cover anything at all, as long as lovers can share or reconcile them.

However, Beauvoir seems to think very highly of humanitarian struggles. Jean-Pierre in *Who Shall Die?* indicates to Clarice that together they will fight against patriarchal injustices, thereby galvanizing their passion for life and each other.[78] The problem with the relationship between Blomart and Hélène in *The Blood of Others*, readers are led to believe, is that they have nothing in common – not even the desire to be in a relationship. Blomart reluctantly gives in to Hélène's persistence, but the relationship does not last. Without Blomart, Hélène seeks meaning through the resistance, and it is this comradeship, the two acting as allies and accomplices, that finally gives license to an authentic loving relationship. As Hélène prepares for a fatal mission, Blomart says: "Now, nothing will separate us, ever".[79]

This dream of unity conflicts with Beauvoir's philosophy of independence. Philosophically, Beauvoir accepts individuals as separate and advises against unions whereby lovers become dependent. Yet, here she also subscribes to a kind of transcendental betrothal. Nevertheless, Beauvoir's formulation sounds in principle like a modification of Stirner's union whereby people come together to achieve more than they could alone. The difference is that Beauvoir suggested for lovers to work with a group toward a cause greater than themselves. Yet how can one presume to know what is in humankind's or society's best interest? Her view presupposes an objectively defined good and glosses over the fact that individuals can disagree on productive endeavors.

Beauvoir seemed to be proposing a modified Kierkegaardian leap from hedonistic and immanent living to an ethical life through a common struggle. However, she abolished Kierkegaard's focus on duty and marriage and instead emphasized the importance of commitment to a cause. Beauvoir dismissed as selfish or egotistical the possibility of two lovers struggling together for their individual projects that happen to be mutually beneficial, but there is no existential justification for doing so. Fighting together need not be for an "objectively" noble or heroic cause.

Key considerations

Despite Beauvoir's metaphysical utopia of authentic loving, there are problems with achieving it in practice. While some of the problems with Beauvoir's philosophy have already been addressed, the aim of this section is to indicate in more detail some of the more pertinent objections to her construction of an existential philosophy of loving.

Narrow view of power and domination

Although the greatest aspiration in authentic living for existential thinkers is freedom, Beauvoir's philosophy demands limited freedom to establish relationships. When Beauvoir suggested that violence is sometimes required to overcome those who are obstacles to freedom, she means that increasing freedom for some entails simultaneously limiting freedom for others. Here she slides toward a utilitarian view of the greatest good for the greatest number.[80] Yet, this is not existential, especially for those individuals against whom violence is waged.

Beauvoir also assumed power struggles in relationships are necessarily pejorative and hostile. This ought not to be the case, because she said explicitly that to live and to become is to struggle and that freedom must constantly be fought for. This should be no different in loving relationships. Although Beauvoir encouraged lovers to accept themselves as subject and other, she did not give credence to the idea that Nietzsche and Sartre alluded to: friction in relationships can be constructive and motivating. There is no reason why Beauvoir should not support power applied in a manner similar to Nietzsche's star friends. Beauvoir seems to be heading toward this idea when she advocates choosing a cause to work toward together, but she did not go this far.

Love can justify life

Notwithstanding Beauvoir's argument that lovers cannot validly justify each other's lives, for some people, the ideal of love does include this criterion. Love is such an invigorating activity that it tends to take over the lovers' worlds and gives their lives meaning. Anne in *The Mandarins* expresses a theme that Beauvoir repeated throughout her writing: "being loved isn't an end in itself, a *raison d'être*; it changes nothing, it leads nowhere".[81] The question one might ask is: for whom does it change nothing? Beauvoir's assumption is that it changes nothing for society because it produces nothing of commercial or objective value. Yet, if we consider the individual, subjective, existential experience, would any lover say it changed nothing? Not only the joy but also the depth of emotion, passion, enthusiasm, and experiences necessarily change lovers' lives. At times, Beauvoir seems to want to play down the importance that loving has in making many people's lives worth living.

In her letters to Sartre around 1939–1940 (a few years before she published her first novel), she said that he was her "sole reason for living", that she needed him, and that her life was nothing and had no meaning without him.[82] Later, in her philosophy, she portrays such an attitude as unexistential because it is invalid to use another person as one's reason for living. Beauvoir is warning women not to fall into her trap, and yet such an attitude tends to be part and parcel of romantic passion. Based on her comments in *Must We Burn Sade?* some emotional intoxication should be encouraged. Furthermore, if one is free to choose passion, it ought to be valid to choose passion for a lover. A simple common bond of attachment is sufficient in Beauvoir's philosophy.

Returning to her idea of transcendence, Beauvoir praised projects that contribute to society at large.[83] She implies that contributing on a family level does not make a worthwhile difference in the world. Firstly, society is a collection of people, so if it is authentic to justify one's existence in doing something for society, then it should also be authentic to do something for a particular individual for whom one happens to care, such as a lover. Secondly, her emphasis on contributions to society reflects her flirtation with Marxism and even latent elements of Kierkegaard's leap of faith into the ethical or spiritual sphere. Kierkegaard advocates loving everyone equally rather than one preferred individual. Similarly, Beauvoir advocates contributions toward humanity rather than devotion to an individual. In *The Ethics of Ambiguity*, she explained one's justification is to be found in others only, but she did not seem to consider lovers to be eligible for this.

The issue of transparency

Another question that arises from Beauvoir's philosophy, life, and loves, is: how do we reconcile freedom and fidelity and "at what price?"[84] If freedom is paramount in an existential romantic loving relationship, then it could include freedom to engage in other relationships. It would be considered bad faith to say that one would not engage in other intimate relationships because one is married, that is, a choice ruled by a contract. Likewise, the virtue of fidelity is externally imposed and limits one's freedom by not engaging in other loving relationships when one wishes. According to Beauvoir, most people are hypocrites when it comes to fidelity. Society upholds fidelity as a virtue, but people either do not practice it, martyr themselves for it, or comfort themselves with alcohol.[85]

Automatically classifying infidelity as a sin is also bad faith. Hence, freedom in relationships is essential to loving existentially. Nevertheless, Beauvoir's view was that it is crude to use freedom as an excuse for promiscuous sex. This is why Beauvoir and Sartre's freedom included the opportunity to love others. The traditional view is that Sartre instigated the open relationship. However, it has been suggested that Beauvoir wanted such freedom because Sartre could not satisfy her.[86] In a letter to Nelson Algren, Beauvoir explained that the physical side of her relationship with Sartre did not last long because Sartre was not interested in sex and that she and Sartre had become just very good friends.[87]

Beauvoir embraced the freedom to fall in love with other people. She often pursued romantic relationships with female students who were in awe of her freedom and wanted to be like her.[88] Beauvoir would also introduce them to Sartre, knowing that he would try to seduce them, often successfully. Beauvoir and Sartre spoke of each other in such a way that made their secondary lovers jealous of and enraptured by the other.[89] Such a relationship gave them freedom to experience the world rather than isolate themselves from it.

Beauvoir and Sartre had identified jealousy as the biggest risk in a free relationship since one is excluded from parts of the other's life. This is why they agreed to be transparent, that is, to provide a secure basis of trust for their love. However, their pact of transparency could also be viewed as demanding and limiting their freedom to lie or complain.[90] Beauvoir was not dogmatically tied to telling the truth, and it would appear that Sartre did not accept transparency as a limitation despite the pact, since he admitted lying to her. Indeed, Sartre has no philosophical justification for transparency: the other is a threat, so there is no obligation to be honest.

Beauvoir also suggested that some things are better left unsaid. Lying to lovers is not only acceptable but also sometimes preferable because while trust is noble in theory, it can be used as a weapon. The confessor aims for redemption, but the effect is rather to "bludgeon someone with an indiscreet truth".[91] For example, Anne tells Nadine in *The Mandarins* that ideal relationships are not those in which lovers tell the truth at all costs but rather those in which there is no need to lie.[92]

The issue, Beauvoir illustrated, is not infidelity but rather hurting each other. Hurt can be inflicted both through lying and reckless truth telling. If a certain type of relationship is agreed to up-front, or adapted to change as the couples change, then there should be no issue with an agreement regarding (in)fidelity as part of a relationship if lovers so choose. Nevertheless, there often are issues with fidelity, which will now be addressed: the complication of the third person and the fact that lovers often *want to* restrict their freedom.

The issue of the third person

Beauvoir and Sartre neglected to consider the impact of their freedom on others. Beauvoir said that they deliberately avoided the question and called it a "defect" in their approach.[93] Their secondary lovers paid the price with lies, disappointment, hurt, and unhappiness. After affairs with Beauvoir and Sartre, Bianca Bienenfeld had a nervous breakdown and Evelyne Rey killed herself. Beauvoir told Sartre that she felt responsible and remorseful for Bienenfeld's suffering.[94]

While Sartre told his lover "M." (Dolores Vanetti) about his situation with Beauvoir from the very beginning, this did not prevent M. from being disappointed later on. The reason was, according to Beauvoir, women believe that love conquers all. Beauvoir blamed Sartre for underestimating the expectations involved in saying he loved her and criticized M. for assuming that Sartre would change his mind and for not telling Sartre this. The question Beauvoir asked is significant: "But if he loved her, how could he bear not to see her for months at a time?"[95]

Loving restricts freedom

The problem for existential thinkers, who revere freedom without limitation, is that the phenomenon of loving tends to restrict freedom because the common approach is exclusivity and acting as a "we". However, as already mentioned, consenting to restricted freedom constitutes a moral fault in Beauvoir's philosophy.

Not only was Beauvoir and Sartre's pact of transparency a limitation, but so too was their pact to remain primary to one another. Owing to this pact, Beauvoir chose to remain in Paris with Sartre rather than move to Chicago for Algren or expand her inner circle to include another lover, Jacques-Laurent Bost, who almost reached primary status in her life. We have seen that Beauvoir scorns the idea of being necessary to a lover. Susan J. Brison argued correctly that the concept of an essential love is bad faith because it implies permanence. Yet authentic loving insists on the freedom to transcend in ways that potentially lead away from being in a relationship because people are free to break up and to choose other lovers and projects.[96] Sartre once said, "existentialism never admits that the chips are ever down", meaning that life is never determined or fixed.[97]

On the one hand, making a commitment to another person is a constraint if lovers take it seriously. Being a couple means that each considers the other in many decisions. Lovers expect and demand consideration and modify their plans in light of each other. In *The Woman Destroyed*, André considers spending time apart from his wife because he finds being a "we" tiring: "Life as a couple implies decisions. 'When shall we eat? What would you like to have?' Plans come into being. When one is alone, things happen without premeditation: it is restful, I got up late".[98] André realizes that the only way to restore his freedom is separation from his lover. Yet, André's comments also highlight the fact that with a partner one has to make conscious decisions and commitments, whereas alone it is easy to slip into immanence and not to reflect on everyday activities.

On the other hand, being free from commitments does not make one free either. Jean-Pierre in *Who Shall Die?* tries to uphold his freedom from everything, including love, on the basis that "Any vow is a prison".[99] However, being free from commitments stifles him. The moral of the story is that one is responsible for action and inaction alike, and only by engaging in the world can one create a meaningful life. Jean-Pierre's life is meaningless until he learns that Clarice has been classified as a useless mouth and is condemned to certain death. When he imagines that his life without her would be worse, he changes his tune:

> *Jean-Pierre:* ...I simply cannot bear to go on living if you die. I love you, Clarice.
> *Clarice:* Yesterday you said that this word has no meaning.
> *Jean-Pierre:* Was that yesterday? It seems so long ago.
> *Clarice (bitterly):* It was yesterday, and you did not love me.
> *Jean-Pierre:* I did not have the courage to love you because I did not have the courage to live. The world seemed unclean to me, and I did not want to defile myself. What stupid arrogance!
> *Clarice (with irony):* And does this world seem more pure today?[100]

Jean-Pierre realizes that by doing nothing, he has condoned Clarice's death. Doing nothing is still a choice. Not wanting her to die, he declares his love and implores her to give him a chance.

The curious nature of loving is that limitations are happily accepted. Fidelity can be an unintended side-effect of loving, as Beauvoir and Algren discovered. Beauvoir referred to him as her husband, and herself as his wife, even though they never married. Beauvoir said that she would be completely faithful because she loved Algren so much that it would be inconceivable for her to be intimate with anyone else.[101]

While Beauvoir insisted on Algren's freedom to pursue relationships with other women, she playfully revealed that she would prefer otherwise: "I will interfere with your freedom: I'll put an electric fence around [your] Wabansia home; I'll poison your skin and lips so that if you touch any woman, she'll fall dead".[102] This highlights the difference between theory and practice: in theory they were free to have other affairs but in practice neither wanted to.

These examples bring to light the conflict between freedom and love: in a relationship, lovers are constantly torn between self-government and compromise. Existential philosophers value freedom but as we see here, lovers are always attempting to rob the other of it.

Love requires devotion

Not only do lovers want to restrict their freedom, but also notwithstanding Beauvoir's insistence that it is inauthentic to put one's loving relationship as the most important priority in one's life, lovers often want to and do. In contrast to her work that condemns devotion and the giving of one's whole life to another, Beauvoir knows that lovers expect it, and not to do so is a risk. She ruminates in a letter to Algren: "But do I deserve your love if I do not give you my life?... Is it right to give something of oneself without being ready to give everything?... I could never give everything to you, and I just feel bad about it".[103]

True to her philosophy, Beauvoir made it clear that her work was more important than her love for Algren, and she did not think that she would be able to write successfully and meaningfully in Chicago. It was not a question of what made her happy. Happiness was not Beauvoir's goal in practice or theory. If it were, she said that she would have chosen Algren.[104]

This example shows that it is not only women who want to place love as the top priority, as Beauvoir suggested in much of her work. The relationship seems to have been extremely important for Algren, who wanted to marry her and for her to live with him in Chicago. All the same, Algren was not willing to move to Paris to be with Beauvoir, which is perhaps unsurprising given her later admission that it was not only her work that held her back, but also her love for Sartre. She explained to Algren that she could not abandon Sartre because he was lonely and needed her, and she felt obliged to stay with him.[105]

Besides the difficulty in imagining that Sartre was ever lonely, it is also difficult to accept philosophically because Beauvoir says that she is necessary to Sartre, which as we have seen is a characteristic of inauthentic loving. Beauvoir repeatedly said love is not everything, and one must not give up anything for a lover, but she was certainly devoted to Sartre. Algren found the situation too difficult to accept and ended the relationship after two years. While we might consider her explanation to be an excuse to break up with Algren, she did seem devastated when he falls out of love with her, and she starts taking a medication called orthedrine to help her relax.[106] She would forever wear a ring that Algren gave her early in the relationship. Beauvoir made a choice, Sartre over Algren, but painted a picture as if she had none. She decided to limit herself and her possibilities for the sake of her love for Sartre.

Although Beauvoir often paints men as the ones who want to make use of their freedom for multifarious sexual activities, the desire for fidelity is not exclusively female. Existentially, we are free to create our essence, so there is no a priori fidelity compulsion – or even if there is, it is up to individuals to choose whether to act on their impulses. In *The Mandarins*, Anne (based on Beauvoir) would not give up life back in France, and Lewis Brogan (based on Algren) tells her, "you can't love someone who isn't all yours the same way as someone who is", and he stops loving her.[107]

Similarly, while Françoise in *She Came to Stay* philosophically supported the pact of freedom that she and Pierre forged, she finds it difficult to do in practice. She is constantly suppressing her relationship doubts, reassuring herself, and reminding herself to be strong. This becomes especially critical when Pierre exercises his freedom to be with other women. Later in the novel, Françoise concedes that she was overly optimistic about how they would handle that much freedom.[108]

A pact of fidelity is reached, ironically, within the *ménage-à-trois* when Pierre proposes that they relish in their love triangle without distractions.[109] According to Beauvoir's ethics, to limit one's freedom voluntarily is not existential, but this example highlights the fact that lovers do often want to impose constraints since romantic loving relationships require time, energy, and attention.

Even though Beauvoir's life was freely chosen, murdering Xavière in *She Came to Stay* suggests that she did have difficulty with free love. Nevertheless, if lovers do away with those expectations, shaking free from familial, societal, and cultural customs and mythologies, then the relationship can be built upon a platform of *tabula rasa* on which the couple decides their own goals. This is what Sartre and Beauvoir did: they went against social norms and created a new relationship based on what was important to them, embracing freedom to the greatest possible extent.

Devotion and transcendence are not mutually exclusive

Beauvoir saw devotion and transcendence as incompatible, so she dismissed devotion entirely. Yet, there is no reason why both cannot be integrated into an authentic existence. There is no existential rule to suggest that devotion has to be absolute and focused on only one thing.[110] One can still be devoted to one's lover and have other interests. Being a lover, wife, or mother can be all-consuming, but to be prudent, it can only be a temporary *raison d'être* or one of many.

Devotion is consistent with existentialism in the context of dedicating oneself passionately to a freely chosen project. Therefore, Beauvoir's objection should not be with devotion but rather with devotion to a single project that limits one's possibilities to engage in other projects, which is consistent with her earlier warning not to invest oneself entirely in a lover. However, Beauvoir made a sensible point with respect to relationship breakdowns and empty nests: lovers need other interests. Having other interests is not only a safety net but also enhances one's being, enriches life, and makes for more interesting couples. So if what Beauvoir meant about going beyond the family means to engage in a broader world than one's own sheltered little nest, then that is certainly sage advice.

A problem of value

Another problem is the underlying values that support Beauvoir's ideal of authentic loving relationships. Beauvoir proposed that authentic loving is possible only if men and women are equal, and yet there are issues with achieving the required conditions for authentic loving to flourish. For example, Beauvoir argues that change must be collective. There is little that individual women can do to change ideas about femininity, and any attempt to do so is futile.[111] Such statements are defeatist because existential thinkers propose that values do not exist inherently in the world; they are chosen and created by humans, and they do not have biological roots. While there are still structural impediments and habitual thinking regarding expectations and women's subordination, making it what some refer to as "a man's world", existentially, it is up to each individual to challenge those obstacles as they arise and make changes. Beauvoir thought it would take more than a few individuals to do this because many women do not believe themselves equal, actively perpetuating their submissive roles. Beauvoir doubted women's ability to change their situation. She implies that women will have to wait quietly for socialism or for men to change things for them. Existentially, this view is debilitating and flawed if individuals define themselves through their projects.

Furthermore, Beauvoir suggested that in order for women to be in a position to love authentically, they need to engage in the world as men do: "thinking, acting, working, and creating".[112] Besides the fact that these are not inherently male engagements, she looked down upon the ways in which women do gain power. Women's alternative activities are not necessarily inferior to men's. On the one hand, Beauvoir commends women for lacking negative male qualities such as "self-importance, the fatuousness, the complacency, and the spirit of emulation" and for being more truthful, caring, and generous than men.[113] But in her philosophy, she did tend to undervalue traditional feminine activities, such as creating and nurturing life and being manipulative and deceptive, which Nietzsche recognized as powerful.[114]

The key point is that it is up to individuals to create their own values, irrespective of sex, gender, historical attributions, or utility in order to live authentically. Thus, it is up to women to create new values, embracing transcendence and femininity, free from the objectifying gaze of men. Living by self-chosen values will be more difficult for some than for others, but it is open to every human in potentially every endeavor.

Money can't buy us love

Further to this issue of masculine and feminine values, Beauvoir argued that economic independence is a requirement for authentic loving. Beauvoir assumed that money increases freedom, and this is why women need to be economically independent. This stems from her inclusion of situation as a factor that restricts freedom. There are three key issues with this, however.

First, Beauvoir suggested that transcendence comes hand-in-hand with economic independence.[115] This is a necessary but insufficient condition. Neither work nor economic independence entails freedom. This is a point that Beauvoir portrayed in the characters of Anne and Françoise, who were economically independent and yet dependent on their lovers for their sense of self-worth.

Second, Beauvoir is absolutist about being either economically independent or doomed to immanence. She considered only paid work to provide the means for self-development and transcendence. Housework and childcare are considered to be unexistential, and husbands' historical parasitical dependence on their wives is ignored.[116] Beauvoir's argument is that husbands are transcending in non-domestic areas, and thus their dependence on wives relegates women to immanence and is a form of patriarchal oppression. Nevertheless, transcendence can be found in any activity and is not only a result of working and making money. The transcending moment is found when one surpasses, overcomes, or reaches beyond oneself and one's given situation. It is the active choice not to be determined by one's role or facticity. Paid work can be just as repetitive and boring and can be just as defined by one's roles as housework. Even creative jobs have elements of repetition. Housework and childcare can be just as creative as some jobs in finding new, more efficient, or more fulfilling ways of doing things. Beauvoir acknowledged that more transcendence can be found in housekeeping than in some paid jobs, but it contradicts her dominant view.

Third, pursuing economic independence is not necessarily an authentic activity. It is not an easy task to find a job that nourishes one's passion and returns enough money to establish independence. Those who are able to find jobs they truly love are the rare and lucky few. Many people work in order to survive and to buy time to do more fulfilling things. It is conceivable that someone is poor but is being more authentic by doing an activity that makes little or no money than a person who is making a lot of money but is working at a job that is neither creative nor inspiring. For example, a struggling artist or writer might represent the epitome of freedom, transcending and projecting into the future courageously, adventurously, and committedly. Yet by Beauvoir's criteria, if no one buys the artist's creations, then financial dependence on a lover also means disqualification from an authentic loving relationship. Such people may not have financial security, but they are conceivably much freer than organizational men and women who earn more money but engage in joyless striving.

These examples show that Beauvoir has failed to prove that work alone guarantees freedom. Money provides the power to withdraw from a relationship of dependence with comfort and without poverty. However, for Beauvoir to advocate a safety net to avoid poverty is pragmatic and not an existential description of authentic loving.

Leaping does not relieve anxiety

There is one final issue: loving requires a leap. Beauvoir portrayed love as an elusive concept. Love is manifested and revealed through loving actions but sustained by the faith that it has a future. Faith in love is supposed to provide lovers with a sense of security, but Beauvoir describes it as false, flimsy, and hollow. For example, Pierre tells Françoise in *She Came to Stay* that he loves her, but only she can choose to believe him. Françoise laments that there is no proof, and believing him requires an enormous leap of faith.[117]

Actions present only the façade of love. One never knows what lies beneath and beyond the actions, that is, the reasons for the actions and whether the actions will persist into the future. Faith is what sustains Paula in wrongly believing she and Henri still have a loving relationship in *The Mandarins*. In *She Came to Stay*, Françoise mourns about how magnificent loving relationships appear superficially, but there is nothing tangible to support feelings. She bemoans that feelings "dazzle outwardly. They're firm, they're faithful, they can even be whitewashed periodically with beautiful words...Only, they must never be opened. You'll find only dust and ashes inside".[118]

Beauvoir also exposes the inadequacy of love orchestrated in this way in *The Blood of Others*. Blomart does not love Hélène. He behaves lovingly, he tells her he loves her, he gives up his other mistress, and he proposes marriage. He wants to see her happy, is very fond of her, likes her body, finds her charming, and feels tenderness and esteem for her. Yet, none of these things amounts to truly loving her. He has reduced love to a functional role. Simply choosing to love is insufficient for Blomart.

Finding evidence of loving in actions says nothing about the future. For Beauvoir, loving is projecting together into the future. Anything beyond the moment, beyond concrete actions, requires faith. "And is faith courage or laziness?" asks Françoise.[119] Furthermore, love requires repeated leaps of faith and constant reaffirmations. Françoise agonizes over the huge effort required to leap to love and the difficulty she has with suspending her disbelief, that is, to continue to believe that Pierre loves her without any concrete evidence.[120]

Notwithstanding the depressing realization that all we might find below the surface is dust and ashes, Beauvoir urges us to embrace loving because there is no certainty in anything in life. Everything is ambiguous, and we must act and choose regardless. Beauvoir urges us to love in spite of the anxiety that it will fail and to embrace its ambiguous nature.[121]

Anguish and risk are conditions of life, and we cannot let it stifle us into inaction, because inaction is still a choice, and we are responsible for all the choices we make. While we can never be sure of the consequences of our actions and the associated risk and anguish, it is fundamental to our human condition. Jean-Pierre asks rhetorically at the end of *Who Shall Die?*: "But why should we wish for anything else?"[122]

Beauvoir works in the space of ambiguity by exploring the contradictions of existence, that is, between free and limited, separate and united, rational and intoxicated, and for and against submission. However, Beauvoir retreated too far and made too many concessions for her to be strictly existential in her venerated goal of freedom to remain solidly intact.

Beauvoir emphasized that romantic loving is so important that it tends to become a major part of our lives, but if individuals have no other interests, there is a risk of inauthentic loving due to the power struggles that emanate from dependence. She gives us no definite formula as to how to balance one's love interest within her recommended diversified portfolio of life. However, she highlighted the fact that love is a high-risk game and what is really important is that lovers strive toward authentic projects and also respect and support each other in their individual quests, even if it means that lovers are not always each other's top priority, and even if it risks the death of love. Being supportive in this sense need not be submission but rather together tackling the world and opening up possibilities for each other. She granted that it is not easy, and it is up to each couple to work it out together.

This chapter focused on the ways in which Beauvoir attempted to create a framework for authentic loving that Sartre failed to do. She accepted that others modify one's choices through infusing the world with opportunities and meanings. Beauvoir highlighted many of the difficulties in traditional ideas of romantic loving, particularly that they tend to be incompatible with authentic living. Like Nietzsche, she pointed out that, historically, women have not been authentic, because they have tolerated oppression and compromised their freedom for the sake of romantic relationships and an easier life. Like Sartre, she pointed out that lovers want to form a "we" to become a whole, but this is undesirable existentially because it induces dependency. Also like Sartre and Nietzsche, she described love as the desire to possess the other but this desire is also bad faith not only because is it impossible but because it is inauthentic to usurp another's transcendence. For Beauvoir, friendship is a much better basis for a relationship than one built on merging because it respects the other as a free subject and accepts that the other has independent projects. It recognizes otherness, but it does not treat the other as an object to be dominated or subordinated. Authentic romantic loving is possible if lovers recognize each other as and act as free, equal, and transcending subjects. Such relationships will be richer and more interesting, lovers will better understand each other, and durability will be strengthened through pursuing common goals.

7
Conclusion

This book has undertaken an existential quest to understand the meaning and nature of heterosexual romantic loving relationships. Existential philosophies provide the narratives to interrogate implicit assumptions about romantic loving behaviors and expectations, and to bring into question saccharine romantic fictions. Although critical of romantic loving, the five existential philosophers in this book did not dismiss it, but instead highlighted flaws in romantic ideals and problems that arise from misplaced expectations.

For example, they point out that the ideals of romantic loving can be perplexing because dreams of oneness and unity are illusions; it feels like it will last forever but there are no guarantees that it will last the night; and lovers hope for harmony, but quarrels are inevitable. The pursuit of the ideals of happiness and longevity in relationships is fraught with danger because, according to the existential philosophers, lovers are bound to set themselves up for failure. Instead, the existential approach suggests that pursuing authentically meaningful relationships is more worthwhile and rewarding.

The existential philosophers are more descriptive than prescriptive. It would be bad faith blindly to follow someone else's rules. Existentially, it is up to individuals to make their own choices. However, from the existential philosophers one can derive important principles to be aware of – if one is interested in making more enlightened choices about relationships.

The existential attitude does not guarantee that lovers will not be hurt or disappointed. Still, with a deeper understanding of loving behavior, dynamics, and expectations, lovers would be more attuned to sources of conflicts and disappointments, more aware of their freedom, and better able to create authentically meaningful relationships. In this way, existential philosophies uncover a fresh approach that reinvigorates and revitalizes romantic loving.

This concluding chapter summarizes the philosophers' views, explores the key problems that existential philosophies pose for romantic loving, and illuminates existential suggestions to overcome these problems.

The existential philosophers' key points about romantic loving

The existential philosophers' central observations regarding the problems of romantic loving and associated solutions are as follows. Max Stirner considered romantic loving to be problematic due to associated obligations and façades of unselfishness. Instead, he recommends self-love, whereby one owns, accepts, and takes an egoistic interest in oneself. Not until one has freed oneself from the expectations of others can one create one's own enjoyable and interesting loving relationships.

Søren Kierkegaard suggested that romantic loving is inherently disappointing due to its unstable nature, rendering it a fleeting and meaningless erotic encounter. He sought to establish loving relationships as more secure through such commitments as marriage and faith in God. Freeing oneself from erotic impulses and loving independently of the beloved were his preferred solutions to avoiding disappointment in relationships.

Friedrich Nietzsche declared that the problems in romantic loving stem from outdated Christian values, inappropriate social conventions, and petty power dynamics. Freeing oneself from these chains enables one better to strive toward the ideal of the *Übermensch*. His advice on how to overcome these restrictions is wide and varied, but primarily he advocated raising awareness about one's power and self-mastery, celebrating the passions, and becoming great friends.

Jean-Paul Sartre proposed that the allure of romantic loving is that it seems to be a means of becoming oneself, but it is inherently disheartening because the ideal is unattainable, leaving loving relationships to wallow in sadomasochistic dialectics. Sartre did not comprehensively articulate solutions, but his suggestions for dealing with the frustrations – even if they cannot be resolved – include recognizing that loving behavior is a choice, accepting the other as they are, and treating the other as the most important person in one's life.

Simone de Beauvoir argued that problems in romantic loving stem from such degenerate behavior as idolizing, submitting to, dominating, attempting to merge with, possessing, devoting oneself to, and justifying oneself in the beloved, as well as blindly accepting pre-established social roles and conventions. More harmonious relationships can be achieved, she maintained, through reciprocal recognition of two freedoms. This requires being free from oppression and fixed roles, and it enables the pursuit of authentic projects.

The following section explores the key problems that existential philosophies pose, by addressing each of the key features of romantic loving as defined in the introduction.

Problems that existential philosophies pose for romantic loving

In the introduction, romantic loving was defined as being passionate, includes the hope that it will last, involves the concept of individuals uniting or merging and creating a "we", and is personal. Some definitions also include companionship, intimacy, and concern for each other's welfare.

The existential philosophers overwhelmingly agree that four of these elements are largely to blame for misplaced expectations and flawed ideals about the nature of, and behavior associated with, romantic loving. Problems arise, in particular, when lovers become slaves to their passions, when they form unrealistic expectations about the longevity of romantic relationships, when they engage in behavior that aims to merge, and when they realize that the intimacy they strive for is slippery at best. The other features of romantic loving – that it is personal and involves companionship and concern for each other's welfare – are less controversial.

When unbridled passion takes over

The existential philosophers do not have a problem with the fact that romantic loving is based on sexual passion. However, they do have issues with unbridled and uncontrolled passion. To lead a hedonistic life ruled by immediate gratification means that one is a slave to one's desires, or in other words, ruled by natural urges and drives.

While there are hedonistic elements within Stirner's philosophy, such as his focus on pleasure, he strongly opposes allowing oneself to be ruled by one's love, or any other passion, because it indicates that one is subordinating oneself to one's desires. Kierkegaard criticized Don Giovanni for being unreflective and for being a prisoner to his sexual urges. For Nietzsche, allowing oneself to be swept away with the frivolity of loving is delusional and deceptive since beauty blinds judgment. It is not only reflective of a weak will but also problematic if it is the basis for such important decisions as marriage and procreation because all too often they end up being mistakes. Beauvoir was particularly worried that lovers, wallowing in the euphoria of their desires, risk losing themselves and sinking into immanence. Although Sartre was more resigned to capricious loving behavior, he also argued that behavior is a choice, even if it is a pre-reflective choice, since there is no escape from responsibility for our actions.

The existential issue with lovers allowing their passions to run wild is that although they satisfy their sexual urges, it is decadent, weak willed, shallow, reactionary, animalistic, and immature to indulge without restraint in one's primal instincts.

When merging descends into tyranny

The existential philosophers were well aware that the temptation for lovers to try to merge is strong. Merging and uniting are ways of being in loving relationships, but it is existentially precarious if it involves slavish or possessive behavior or if lovers expect to achieve lasting perfect harmony and oneness. The definition of romantic loving includes a shift in lovers' perspectives from considering themselves as two "I"s to a single "we". The existential philosophers acknowledge that this feeling of solidarity and connectivity is part and parcel of romantic loving. However, they also agree that merging with another is impossible if it is understood sentimentally as fusing with one's other half, creating a single entity, and being one.

Stirner abhorred the very idea of being tied to another because it is restrictive. Similarly, Nietzsche observed that lovers all too often smother each other and hold each other back from greatness, and so he recommended regularly cutting one's ties. Sartre acknowledged that lovers sometimes do feel as if they have achieved the ideal, but any respite is brief because escaping the vicious cycle of assimilation and appropriation is nearly impossible. Beauvoir argued that the sense of oneness established and the concept of "we" are misplaced because people will have differences in thinking. Harmony cannot be taken for granted, because it is inherently unstable. Although lovers can feel as if they have merged into a harmonious entity, the existential view is that connections are unreliable.

The existential portrayal of romantic loving builds on Hegel's master-slave dialectic. According to Hegel, encounters with others result in one's seizing the status of a master and the other, more fearful, retreating to the status of a slave. Nevertheless, masters need slaves in order to assert their masterly status, rendering a paradoxical dialectic whereby slaves hold the power to define their masters. The existential philosophers agree that a similar dynamic is at play in romantic relationships, and they point out that slavishness and possessiveness are both strategies that are liable to create problems for lovers.

For Stirner and Nietzsche, romantic loving, like all relations, is possessive in nature. They both allude to love as war, but they also suggest that possessiveness for the sake of such desires as jealousy or avarice is weak and indicative of one who is not master of oneself. Stirner and Kierkegaard described romantic loving as the attempt to conquer and possess the other for the interesting and enjoyable experience. However, Kierkegaard indicated that this dynamic becomes a source of frustration because possession can never be fully realized. Kierkegaard thought marriage would annul such power dynamics because it implies already having conquered one another.

For Sartre, merging is the ideal of romantic loving. However, it is very risky business. The goal is to possess the other's freedom while not having one's own freedom possessed and one's very being is at stake. Slavishness is a masochistic strategy and possessiveness is a sadistic strategy that lovers utilize to try to achieve this ideal. Nevertheless, Sartre pointed out that if it were possible, it would destroy what one values in the other: their otherness.

Beauvoir agreed with Nietzsche that sexual loving is characterized by a craving to possess and control the lover. She also agreed with Nietzsche that the traditional feminine ideal of love is to relinquish and devote oneself to a male lover and that such an attitude is actually egoistic because it is a subtle strategy either to escape responsibility for an independent existence or to satisfy their unbridled urges. Moreover, Beauvoir agreed with Nietzsche that lovers who act as adoring chattels actually lace their generosity with tyranny.

For Beauvoir, if the attempt to merge occurs in the context of a lover's trying to control the beloved's actions, it neglects the fact that the other is a sovereign subject, and choices cannot be authentically made on the beloved's behalf. Beauvoir scorned the possessiveness that merging encourages because it treats the other as an object and is disrespectful since it is an attempt to hijack the beloved's freedom. Alternatively, if it is a form of romantic rent-seeking – that is, a means of lazily trying to define oneself through another's actions or as a derivative of the other's identity – then this is also inauthentic because individuals are responsible for their own actions. Certainly, actions occur in webs of relationships, but for them to be entirely defined by others is problematic because it corresponds to a loss of independence and is a corrupted means of self-definition. Beauvoir and Sartre both agree that the trophy of the game is to become complete. For Sartre, the goal is completed self-knowledge, that is, to be one's own foundation. For Beauvoir, it is to take control of the beloved for justification of one's life so that one does not have to strive for one's own transcendence. Nietzsche and Sartre, however, both thought that men are just as likely as women to attempt to rob others of their freedom.

Merging behavior that manifests as slavishness or possessiveness is problematic for the existential philosophers because both attitudes alike foster unproductive power struggles that thwart lovers in their personal endeavors. Being a slave either to the ideal of love or to a lover is problematic if it involves annihilating oneself as a self-determining and self-creating sovereign subject. Existentially, even though others are a condition of one's existence, this does not mean that one should subsume oneself into others, because that is to lose oneself.

When love fades

The allure of romantic loving as a merging is strong because, if it were possible, it would overcome the anguish of existence by finding completeness in each other. In finding a complementary being, lovers gain a sense of fullness and an end to anxiety about being alone. Indeed, loving relationships can relieve anxieties regarding self-worth and self-esteem because one is valued, accepted, and desired by another.

It is no wonder that lovers want love to last. It is no wonder that lovers want to promise "Till death us do part". Lovers tend to want some kind of assurance of the future with each other for better or for worse, that is, no matter what other changes occur. Romantic relationships seem to promise certainty and comfort in an unpredictable and changeable world.

The existential philosophers were well aware that one of the fundamental charms of romantic loving is that lovers hope that it will relieve anxiety. For example, Kierkegaard suggested that secure relationships give life continuity; Nietzsche proposed that romantic loving is like a medicine that relieves the pain of life; for Sartre, love's joy is the feeling that one's life is justified; and similarly for Beauvoir, lovers find solace in the illusion of harmony and feeling of oneness. Stirner is the notable exception since he argued that being anxious about anything is counterproductive.

The five existential philosophers saw nothing wrong with hoping love will last, but problems start when lovers turn their hope into an absolute. The existential point is that if romantic loving is based on whimsical, uncontrolled desires, then change is inevitable, and couples will thus find themselves wanting to part well before death.

Stirner focused his attack not on enduring relationships, but on the expectation that they *should* endure. Like wine, one can have too much of a good thing and lose interest, or the object of affection changes its qualities and loses what made it desirable in the first place. The issue for Kierkegaard and Nietzsche was that loving relationships based on sensuality and instant satisfaction are fickle and fleeting. Kierkegaard thought that a lack of serious definitive choices makes romantic relationships meaningless. Moreover, he suggested that lovers who are slaves to their passions are prone to being caught up in monotonous cycles of serial romances. This is the idea implicit in his description – but not his recommendation – of crop rotation in *Either/Or*, when he suggested that as soon as the current crop enters maturity, or one tires of relationships, one starts seeking out new possibilities and preparing for the next. Nietzsche was more concerned that lovers do make serious choices based on an unstable and delusional affectation that all too often tires with age and frequency of contact, and broken promises and reckless choices turn lovers into liars and hypocrites.

The issue for Sartre and Beauvoir alike was that because lovers believe that love will last a lifetime, they establish each other as a primary source of meaning in their lives. Yet Sartre highlighted that absolute security is unachievable because individuals are creative nothingnesses, and they are free to change in unpredictable ways. One never knows with perfect confidence whether and to what extent loving will be requited, and although we do not want it to end, the possibility looms over us. Beauvoir showed that once the novelty of admiration wears off, power struggles and boredom tend to kill romance. Thus, it is risky to found one's being in something so unpredictable, and lovers are left void of meaning if the relationship ceases.

Romance wanes because life is impermanent. Existentially, we are thrown into an ever-changing, unstable existence, and in it we are creative nothingnesses, always becoming and evolving and free to define ourselves as we choose. At every moment, possibilities lie before us, meaning that lovers and feelings are liable to change. This makes romantic loving inherently insecure, which goes some way to explaining why the ideal that romantic love should last is so elusive and why it is a major source of frustration in relationships.

When intimacy fails

Intimacy is a highly desirable feature of romantic loving, but the existential philosophers point out that it is highly unreliable. All five philosophers emphasize the importance of being with others in being human, in self-discovery, in self-creation, and in enjoying oneself. Relationships are a primordial existential category: we are for-ourselves, but we exist in a world with others, and we define ourselves through our relationships. Romantic partners are particularly valuable because they engage on a more sensual level than other relationships do. Romantic relationships seem to promise complete disclosure between the couple because such closeness fosters senses of unparalleled intimacy and completion or, as Sartre called it, the being-in-itself-for-itself.

Nevertheless, the five existential philosophers bring to light the limitations with respect to defining ourselves with and through others. Following from the earlier problems, if two people cannot merge, and the sense of oneness is an illusion, then this brings into question how intimate lovers can be, that is, how well lovers can know each other and how much they can know about themselves through each other.

Nietzsche and Stirner were wary of being too intimate. They thought it to be dangerous to get too close to others because it gives others the power to mislead, beguile, and entrap. Kierkegaard thought that God was the only one who could really know an individual intimately, but later, he gave his ex-fiancé Regine some credit for paving the way toward deepening his self-understanding. While Sartre argued that people could know themselves better through being intimate, he also granted that this is unreliable because people lie. Beauvoir, who had first-hand experience with Sartre's lies, proposed that an intimate connection between lovers could be achieved through great sex. However, the problem remains that even if lovers can establish an understanding, they cannot control each other's views, and this is what led to Xavière's murder in *She Came to Stay*.

Thus, the existential answer to how well lovers can know each other and themselves is that it is uncertain. Since lovers cannot merge, they cannot fully trust or comprehend each other beyond all doubt; nor can they control each other's views. Lovers long for connections between them, but the bridges we build are fragile.

The less problematic elements of romantic loving
Romantic loving is personal

Kierkegaard, unlike the other four philosophers, took particular issue with the personal nature of loving. According to Kierkegaard, romantic loving's preferential nature is problematic because it requires the beloved to reciprocate, and that makes romantic loving insecure. Thus, Kierkegaard sought to overcome the problems outlined above by leaping to faith and loving independently of the beloved. Yet this solution raises other issues, in particular that it is a leap out of romantic loving and into spiritual loving.

Romantic loving includes companionship

If companionship is understood as deep and meaningful friendship, as opposed to keeping each other company, then the existential philosophers were supportive of romantic loving's including it. However, they were skeptical that lovers would actually be capable of it because they saw that lovers tend to descend quickly into power games. Sartre was less interested in friendship because he placed great importance on the role of carnal knowledge in self-understanding. Nietzsche and Stirner noted the problem that friendships are also at risk of petty power struggles, although really great friends strive to overcome them.

Romantic loving includes concern for the other's welfare

The five existential philosophers endorse the idea that romantic loving includes concern for the lover's welfare, but they disagree on whether it is for the lover's sake or one's own sake. Stirner and Nietzsche proposed that lovers are hypocrites if they think concern for the other is unselfish or unegoistic since by helping others they are actually serving their own interests. For Sartre, since love is a project to discover secrets about oneself, one values the other's welfare insofar as one values their opinion. Kierkegaard and Beauvoir wanted to avoid such attitudes as these, which descend quickly into selfishness. This is why Kierkegaard recommended religious loving, and in her fiction, Beauvoir dismissed such an attitude as tainted loving, though still technically romantic, because it treats the lover as an object.

Given the raft of issues that existential philosophies pose for romantic loving, it is unsurprising that they associate such relationships with anxiety. Kierkegaard suggested that because romantic loving is insecure, melancholy plagues it. Nietzsche suggested that the feeling of security in love is delusional, and Sartre proposed that any relief would be short-lived as a result of a myriad of factors working toward love's destruction. Beauvoir's writings suggest even more skepticism when she argued that it is inauthentic to seek meaning through a lover. Nevertheless, it was shown that there is no reason why it cannot be one among others or a temporary one.

Anxiety stems from the acknowledgment that one cannot rely on the lover to provide absolute meaning in one's life, the insurmountable abyss between lovers, awareness of the tensions that loving relationships create, and the recognition that there is no security in the relationship – such as how long it will last, if it will be requited as one wants, whether one is a means to another end and what that end might be, and how reliable the other person's gaze is.

The anxiety of love lies in its vagaries. Love can relieve anxieties by infusing one's life with meaning, but such relief is inherently precarious given the problems outlined above and is likely to be temporary, unreliable, or illusory. The existential message is for lovers to be aware that passions change, lovers evolve, and it is unrealistic to expect the initial phases of love to last naturally. To make major life decisions based on romantic whims is naïve if not negligent.

Existential advice for overcoming problems in romantic loving

The key to unpacking existential solutions in order to overcome these issues outlined above is freedom, which can be understood in terms of freeing oneself *from* both external and self-imposed constraints in order to be free *to* act in accordance with one's choices and establish oneself as self-determining and self-creating. Stirner and Nietzsche understood that this is determined by whether one has the *power* to act as one chooses. Specifically, the existential philosophers suggest that lovers free themselves from being slaves to their passions, from petty power games, and from pre-established romantic ideals in order to be free to choose behavior and priorities and in order to create authentically meaningful relationships.

Free from being a slave to one's passions

The existential philosophers are careful not to discount the gravity of romantic loving's passionate and intoxicating nature. There is nothing wrong with love-fueled ecstasy, excitement, elation, and enthusiasm. For example, Stirner emphasized frivolity and the enjoyment of loving. Through the eyes of Johannes, Kierkegaard described the beauty and exhilaration that romantic loving sparks. Nietzsche was acutely concerned that suppressing passions can wreak havoc, and he impressed upon the importance of passionate expression and intoxication so as not to be overwhelmed by the storms within. In one of Sartre's later works, he referred to the value in allowing oneself to be overcome by one's love. Beauvoir took the idea to the extreme by suggesting that not all passions can be mastered and that intoxication is an essential element of authentic loving. For the existential philosophers, it is clear that passionate expression is a vital part of living and loving.

Nevertheless, it was also seen that the five existential philosophers emphasize that it is important to be free from being a slave to one's passions so that one's impulses do not determine one's behavior. Contra Dostoyevsky's notorious line, anything does not go, because existentially, one does not debase oneself to petty whims and act upon immediate impulses. Instead, Stirner and Nietzsche affirmed the importance of self-mastery, whereby one rules one's appetites, emotions, and sensuality. Passions, although essential, can and should be directed. Kierkegaard also encouraged lovers to reflect on their moods, master their desires, and free themselves from making impulsive or reactionary choices in order that they own themselves. The key existential message is that being tipsy on love is beautiful and wonderful, but getting blind drunk is ugly and debauched, although it is easier said than done.

Free from petty power games

The existential philosophers ultimately recommended that lovers stop playing power games in order to live a more noble and worthwhile existence and to achieve authentically meaningful relationships. This does not mean that conflict is eliminated altogether but rather that the pettiness of trivial possessive games is left behind. An example would be lovers who are critical in a constructive manner, such as through discussing and arguing issues, which encourages reflection on each partner's mode of being in the world and fosters a greater understanding of it via new perspectives. Such lovers are more like friends, and their love is a rich and fertile battlefield.

Stirner proposed that unique ones come to understandings through unions. The purpose of such unions is not to know oneself but instead to enjoy oneself and extend one's power. Nietzsche expressed this idea through the star friendship, whereby partners inspire and push each other to achieve more than they could have imagined alone and to get closer to the ideal of the *Übermensch*. Nietzsche and Beauvoir were particularly fond of great friendships. They saw such relationships as having overcome power games because friends support and respect each other and their individual striving and are more amenable to constructively challenging one another than are lovers. While Nietzsche was skeptical that lovers could be friends, Beauvoir thought it to be not only possible but also highly preferable. Although Beauvoir strove for harmony, she realized that it had to be constantly worked for, suggesting that struggling is a fundamental part of understanding one's being in the world.

In his fictional works, Sartre, like Nietzsche, finds the intolerance and resistance that enemies provide to be of greater value than what lovers provide. They both highlighted the benefits of alterity – that is, taking on the role of enemy when challenge, criticism, and competition are appropriate. Sartre alludes to the constructive nature of tension in *Huis Clos* when Inez challenges Garcin, in *Lucifer and the Lord* when Goetz rejects Hilda's hollow gaze, and in *Being and Nothingness* when Sartre argues that a situation of intolerance sparks opportunities to assert oneself.

The existential perspective reveals that loving can mean war; however, as lovers rise above power struggles of domination, subordination, and oppression, rivalry still exists, but it is a constructive and inspiring engagement, as opposed to one that leaves a trail of destruction in its wake. Tolerance is not an admirable quality, and challenging each other provides a more helpful basis for transcending, self-fulfillment, and self-discovery than does unquestioning acceptance. Although being at loggerheads all the time would be exhausting, a healthy dose of adversity is sure to keep lovers on their toes. This is not to say that lovers in a destructive relationship should stick together, but rather let us recognize that there will be opportunities to galvanize the antagonism and channel efforts and conversation into being constructive.

Although being with others is an integral dimension of being human, the existential philosophers acknowledge the benefits to be had through appreciating distance, differences, and otherness, such as different perspectives, ideas and challenges and also keeping a little mystery, surprise, wonder, and sense of discovery alive. Nietzsche suggested that relationships would be stronger if lovers were to give each other space and regularly spent time apart. Ideally, he advised, living apart would help to keep the relationship fresh and sparkling, and presumably it would help to avoid taking each other for granted. It is a matter of creating a mode of being with lovers that is creative and opens up possibilities for one another.

Free from pre-established romantic ideals

The five existential philosophers are also critical of preconceived expectations about how romantic lovers ought to behave. Just as instinctively responding to one's impulses is indicative of a weak, undeveloped, unreflective, and immature individual, so too is instinctively accepting preestablished ideals indicative of a herd animal or someone who hides in the crowd. It is not authentic, since one is not choosing one's own values and relationships.

Stirner criticized any expectation that a lover ought to behave in a certain manner, but he specifically condemns the expectations that romantic loving ought to be unselfish, unconditional, and forever.

Instead, he advocated owning oneself rather than being owned by norms and values created by others. Sartre advocated being free from illusions and from belief in determinism – for example, the belief that soul mates exist who are uniquely destined for one another. Since existence precedes essence, we create our relationships and are responsible for our romantic choices. Beauvoir accentuated being free from such sentimental notions as love's all-consumingness and its ability to conquer all obstacles. She was also critical of loving behavior, particularly women's, in blindly accepting their conventional roles and customs, that is, in subordinating themselves to male lovers and unquestioningly accepting the traditional destiny of being a wife and mother. This is also why the existential philosophers have a problem with the assumption that a good relationship is a long one.

While Stirner, Sartre, and Beauvoir objected to the ideal of romantic loving culminating in marriage because it incorporates accepting pre-established social roles and values, Kierkegaard and Nietzsche did not. Kierkegaard and Nietzsche saw it as a worthwhile institution for elevating romantic loving into something more serious, stable, and durable. Nevertheless, Nietzsche was not wedded to this view, and he oscillated between advocating marriage for all and arguing against it as being unnatural and irrational when built on an anemic foundation of romantic loving. Beauvoir and Nietzsche criticized both men and women's loving behavior that manifests as instinctively acting out and conforming to masculine and feminine ideals and images.

One can live a life of being a victim of circumstance: blindly stumbling along, going with the flow, being a slave to social, biological, and cultural processes. Such a life is what Beauvoir called "immanent" living and what Sartre called "bad faith". The existential moment is realizing that such a life is not good enough and not worth living. The moment of conversion is recognizing one's situation and possibilities and then acting bravely in a way that upholds the principles by which one chooses to live. It is the resolve to do and to act rather than being blown where the wind takes one. It is assertively leaping from possibility into actuality, as Kierkegaard would say.

In loving relationships, the existential leap is the Nietzschean "yes" to the lover – or in other words, a decisive declaration that "I choose you" – and behaving in ways that support that decision. We saw this in Sartre's *Nausea* when Anny spoke of delving into the relationship without looking back and in Beauvoir's *Useless Mouths* when Jean-Pierre embraced the absurd world and undertook to change it so that it exists with his lover Clarice in it. It is refusing to live by the rules, roles, and expectations of society. It is a matter of choosing oneself rather than being chosen for. It is clear why Kierkegaard and Nietzsche saw marriage as a suitable forum for making such a choice: it ought to be one of the most meaningful and life-changing decisions people make, although it is rarely taken seriously enough.

Nevertheless, freeing oneself from such chains as instinctive loving behavior and blind acceptance of problematic romantic ideals is not sufficient for the existential philosophers. The question becomes: what will lovers have freed themselves to do? Or, since for Stirner and Nietzsche freedom is not the issue, they would have asked: what do lovers have the power to do? Freeing themselves from the fetters identified thus far, lovers will have empowered themselves to be self-determining and self-creating, which means that they will be able to reinvigorate romantic loving in a way that allows for authentically meaningful relationships. This dimension is explored through the roles of choice, freedom, and authenticity in romantic loving below.

Free to choose loving behavior

We cannot be free from everything, because some things are beyond our power. Stirner said that we can free ourselves from most things, but not from everything; Kierkegaard considered the lack of ability to control another's love to be problematic; Nietzsche suggested that it is too easy to lose control of ourselves if passions are suppressed; Sartre argued that some things limit our possibilities if we see them as obstacles; and Beauvoir argued that situations can be oppressive. However, there are many aspects of one's life within one's power, notably one's behavior.

The existential view is that individuals are free to choose romantic behavior. Romantic loving is revealed through actions, and those actions are not pre-defined. Lovers are creative nothings, and just as they create themselves, so too do they create their loving relationships and choose themselves as people who do loving things. If the romantic elements fade, it is because lovers choose not to behave lovingly and choose not to engage in a romantic way.

In Sartre's words, loving actions reveal one's love, and romantic loving is the sum of loving actions. To proceed to a higher, existential mode of living, Kierkegaard suggested that lovers need actively and assertively to choose their relationships. Kierkegaard and Nietzsche conceded that marriage would not provide a strong enough platform to establish authentically meaningful relationships, because married couples are just as likely to engage in frivolous power games. Thus, Kierkegaard turned to religious love, whereas Nietzsche and Beauvoir advocated friendship as a means of sublimating sexual impulses into more productive relationships that promote self-overcoming and nourish and strengthen the individuals so that they can better strive toward their goals. Stirner advocated egoistic unions to a similar end. Although Stirner thought that power dynamics were a fact of relationships, unique ones embrace this fact and use their power to create and negotiate relationships that interest them.

There are three key points to note with respect to the emphasis on the role of choice in romantic loving. First, if existentially we are condemned to choose, how can we reconcile it with the passionate elements of loving? The answer is that lovers choose their passions, choose to master them, and choose themselves as loving people. Loving feelings can seem overwhelming, and while some elements of the relationship may seem uncontrollable, such as physical and sexual attraction, the decision to be in and stay in the relationship *is* controllable, as is the decision whether or not to act upon those seemingly uncontrollable drives, and if so, to what extent.

A second point is whether it is unromantic to suggest that romantic loving can be chosen since that means everyone is a potential lover. Romantic loving conceived as a choice does mean that everyone is a potential lover, but that does not make it unromantic. Although it means that lovers are not destined to find their "other half" or their "soul mate" and that they are not "made for each other", romantic loving is an appreciation of an individual's unique qualities. To be loved independently of one's distinctiveness (as Kierkegaard suggested) is to depersonalize the relationship, and that would make it unromantic. Since lovers are creative nothingnesses, it is possible that both lovers evolve and that what they find lovable in the other changes over time. It is up to the individuals to choose their criteria and to create their own relationships.

The third key aspect of loving conceived as a choice is that it is not a one-off choice. The idea that cupid's arrow need pierce its target's heart only once for love to strike is a cute myth. The existential approach exiles cupid and recognizes that love does not happen in an isolated moment. A loving relationship is a series of choices requiring reaffirmation – that is, perpetually choosing oneself as one who acts lovingly toward another. Just as a relationship is a series of actions, so too is it a series of leaps into an unknown future. Sartre's character Annie in *Nausea*, Beauvoir's character Françoise in *The Mandarins*, and Kierkegaard's pseudonym Climacus in *Concluding Unscientific Postscript* all describe the anxiety and the herculean courage involved in making such leaps. Nevertheless, the existential philosophers do not recommend seeking safety and comfort but instead advise lovers to leap passionately into relationships.

Free to choose priorities

The problem with romantic loving is not only that being with a lover calls for lovers to restrict their freedom, but also that lovers often want to restrict their own freedom. This is potentially contradictory since the five existential philosophers also bring to light the urgency of freeing oneself from self-imposed limitations. They overcome this issue not by denying that they are free, but rather by accepting responsibility for their choices and by prioritizing their passions. Being conscious of the chains that threaten to encapsulate lovers allows lovers more carefully to choose their ties.

The five existential philosophers suggest that romantic relationships do tend to call for lovers to restrict their freedom or modify their choices because the relationship is more important than absolute freedom. They barter certain liberties, such as sexual freedom, for other expected benefits, such as trust, security, or depth of experience. Since loving behavior, passions, and ties are chosen, lovers are also in a position to choose to prioritize, and this can be understood as foregoing certain possibilities because one wishes to maintain a loving relationship. There is no issue with compromising and sacrificing for the other's benefit, as long as lovers do not surrender themselves and as long as they master their loving behavior. Such a relationship is built on the strength of two individuals striving together instead of being weak and slavish and weighing each other down with dependencies and deficiencies.

Stirner argued that lovers can choose whatever limits and obligations they like, as long as they own them and are ready to break them if those limits and obligations compromise one's ownness. Kierkegaard suggested that by making commitments, one opens up possibilities for oneself and gives meaning and purpose to existence. Although Nietzsche recommended breaking ties with others to reassert oneself as self-defining, he also welcomed the challenges that only great lovers can provide.

Beauvoir argued that it is bad faith voluntarily to renounce freedom, but she was referring to being a slave and escaping responsibility for self-determination through becoming an other for the male lover. Restricted freedom in the form of fidelity was a consequence of Beauvoir and Algren's relationship, but it was not bad faith, because it was freely chosen, was not imposed externally, and did not involve abdicating themselves.

Beauvoir and Sartre's experience would seem to indicate that although they attempted to maintain freedom in their relationship, there were still such conditions as transparency and maintaining each other's status as essential. Nevertheless, it was also seen that transparency does not appear to have been a constraint that Sartre took seriously. According to Sartre, denying one's freedom by turning away from possibilities is a form of bad faith, but the way one engages with the world determines whether something is a restriction, and thus limitations are actually freely chosen priorities.

Free to create authentically meaningful relationships

Pursuing one's own authentic projects while being in a romantic relationship can be complicated since lovers make concessions, sacrifice, negotiate, modify goals, shift priorities, and forego possibilities for the sake of each other. However, it has been shown that romantic relationships are no excuse for limiting lovers' freedom or authentic pursuits. Romantic relationships that do not allow for authentic self-chosen projects can and do exist but are problematic existentially since lovers then are not free from being a slave to their passions, problematic romantic ideals, or, as Beauvoir emphasized, oppression. For Beauvoir, authentic loving is not possible under oppression, and women who play to their strengths within oppression are inauthentic. The existential challenge for romantic lovers is to create more satisfying relationships that complement and enhance their personal, authentic endeavors. It is not the case that the gain in possibilities offsets the losses, but rather the existential attitude is to search for possibilities that open up in and through the relationship. It is a matter of making the most of love's fertile battlefield and creating and seizing new opportunities.

Such an attitude is evident in Beauvoir's emphasis on the importance of lovers working together toward a common goal. Similarly, it is seen in Stirner's union to pursue mutually beneficial goals and in Sartre's authentic loving that supports each other's ends. It is further seen in Nietzsche's idea of two strong individuals who act as catalysts for each other's striving toward the ideal of the *Übermensch* and in Kierkegaard's eventual realization that he could have had a romantic relationship with Regine if he had had faith in God. It is up to lovers to reinvigorate their romantic behavior in a way that allows for authentically meaningful relationships.

Despite the existential philosophers' suspicion about the impact that romantic relationships have on individual freedom, authenticity, and power, they suggest that the most fulfilling and satisfying existence can be achieved only through leaping into romantic loving because it is enriching and enables individuals to engage more intensely in the world. It seems fitting to give the philosophers the final word: Stirner wrote that someone who loves is richer than someone who does not; Kierkegaard suggested that loving others is the only thing worth living for; Nietzsche advised that we need lovers like bitter medicine to be able better to strive toward the ideal of the *Übermensch*; Sartre held that lovers are the key to revealing deeper dimensions of our being; and, according to Beauvoir, the world takes on meaning by throwing oneself into loving.

Notes

1 Introduction

1. For example, Singer *The Pursuit of Love* 166.
2. Joseph, Reynolds, and Woodward *The Continuum Companion to Existentialism* 3.
3. Bergmann *The Anatomy of Loving: The Story of Man's Quest to Know What Love Is* 96–97.
4. Solomon "The Virtue of (Erotic) Love" 508–509 and Solomon and Higgins *The Philosophy of (Erotic) Love* 56.
5. Honderich *The Oxford Companion to Philosophy* 778.
6. Badinter *Dead End Feminism* 1, 51–52.
7. Solomon *Love: Emotion, Myth, and Metaphor* xxix, 54–55.
8. Adapted from Hendrick and Hendrick "Romantic Love" 204–210.
9. Dillon *Beyond Romance* 55.
10. Nozick "Love's Bond" 417–419.
11. Ben-Ze'ev and Goussinsky *In the Name of Love: Romantic Ideology and Its Victims* xi–xii.
12. Singer *The Pursuit of Love* 23.
13. Singer *The Pursuit of Love* 165–166.
14. Solomon *Love: Emotion, Myth, and Metaphor* xxx, 13–14, 148, 263.
15. Sternberg *Love is a Story* x.
16. Secomb *Philosophy and Love: From Plato to Popular Culture*.
17. Hendrick and Hendrick "Romantic Love" 204–205 draw on Berscheid and Walster's analysis in *Interpersonal Attraction*.
18. Sternberg "A Triangular Theory of Love" 119–124. Robert Sternberg draws on Hatfield and Walster, who define passionate reciprocated love as desire for a euphoric and fulfilling union with the beloved (*A New Look at Love* 9).
19. Aron and Aron *Love and the Expansion of Self*.
20. Koestenbaum *Existential Sexuality: Choosing to Love* 36.
21. Lindholm "Romantic Love and Anthropology" 10, 17.
22. Hendrick and Hendrick "Romantic Love" 207.
23. Solomon and Higgins *The Philosophy of (Erotic) Love* 128.
24. Harry Frankfurt argues that "disinterested concern" characterizes the essential nature of loving and dismisses romantic loving relationships as impure because there are too many confusing and distracting factors (*The Reasons of Love* 43). This book seeks to explore such distracting and confusing elements.
25. Cox *The Existentialist's Guide to Death, the Universe and Nothingness* 114.
26. Nietzsche "Schopenhauer as Educator" 161.
27. Nietzsche *The Gay Science* 228.
28. Nietzsche *The Will to Power* 423–424, 513.
29. Sartre *Being and Nothingness* 475, 477, 478, 479, 481, 483.
30. Joseph, Reynolds, and Woodward *The Continuum Companion to Existentialism* 3 and Macquarrie *Existentialism* 14.

31. Spillane *An Eye for An I: Living Philosophy* 315.
32. For example, Spillane *An Eye for An I: Living Philosophy* 317–318.
33. Joseph, Reynolds, and Woodward *The Continuum Companion to Existentialism* 345–348.
34. Beauvoir *The Prime of Life* 112.
35. Beauvoir *The Ethics of Ambiguity* 35.
36. Sartre *Being and Nothingness* 186.
37. Erich Fromm notes the important difference between "freedom to" and "freedom from" in *Escape from Freedom* 35.
38. Solomon *Love: Emotion, Myth, and Metaphor* 140.
39. Koestenbaum *Existential Sexuality: Choosing to Love* 162.
40. Mikulincer, Florian, and Hirschberger "The Terror of Death and the Quest for Love: An Existential Perspective on Close Relationships" 287–290.
41. See, for example, Spillane *An Eye for An I: Living Philosophy* 324 and Reynolds and Woodward "Existentialism and Poststructuralism: Some Unfashionable Observations" 265.
42. Sartre *Being and Nothingness* 703.
43. Adapted from Koestenbaum *Existential Sexuality: Choosing to Love* 13–14.
44. Macquarrie *Existentialism* 206.
45. For example, John Macquarrie proposes that interpersonal relations are problematic for existential philosophers because not all being-with-others is authentic, and although they acknowledge our communal existence, their primary concern is with individual being (*Existentialism* 16–17).
46. Cooper *Existentialism: A Reconstruction* 106.
47. Sadler Jr *Existence and Love: A New Approach in Existential Phenomenology* 166, 173, 185.
48. Koestenbaum *Existential Sexuality: Choosing to Love* 29.
49. Segal "The Yearning for Philosophy Today: Its Transformational and Therapeutic Value" 8.
50. Joseph, Reynolds, and Woodward *The Continuum Companion to Existentialism* 343–344.
51. McKinnon "Kierkegaard and the 'Leap of Faith'" 117.
52. Christopher Hodgkinson argues for such a structure applied to leadership in *The Philosophy of Leadership* 38.
53. Sartre *War Diaries: Notebooks from a Phoney War 1939–1940* 62.
54. Szabados "Autobiography and Philosophy: Variations on a Theme of Wittgenstein" 64.
55. Monk "Philosophical Biography: The Very Idea" 3–6.
56. See Nietzsche *Human, All Too Human* 182 and *Beyond Good and Evil* 37–38.
57. Cooper *Existentialism: A Reconstruction* 10.
58. Camus *Lyrical and Critical Essays* 345.
59. Padgett and Wilkens *Christianity and Western Thought: A History of Philosophers, Ideas and Movements* 83.
60. For example, see Daigle *Existentialist Thinkers and Ethics* 4 and Reynolds *Understanding Existentialism* 110.
61. Daigle *Existentialist Thinkers and Ethics* 5 and Joseph, Reynolds, and Woodward *The Continuum Companion to Existentialism* 5.
62. For example Joseph, Reynolds, and Woodward *The Continuum Companion to Existentialism* 5, 290, Cox *The Sartre Dictionary* 146, Daigle *Existentialist*

Thinkers and Ethics 5, Cooper *Existentialism: A Reconstruction* 9, and Solomon *Living with Nietzsche* 206–207.
63. Carroll *Break-Out from the Crystal Palace* 39.
64. Cooper *Existentialism: A Reconstruction* 6.
65. Simons, Benjamin, and Beauvoir "Simone de Beauvoir: An Interview" 338.
66. Joseph, Reynolds, and Woodward *The Continuum Companion to Existentialism* 310–311.
67. Johnson *The Psychology of Romantic Love* xi.
68. See Nietzsche *The Will to Power* 261 and *Thus Spoke Zarathustra* 67.
69. Joseph, Reynolds, and Woodward *The Continuum Companion to Existentialism* 8.
70. Davis "Existentialism and Literature" 138–140.

2 Max Stirner and Loving Egoistically

1. From Goethe's play *Vanitas! Vanitatum Vanitas*: "Ich hab' Mein' Sach' auf Nichts gestellt", which literally translates as: "I have set my affair on nothing" (Stirner *The Ego and His Own* 3, 366).
2. Stirner *The Ego and His Own* 10.
3. Stirner *The Ego and His Own* 296–297.
4. For example, Welsh *Max Stirner's dialectical egoism: a new interpretation* 4.
5. For example, R.W.K. Paterson argues that the existential thinkers either ignored or did not recognize the similarities (*The Nihilistic Egoist: Max Stirner* 170–171). Similarly, John Welsh is surprised that the existential thinkers do not acknowledge Stirner, even though he ultimately dismisses similarities as superficial (*Max Stirner's dialectical egoism: a new interpretation* 24).
6. Many authors have identified theoretical links. For example, Carroll *Break-Out from the Crystal Palace*, Clark *Max Stirner's Egoism*, Paterson *The Nihilistic Egoist: Max Stirner*, and Welsh *Max Stirner's dialectical egoism: a new interpretation*. According to Herbert Read, "Stirner is one of the most existentialist of all past philosophers, and whole pages of *The Ego and His Own* read like anticipations of Sartre" (*Anarchy and Order* 165).
7. For example, Stepelevich "Max Stirner as Hegelian" 604 and Löwith *From Hegel to Nietzsche* 103.
8. Stirner *The Ego and His Own* 292–293.
9. Stirner *The Ego and His Own* 311.
10. Stirner *The Ego and His Own* 324.
11. Stirner *The Ego and His Own* 236–237.
12. Stirner *The Ego and His Own* 190.
13. Stirner *Kleinere Schriften und seine Entgegnungen auf die Kritik seines Werkes "Der Einzige und sein Eigenthum" aus den Jahren 1842–1848* 414.
14. John Clark, for example, criticizes Stirner for neglecting communal values (*Max Stirner's Egoism* 97).
15. Stirner *The Ego and His Own* 291.
16. Stirner *The Ego and His Own* 209.
17. Stirner *The Ego and His Own* 361.
18. Stirner *The Ego and His Own* 5.
19. Stirner *The Ego and His Own* 358.
20. Camus *L'Homme révolté* 87.

21. Stirner *The Ego and His Own* 169.
22. Stirner *The Ego and His Own* 251.
23. Stirner *The Ego and His Own* 60, 76.
24. Stirner *The Ego and His Own* 164.
25. Stirner *The Ego and His Own* 158.
26. Stirner *The Ego and His Own* 157.
27. Stirner *The Ego and His Own* 185.
28. Stirner *The Ego and His Own* 358.
29. Stirner *The Ego and His Own* 37.
30. Stirner *The Ego and His Own* 5.
31. Stirner *The Ego and His Own* 336.
32. Stirner *The Ego and His Own* 154.
33. Camus *L'Homme révolté* 84–88.
34. Stirner *The Ego and His Own* 359.
35. Stirner *The Ego and His Own* 164.
36. For example, Hartmann *Philosophy of the Unconscious* 97, Clark *Max Stirner's Egoism* 31–32, and Camus *L'Homme révolté* 87.
37. Stirner *Kleinere Schriften und seine Entgegnungen auf die Kritik seines Werkes "Der Einzige und sein Eigenthum" aus den Jahren 1842–1848* 348.
38. Sartre *Being and Nothingness* 511.
39. Stirner *The Ego and His Own* 163.
40. Stirner *The Ego and His Own* 13.
41. Stirner *Kleinere Schriften und seine Entgegnungen auf die Kritik seines Werkes "Der Einzige und sein Eigenthum" aus den Jahren 1842–1848* 357.
42. Stirner *The Ego and His Own* 13.
43. Stirner *The Ego and His Own* 295–296.
44. Stirner *The Ego and His Own* 315.
45. Stirner *The Ego and His Own* 319–320.
46. Stirner *Kleinere Schriften und seine Entgegnungen auf die Kritik seines Werkes "Der Einzige und sein Eigenthum" aus den Jahren 1842–1848* 373–374.
47. Stirner *The Ego and His Own* 291.
48. Stirner *The Ego and His Own* 170–171.
49. Stirner *The Ego and His Own* 292.
50. Stirner *Kleinere Schriften und seine Entgegnungen auf die Kritik seines Werkes "Der Einzige und sein Eigenthum" aus den Jahren 1842–1848* 375.
51. Stirner *The Ego and His Own* 290.
52. Stirner *The Ego and His Own* 291.
53. Stirner *The Ego and His Own* 291–292.
54. Stirner *The Ego and His Own* 293–294.
55. Stirner *The Ego and His Own* 290.
56. Stirner *The Ego and His Own* 290.
57. Stirner *The Ego and His Own* 295.
58. Stirner *The Ego and His Own* 164.
59. Paterson *The Nihilistic Egoist: Max Stirner* 6–10.
60. Mackay *Max Stirner: His Life and His Work* 12.
61. Mackay *Max Stirner: His Life and His Work* 205.
62. Camus *L'Homme révolté* 87–88.
63. For example, John Carroll maintains that the union is an illogical extension of Stirner's philosophy (*Break-Out from the Crystal Palace* 80) and Robert

182 Notes

Paterson argues that an egoist would be better off being alone rather than risk being exploited by other egoists (*The Nihilistic Egoist: Max Stirner* 270).
64. Stirner *The Ego and His Own* 310–311.
65. Stirner, being the German translator of Adam Smith's *Wealth of Nations*, knew more than a little about it. However, there are some strong links between Stirner's philosophy and capitalist principles. For example, both emphasize individual self-interest, exploitation of resources, competition, and property, and success is measured by the accumulation of assets (Clark *Max Stirner's Egoism* 57).
66. Stirner *The Ego and His Own* 179.
67. Stirner *The Ego and His Own* 311.
68. Stirner *The Ego and His Own* 313.
69. Stirner *The Ego and His Own* 306.
70. Stirner *The Ego and His Own* 164.
71. Hegel "A Fragment on Love" 117–118.
72. Stirner *The Ego and His Own* 134.
73. For example, with reference to Stirner and other Romantics, Dmitri Shalin argued that Romantic introspection is the antithesis of narcissism. Narcissism is a passive obsession with a static idea of oneself, while the Romantic attitude involves a willingness to actively lose and recreate oneself ("The Romantic Antecedents of Meadian Social Psychology" 47–48). Robert Spillane argues along similar lines that Stirner is not a narcissist, "because the narcissist is in love with his cozy 'I', whilst the Romantic actively projects 'I' into the world" (*An Eye for An I: Living Philosophy* 353).
74. For example, John Clark (*Max Stirner's Egoism* 41) and Eduard von Hartmann (*Philosophy of the Unconscious* 97) argue that Stirner's philosophy is tautological.
75. Psychological egoism is "The theory that all human actions are motivated by self-interest...[and] considers only the influence of present desires on choice" (Honderich *The Oxford Companion to Philosophy* 220–221).
76. Stirner *The Ego and His Own* 294.
77. Stirner *Kleinere Schriften und seine Entgegnungen auf die Kritik seines Werkes "Der Einzige und sein Eigenthum" aus den Jahren 1842–1848* 395–396.
78. Marx and Engels *The German Ideology* 287.

3 Søren Kierkegaard and Loving Aesthetically

1. Kierkegaard *Either/Or* 275, 315, 341.
2. Kierkegaard *Either/Or* 518.
3. Kierkegaard *Fear and Trembling* 35.
4. Kierkegaard *Works of Love* 344.
5. Kierkegaard *Concluding Unscientific Postscript* 34.
6. Kierkegaard *Concluding Unscientific Postscript* 49–50.
7. Kierkegaard *Søren Kierkegaard's Journals and Papers (Volume 6)* 9.
8. Sartre *Between Existentialism and Marxism* 152. However, Sartre also criticizes Kierkegaard for not starting afresh with Christianity and failing to question religious dogma.
9. Levinas *Proper Names* 76.
10. Flynn *Existentialism* 26.

11. Boesen "Boesen's Account of his Hospital Conversations with Kierkegaard: 14 & 16 October 1855" 132.
12. Kierkegaard *Concluding Unscientific Postscript* 19, 35.
13. Kierkegaard *The Crowd is Untruth*.
14. Kierkegaard *Concluding Unscientific Postscript* 75, 259.
15. Kierkegaard *Kierkegaard's Journals and Notebooks* 19 (1 August 1835).
16. Kierkegaard *Concluding Unscientific Postscript* 1, 552, 553.
17. Kierkegaard *The Point of View* 288.
18. Kierkegaard *Either/Or* 89–90.
19. For example, see Kierkegaard *Kierkegaard's Journals and Notebooks* 107, Croxall "Kierkegaard and Mozart" and Utterback "Don Juan and the Representation of Spiritual Sensuousness".
20. Kierkegaard *Either/Or* 104–105.
21. Sylvia Walsh Utterback provides a comprehensive survey of the different interpretations of Don Juans in "Don Juan and the Representation of Spiritual Sensuousness".
22. Kierkegaard *Either/Or* 69, 80, 107, 111, 135.
23. Kierkegaard *Either/Or* 100, 106.
24. Kierkegaard *Purify Your Hearts! A "Discourse for a Special Occasion"* the first of three *"Edifying Discourses in a Different Vein"*, published in 1847 at Copenhagen 39.
25. Kierkegaard *Kierkegaard's Journals and Notebooks* 21.
26. Widner "Love in *Don Giovanni*" 293.
27. Kierkegaard *Either/Or* 251.
28. Kierkegaard *Either/Or* 310.
29. Kierkegaard *Either/Or* 251–252.
30. Kierkegaard *Either/Or* 321.
31. Kant *The Critique of Judgement* 6.
32. Kierkegaard *Either/Or* 282.
33. Kierkegaard *Either/Or* 276.
34. Kierkegaard *Concluding Unscientific Postscript* 314.
35. Kierkegaard *Either/Or* 305. According to Jane Duran, this is the most disturbing aspect of the *Diary* ("The Kierkegaardian Feminist" 251).
36. Kierkegaard *Either/Or* 341.
37. Kierkegaard *Either/Or* 385.
38. Kierkegaard *Either/Or* 321.
39. Kierkegaard *Either/Or* 306.
40. Kierkegaard *Either/Or* 299.
41. Kierkegaard *Either/Or* 363–364.
42. Kierkegaard *Either/Or* 362.
43. Kierkegaard *Either/Or* 301.
44. Kierkegaard *Either/Or* 298.
45. Kierkegaard *Either/Or* 288.
46. Kierkegaard *Either/Or* 255.
47. Kierkegaard *Either/Or* 56.
48. Kierkegaard *Either/Or* 44.
49. Kierkegaard *Either/Or* 46.
50. Kierkegaard *Either/Or* 130–131.
51. Kierkegaard *Either/Or* 223.

184 Notes

52. Kierkegaard *Either/Or* 543. Climacus also discusses this theme in *Concluding Unscientific Postscript* 262–265.
53. Kierkegaard *Either/Or* 513.
54. Kierkegaard *Either/Or* 528.
55. Kierkegaard *Søren Kierkegaard's Journals and Papers (Volume 5)* 158–159.
56. Kierkegaard *Either/Or* 462.
57. Kierkegaard *Either/Or* 466.
58. Kierkegaard *Works of Love* 46–50.
59. Kierkegaard *Søren Kierkegaard's Journals and Papers (Volume 5)* 221.
60. Kierkegaard *Kierkegaard's Journals and Notebooks* 30.
61. Kierkegaard *Concluding Unscientific Postscript* 182.
62. Kierkegaard *Søren Kierkegaard's Journals and Papers (Volume 3)* 36.
63. Kierkegaard *Søren Kierkegaard's Journals and Papers (Volume 3)* 40.
64. See Adorno "On Kierkegaard's Doctrine of Love" 418–419.
65. Kierkegaard *Works of Love* 282–283.
66. Kierkegaard *The Concept of Anxiety* 61.
67. Kierkegaard *The Concept of Anxiety* 155.
68. Kierkegaard *The Concept of Anxiety* 115.
69. Kierkegaard *The Concept of Anxiety* 137.
70. Kierkegaard *The Concept of Anxiety* 155–156.
71. Kierkegaard *The Concept of Anxiety* 161.
72. Kierkegaard *Søren Kierkegaard's Journals and Papers (Volume 3)* 125.
73. Kierkegaard *Søren Kierkegaard's Journals and Papers (Volume 6)* 194.
74. Kierkegaard *Søren Kierkegaard's Journals and Papers (Volume 6)* 195.
75. Kierkegaard *Søren Kierkegaard's Journals and Papers (Volume 6)* 144, 196.
76. Kierkegaard *Søren Kierkegaard's Journals and Papers (Volume 5)* 176.
77. Kierkegaard *Søren Kierkegaard's Journals and Papers (Volume 6)* 196 and *Søren Kierkegaard's Journals and Papers (Volume 5)* 173.
78. Kierkegaard *Søren Kierkegaard's Journals and Papers (Volume 5)* 233.
79. Kierkegaard *Søren Kierkegaard's Journals and Papers (Volume 6)* 253–255.
80. Kierkegaard *Søren Kierkegaard's Journals and Papers (Volume 6)* 11.
81. Kierkegaard *Søren Kierkegaard's Journals and Papers (Volume 6)* 141.
82. Kierkegaard *Søren Kierkegaard's Journals and Papers (Volume 3)* 126.
83. Kierkegaard *Søren Kierkegaard's Journals and Papers (Volume 6)* 7–8.
84. See Evans *Kierkegaard's Ethic of Love – Divine Commands and Moral Obligations* 46.
85. Kierkegaard *Either/Or* 485.
86. Some interpretations of Don Juan, such as Byron's, portray him as self-aware and striving, but 'A' specifically disagrees with this interpretation (Kierkegaard *Either/Or* 113).
87. Wilfried Greve argues for a hedonistic sphere, in which the goal in life is pleasure, but maintains that it is impulsive (*Kierkegaards maieutische Ethik* 50–51).
88. Kierkegaard *Either/Or* 310.
89. For example, Bradley Dewey argues that leaping into an aesthetic sphere is logically consistent within Kierkegaard's philosophy ("Seven Seducers: A Typology of Interpretations of the Aesthetic Stage in Kierkegaard's 'The Seducer's Diary'" 168).
90. Kierkegaard *Concluding Unscientific Postscript* 350.
91. Kierkegaard *Works of Love* 308.

92. See Jamie M. Ferreira, who argues that neighborly love is abstract because it does not appreciate individual differences ("Equality, impartiality, and moral blindness in Kierkegaard's *Works of Love*" 69).
93. Kierkegaard *Works of Love* 153.
94. For example, see Adorno "On Kierkegaard's Doctrine of Love" 418–419.

4 Friedrich Nietzsche and Loving Powerfully

1. Fuss and Shapiro *Nietzsche: A Self-Portrait from His Letters* 104.
2. See Nietzsche *Daybreak* 158 and "Twilight of the Idols" 35.
3. For example, Reginster *The Affirmation of Life: Nietzsche on Overcoming Nihilism* 3, 290.
4. Nietzsche *The Gay Science* 189.
5. Solomon *Living with Nietzsche* 94.
6. Köhler *Zarathustra's Secret* xiv.
7. For example, Solomon and Higgins *What Nietzsche Really Said* 24.
8. Small *Nietzsche and Rée: A Star Friendship* 138.
9. Hollingdale *Nietzsche: The Man and His Philosophy* 149.
10. Fuss and Shapiro *Nietzsche: A Self-Portrait from His Letters* 51 and Nietzsche "Ecce Homo" 78, 90.
11. For example, see Oliver "Nietzsche's Abjection" 60, 63.
12. Nietzsche *Human, All Too Human* 150.
13. Nietzsche *The Will to Power* 426. This book was published posthumously after being manipulated for anti-Semitic purposes by his sister; however, scholars have since unraveled her interference. There is some debate whether Nietzschean scholars should consider it since Nietzsche did not pursue its publication. However, Jean-Etienne Joullié argues that even if it was provisional for Nietzsche, it gives us further insights into his thinking (*Will to Power, Nietzsche's Last Idol* 10), and thus I have included it because it does enhance understanding of his thinking on the topic of loving.
14. Nietzsche *The Gay Science* 186.
15. For example, see Fuss and Shapiro *Nietzsche: A Self-Portrait from His Letters* 29.
16. Nietzsche *Human, All Too Human* 192. See also Nietzsche *Daybreak* 174 and Fuss and Shapiro *Nietzsche: A Self-Portrait from His Letters* 53.
17. Nietzsche *The Gay Science* 109, 120, 199. To this day, speculation remains about whether Nietzsche had read Stirner's work. While he does not mention Stirner in his writing, he undoubtedly knew of him, since he read books that referred to Stirner, allegedly recommended reading Stirner to a student, and a close friend of Nietzsche's reported that he spoke to her of the affinity he felt with Stirner but did not want to talk about him for fear of accusations of plagiarism. It is also possible that Nietzsche did not write about Stirner for fear of not being seen as a unique and radical thinker. See Brobjer "Philologica: A Possible Solution to the Stirner-Nietzsche Question", Glassford "Did Friedrich Nietzsche (1844–1900) Plagiarise from Max Stirner (1806–56)?", Gilman and Parent *Conversations with Nietzsche: A Life in the Words of His Contemporaries* 114, Löwith *From Hegel to Nietzsche* 187, Camus *L'Homme révolté* 88, and Simmel *Schopenhauer and Nietzsche* 162.

18. Nietzsche "Ecce Homo" 99.
19. Nietzsche "Twilight of the Idols" 33.
20. Nietzsche *Human, All Too Human* 152.
21. Nietzsche *The Gay Science* 73.
22. Nietzsche *The Gay Science* 73.
23. Nietzsche *The Will to Power* 425.
24. Nietzsche *The Gay Science* 226.
25. Nietzsche *Human, All Too Human* 152, 154.
26. Nietzsche *Beyond Good and Evil* 102.
27. Nietzsche *The Gay Science* 73.
28. Nietzsche *Beyond Good and Evil* 163, 167–168.
29. Nietzsche *Beyond Good and Evil* 93, 167.
30. Nietzsche *Human, All Too Human* 154.
31. See Diethe "Nietzsche and the Woman Question" 865–867, Higgins "The Whip Recalled" 2, and Oppel *Nietzsche on Gender: Beyond Man and Woman* 1.
32. Nietzsche *Human, All Too Human* 150.
33. Nietzsche *The Will to Power* 198 and "On the Genealogy of Morals" 135.
34. Nietzsche *Human, All Too Human* 46.
35. Nietzsche *The Will to Power* 183.
36. Nietzsche *Thus Spoke Zarathustra* 87.
37. Nietzsche "Ecce Homo" 105.
38. Nietzsche *The Will to Power* 167.
39. Nietzsche *Daybreak* 48.
40. Nietzsche "Ecce Homo" 105 and *The Will to Power* 197.
41. Nietzsche *The Will to Power* 198.
42. Nietzsche "Twilight of the Idols" 97.
43. Nietzsche *The Gay Science* 40.
44. Nietzsche *Beyond Good and Evil* 106.
45. Nietzsche *Daybreak* 45.
46. Nietzsche *Human, All Too Human* 52.
47. Nietzsche *Beyond Good and Evil* 99–100 and *Human, All Too Human* 153–154.
48. Nietzsche *Daybreak* 91.
49. Nietzsche *Daybreak* 157 and *Beyond Good and Evil* 104.
50. Nietzsche "The Anti-Christ" 20.
51. Nietzsche *The Gay Science* 72.
52. Nietzsche *The Gay Science* 151.
53. Nietzsche *The Will to Power* 426–427.
54. Nietzsche *The Will to Power* 249, 424.
55. Nietzsche *Human, All Too Human* 187.
56. Nietzsche *Human, All Too Human* 38 and "The Anti-Christ" 27.
57. Nietzsche *The Will to Power* 425.
58. Nietzsche *Human, All Too Human* 152.
59. Nietzsche *Beyond Good and Evil* 166.
60. Nietzsche *The Gay Science* 39–40.
61. Nietzsche *Beyond Good and Evil* 117.
62. Nietzsche *The Gay Science* 228.
63. For example, see Singer *The Nature of Love: The Modern World* 86.
64. Nietzsche *The Will to Power* 407.
65. Nietzsche *Human, All Too Human* 42.

66. Nietzsche *The Gay Science* 73.
67. Nietzsche *The Will to Power* 460.
68. Nietzsche "The Case of Wagner: A Musician's Problem" 236.
69. Nietzsche *Human, All Too Human* 159.
70. Nietzsche *Human, All Too Human* 153, 159 and *Daybreak* 205.
71. Nietzsche *Thus Spoke Zarathustra* 90.
72. Nietzsche "Twilight of the Idols" 120.
73. Fuss and Shapiro *Nietzsche: A Self-Portrait from His Letters* 51, 114.
74. Nietzsche "Twilight of the Idols" 33.
75. Nietzsche *The Will to Power* 370.
76. Nietzsche *Thus Spoke Zarathustra* 231.
77. Nietzsche *Beyond Good and Evil* 105.
78. Nietzsche *Daybreak* 45.
79. Nietzsche "Twilight of the Idols" 52, "The Wanderer and His Shadow" 319, and *Human, All Too Human* 76, 188.
80. Nietzsche *Thus Spoke Zarathustra* 81.
81. Nietzsche "Twilight of the Idols" 52.
82. Nietzsche "Ecce Homo" 106 and *Human, All Too Human* 54.
83. Nietzsche "Twilight of the Idols" 53.
84. Nietzsche *Daybreak* 46.
85. Nietzsche *Human, All Too Human* 76.
86. Nietzsche *The Gay Science* 74–75.
87. Nietzsche *Beyond Good and Evil* 97.
88. Kathleen Higgins, for example, suggests that such aphorisms as this reveal his sympathy towards women and their situation ("Gender in *The Gay Science*" 229–230).
89. Nietzsche *Daybreak* 159.
90. Nietzsche *Human, All Too Human* 157.
91. Nietzsche *Beyond Good and Evil* 101.
92. Nietzsche *Daybreak* 21–22.
93. Nietzsche *Beyond Good and Evil* 98.
94. Nietzsche *Daybreak* 21.
95. Nietzsche *Thus Spoke Zarathustra* 96, *Human, All Too Human* 151, and *Daybreak* 150.
96. See Nietzsche *Daybreak* 97, "The Wanderer and His Shadow" 324, and "Twilight of the Idols" 105.
97. Nietzsche *Daybreak* 21.
98. Nietzsche *Thus Spoke Zarathustra* 228.
99. Nietzsche *Human, All Too Human* 42.
100. Nietzsche "Twilight of the Idols" 53, 104.
101. Nietzsche *Thus Spoke Zarathustra* 228.
102. Nietzsche *Daybreak* 172.
103. Nietzsche *Human, All Too Human* 158.
104. Nietzsche "On the Genealogy of Morals" 57.
105. Nietzsche *The Gay Science* 159.
106. Fuss and Shapiro *Nietzsche: A Self-Portrait from His Letters* 62.
107. Salomé *Nietzsche* xlvi.
108. Salomé *Nietzsche* li–lii.
109. Salomé *Nietzsche* li.

110. Safranski *Nietzsche: A Philosophical Biography* 255.
111. Fuss and Shapiro *Nietzsche: A Self-Portrait from His Letters* 76.
112. For example, Lungstrum "Nietzsche Writing Woman/Woman Writing Nietzsche: The Sexual Dialectic of Palingenesis" 144, and Diethe "Nietzsche and the Woman Question" 866.
113. Nietzsche *Thus Spoke Zarathustra* 228.
114. Fuss and Shapiro *Nietzsche: A Self-Portrait from His Letters* 59.
115. Nietzsche *Human, All Too Human* 156.
116. Nietzsche "On the Genealogy of Morals" 107.
117. Nietzsche *Human, All Too Human* 158–159.
118. Fuss and Shapiro *Nietzsche: A Self-Portrait from His Letters* 66.
119. For example, *Ecce Homo*'s subtitle is: *How to Become What You Are*. See also Nietzsche *The Gay Science* 189.
120. Nietzsche *Beyond Good and Evil* 60–61.
121. Nietzsche "Twilight of the Idols" 104.
122. Letter of 23 March 1887 in Kofman "Baubo: Theological Perversion and Fetishism" 47.
123. Nietzsche *Human, All Too Human* 156.
124. Nietzsche "Twilight of the Idols" 105.
125. Nietzsche *Human, All Too Human* 151, 152, 154.
126. Nietzsche *Daybreak* 98.
127. Penn "Arranged Marriages in Western Europe: Media Representations and Social Reality" 637.
128. Nietzsche "Twilight of the Idols" 106.
129. Nietzsche *Human, All Too Human* 152.
130. Nietzsche *Daybreak* 97 and *The Will to Power* 360.
131. Nietzsche *Thus Spoke Zarathustra* 95.
132. Nietzsche *Thus Spoke Zarathustra* 92.
133. Nietzsche *Thus Spoke Zarathustra* 95.
134. Nietzsche *Human, All Too Human* 156.
135. Nietzsche *Thus Spoke Zarathustra* 91.
136. Nietzsche "Ecce Homo" 106.
137. Nietzsche "Twilight of the Idols" 120.
138. Nietzsche "Twilight of the Idols" 120.
139. Nietzsche "Twilight of the Idols" 99.
140. Nietzsche "Schopenhauer as Educator" 161.
141. Nietzsche *Daybreak* 210–211.
142. Nietzsche *Human, All Too Human* 229–230.
143. Nietzsche *Daybreak* 197–198.
144. Nietzsche *Thus Spoke Zarathustra* 93.
145. Nietzsche *Thus Spoke Zarathustra* 92–93.
146. Nietzsche *The Gay Science* 70–71.
147. Robert Ackermann suggested the whip could be to help create distance to enable fantasy about the feminine and inspire creativity (Ackermann *Nietzsche: A Frenzied Look* 124, 129). Jacques Derrida argues that because love is a power struggle, keeping one's distance from a woman is important so as to avoid falling under her spell (Derrida *Spurs: Nietzsche's Styles* 49).
148. Nietzsche *Thus Spoke Zarathustra* 83.
149. Nietzsche *Beyond Good and Evil* 102.

150. Nietzsche *Human, All Too Human* 150.
151. Nietzsche *Thus Spoke Zarathustra* 82–84.
152. Nietzsche *Human, All Too Human* 150–151.
153. Nietzsche "Schopenhauer as Educator" 163.
154. Nietzsche *The Will to Power* 197.
155. Nietzsche *The Will to Power* 506.
156. Christine Daigle, for example, argues that the *Übermensch* is a state of striving, becoming, and overcoming towards a receding goal ("Nietzsche: Virtue Ethics... Virtue Politics?" 8–9).
157. Nietzsche "Ecce Homo" 144 and Fuss and Shapiro *Nietzsche: A Self-Portrait from His Letters* 135.
158. Fuss and Shapiro *Nietzsche: A Self-Portrait from His Letters* 99.
159. For example, Singer *The Nature of Love: The Modern World* 85–86.
160. See MacIntyre *After Virtue* 114.

5 Jean-Paul Sartre and Loving Sadomasochistically

1. Rowley *Tête-à-Tête: Simone de Beauvoir and Jean-Paul Sartre* 20.
2. Contat, Rybalka, and Sartre *The Writings of Jean-Paul Sartre* 361.
3. Sartre *Sartre in the Seventies: Interviews and Essays* 60.
4. Gerassi *Talking with Sartre: Conversations and Debates* 44.
5. Sartre "Interview with Jean-Paul Sartre" 7.
6. Sartre *Being and Nothingness* 5.
7. Sartre "Interview with Jean-Paul Sartre" 9.
8. Sartre *Being and Nothingness* 321–322.
9. Hegel *Phenomenology of Spirit* 113–115.
10. Other scholars who support this interpretation include Evans "Sartre and Beauvoir on Hegel's Master-Slave Dialectic and the Question of the 'Look'" 90, Ogilvy "Mastery and Sexuality: Hegel's Dialectic in Sartre and Post-Freudian Psychology" 201, and Solomon *Love: Emotion, Myth, and Metaphor* 273.
11. Sartre *The Problem of Method* 114.
12. Sartre "Interview with Jean-Paul Sartre" 10.
13. *Existentialism is a Humanism* is a lecture Sartre delivered specifically in order to simplify and clarify some of the key themes he raised in *Being and Nothingness* and to address criticisms that it was overly negative (Sartre *Existentialism is a Humanism* xii). Sartre later regretted the lecture because of the superficial way that it was interpreted (Priest *Jean-Paul Sartre: Basic Writings* 7). For this reason, the essay is referenced where it complements the ideas in *Being and Nothingness*.
14. Sartre "Interview with Jean-Paul Sartre" 9 and Gerassi *Talking with Sartre: Conversations and Debates* 53.
15. Gerassi *Talking with Sartre: Conversations and Debates* 53.
16. Sartre *Being and Nothingness* 29, 152, 432, 559.
17. Sartre *Being and Nothingness* 169.
18. Sartre *Being and Nothingness* 784.
19. Sartre *Being and Nothingness* 139.
20. Sartre *Being and Nothingness* 65–69, 73, 82.

21. Sartre *Being and Nothingness* 23–24.
22. Sartre *Being and Nothingness* 559, 614.
23. Sartre *Being and Nothingness* 12–13 and "Interview with Jean-Paul Sartre" 47–48.
24. Sartre "Interview with Jean-Paul Sartre" 47–48.
25. Sartre *Sartre in the Seventies: Interviews and Essays* 64–65.
26. Sartre *Being and Nothingness* 343.
27. Sartre *Being and Nothingness* 672.
28. Sartre *Being and Nothingness* 674.
29. Sartre *Being and Nothingness* 376.
30. Sartre *Being and Nothingness* 320–324.
31. Sartre *Being and Nothingness* 547–555.
32. Sartre *Being and Nothingness* 343.
33. Sartre *Being and Nothingness* 358.
34. Sartre "Huis Clos" 223 and Contat, Rybalka, and Sartre *The Writings of Jean-Paul Sartre* 99.
35. Sartre *Being and Nothingness* 475.
36. Sartre *Being and Nothingness* 754–756.
37. Sartre *Being and Nothingness* 477–478.
38. Sartre *Being and Nothingness* 387, 478.
39. Sartre *Being and Nothingness* 478–484.
40. Sartre *Nausea* 137.
41. Sartre *Nausea* 157.
42. Sartre *Being and Nothingness* 485.
43. Sartre *Witness to My Life: The Letters of Jean-Paul Sartre to Simone de Beauvoir 1926–1939* 21.
44. Sartre *War Diaries: Notebooks from a Phoney War 1939–1940* 266.
45. Lamblin *A Disgraceful Affair* 39.
46. Sartre *War Diaries: Notebooks from a Phoney War 1939–1940* 284–285.
47. Sartre *Being and Nothingness* 488.
48. Sartre *Being and Nothingness* 491.
49. Sartre *Being and Nothingness* 491–493.
50. Sartre *Being and Nothingness* 515.
51. Sartre *Being and Nothingness* 506–507, 511.
52. Sartre *Being and Nothingness* 511–512.
53. Sartre *Being and Nothingness* 518–527.
54. Sartre *Being and Nothingness* 328.
55. Sartre "The Room" 35.
56. Sartre "Lucifer and the Lord" 142.
57. Sartre *Being and Nothingness* 483.
58. Sartre *Existentialism is a Humanism* 20.
59. Sartre *Existentialism is a Humanism* 29.
60. Sartre *Existentialism is a Humanism* 20.
61. Sartre *Being and Nothingness* 89.
62. Sartre *Being and Nothingness* 665.
63. Sartre *Existentialism is a Humanism* 37.
64. Sartre *Being and Nothingness* 231–232.
65. Sartre *Being and Nothingness* 684.
66. Sartre *Being and Nothingness* 595.

67. Sartre "Huis Clos" 217.
68. Sartre *Being and Nothingness* 227.
69. Sartre *Being and Nothingness* 230.
70. Sartre *Notebooks for an Ethics* 476.
71. Sartre *Notebooks for an Ethics* 476.
72. Sartre *Notebooks for an Ethics* 476.
73. Sartre *Notebooks for an Ethics* 477.
74. Sartre *Notebooks for an Ethics* 477.
75. Sartre *The Emotions: Outline of a Theory* 91.
76. Sartre *Being and Nothingness* 534. Mary Warnock proposes the radical conversion is (unsatisfactorily) Marxism (*The Philosophy of Sartre* 179). David Cooper argues that it is "ethics of reciprocal freedom" (*Existentialism: A Reconstruction* 186). Robert Santoni suggests that it is authenticity (*Bad Faith, Good Faith, and Authenticity in Sartre's Early Philosophy* xxvii).
77. Sartre "Interview with Jean-Paul Sartre" 13.
78. Sartre *Notebooks for an Ethics* 477.
79. Sartre *Nausea* 145.
80. Sartre "The Flies" 246.
81. Sartre "The Flies" 277.
82. Sartre "The Flies" 277.
83. Sartre *The Chips are Down* 63.
84. Sartre *The Chips are Down* 127.
85. Sartre *Notebooks for an Ethics* 508.
86. Sartre *Sartre in the Seventies: Interviews and Essays* 63.
87. Sartre *Notebooks for an Ethics* 414–415.
88. Sartre *War Diaries: Notebooks from a Phoney War 1939–1940* 75.
89. Beauvoir *The Prime of Life* 24.
90. Beauvoir *Force of Circumstance* 134.
91. Beauvoir *The Prime of Life* 24–25.
92. Rowley *Tête-à-Tête: Simone de Beauvoir and Jean-Paul Sartre* 35.
93. Rowley *Tête-à-Tête: Simone de Beauvoir and Jean-Paul Sartre* 337–338.
94. Sartre *Being and Nothingness* 627, 635, 640.
95. Sartre *Being and Nothingness* 680.
96. Sartre *Being and Nothingness* 116.
97. Sartre *Being and Nothingness* 81.
98. Sartre *War Diaries: Notebooks from a Phoney War 1939–1940* 220–221.
99. Sartre *Existentialism is a Humanism* 29.
100. Sartre *Being and Nothingness* 387.
101. For example, Singer *The Pursuit of Love* 76–77.
102. Sartre *Being and Nothingness* 796.
103. Sartre *Sartre in the Seventies: Interviews and Essays* 65. Dmitri Shalin's point is as relevant for Sartre as it was for Stirner. See Shalin "The Romantic Antecedents of Meadian Social Psychology" 47–48.
104. Sartre *Quiet Moments in a War: The Letters of Jean-Paul Sartre to Simone de Beauvoir 1940–1963* 75–76.
105. Rowley *Tête-à-Tête: Simone de Beauvoir and Jean-Paul Sartre* 311.
106. Rowley *Tête-à-Tête: Simone de Beauvoir and Jean-Paul Sartre* 327.
107. Schwarzer *After The Second Sex: Conversations with Simone de Beauvoir* 110.
108. Sartre *Sartre in the Seventies: Interviews and Essays* 64–65.

192 Notes

109. Sartre "Huis Clos" 220.
110. Sartre "Lucifer and the Lord" 163.
111. Sartre *Being and Nothingness* 530.
112. Christine Daigle and Jacob Golomb, for example, highlight this more constructive interpretation of Sartre's and Beauvoir's loving relationship that did not conform to Sartre's description of love in *Being and Nothingness* (*Beauvoir and Sartre: The Riddle of Influence* 6).
113. Sartre "Lucifer and the Lord" 173.

6   Simone de Beauvoir and Loving Authentically

1. Beauvoir "What is Existentialism?" 324.
2. Beauvoir *All Said and Done* 1.
3. Beauvoir *The Ethics of Ambiguity* 11.
4. Beauvoir *The Ethics of Ambiguity* 15.
5. Beauvoir *The Ethics of Ambiguity* 29 and *The Prime of Life* 18, 107, 346.
6. Beauvoir "Pyrrhus and Cineas" 108.
7. Beauvoir *The Ethics of Ambiguity* 70–71.
8. Beauvoir *The Second Sex* 359.
9. Beauvoir "Pyrrhus and Cineas" 138.
10. Joseph, Reynolds, and Woodward *The Continuum Companion to Existentialism* 342.
11. Beauvoir *The Second Sex* 73–74.
12. Beauvoir *The Second Sex* 154.
13. Beauvoir *The Ethics of Ambiguity* 72.
14. Beauvoir *The Ethics of Ambiguity* 72.
15. Beauvoir *Who Shall Die?* 41.
16. Beauvoir *Who Shall Die?* 54.
17. Beauvoir *The Ethics of Ambiguity* 15–16.
18. Beauvoir *The Prime of Life* 430.
19. Beauvoir *The Blood of Others* 130.
20. Beauvoir "Pyrrhus and Cineas" 138.
21. See Beauvoir *The Second Sex* 698.
22. Beauvoir *The Second Sex* 757.
23. Beauvoir *The Second Sex* 749.
24. Beauvoir *The Second Sex* 685, 757, 758.
25. Brison *Beauvoir and Feminism: Interview and Reflections* 191 and Beauvoir *The Second Sex* 17, 721, 749, 750, 761.
26. Beauvoir *The Second Sex* 16.
27. Beauvoir *The Mandarins* 157.
28. Beauvoir *The Mandarins* 31.
29. Beauvoir *The Second Sex* 693–694.
30. Beauvoir *The Second Sex* 691.
31. Beauvoir *The Second Sex* 725.
32. Beauvoir *The Second Sex* 726.
33. Beauvoir *The Second Sex* 691.
34. For example, Beauvoir *Letters to Sartre* 100.
35. Beauvoir *The Prime of Life* 118.

36. Beauvoir *She Came to Stay* 130–131.
37. Beauvoir *Les Belles Images* 87.
38. Beauvoir *The Prime of Life* 208.
39. Beauvoir *She Came to Stay* 208.
40. See Fullbrook "She Came to Stay and Being and Nothingness" for an analysis of the philosophical ideas in Sartre's *Being and Nothingness* that Beauvoir had already raised in *She Came to Stay*.
41. Beauvoir *She Came to Stay* 112.
42. Beauvoir "Pyrrhus and Cineas" 118–122.
43. Beauvoir *The Woman Destroyed* 124, 180.
44. Beauvoir *She Came to Stay* 75.
45. Beauvoir *The Blood of Others* 154.
46. Beauvoir *The Second Sex* 683.
47. Beauvoir *The Mandarins* 31.
48. Beauvoir *A Transatlantic Love Affair: Letters to Nelson Algren* 208.
49. Beauvoir *When Things of the Spirit Come First* 44, 210.
50. Beauvoir *The Second Sex* 57, 723.
51. Beauvoir *The Second Sex* 283.
52. Beauvoir *The Second Sex* 44, 418.
53. Beauvoir *The Second Sex* 706.
54. Brison *Beauvoir and Feminism: Interview and Reflections* 190–191.
55. Beauvoir *Who Shall Die?* 53.
56. Beauvoir *The Second Sex* 733.
57. Beauvoir *The Second Sex* 734.
58. Beauvoir *The Second Sex* 568.
59. Beauvoir *The Second Sex* 766.
60. Beauvoir *The Second Sex* 755.
61. Beauvoir *She Came to Stay* 367, 373.
62. Beauvoir *She Came to Stay* 237.
63. Beauvoir *The Second Sex* 467.
64. Beauvoir *Old Age* 318–319.
65. Beauvoir "Must We Burn Sade?" 32–33.
66. Beauvoir *The Second Sex* 383.
67. Beauvoir *The Second Sex* 415.
68. Beauvoir *The Second Sex* 413, 415.
69. Beauvoir *The Second Sex* 443.
70. Beauvoir *The Prime of Life* 252.
71. Beauvoir *The Prime of Life* 270–271.
72. Beauvoir *Force of Circumstance* 283. Hazel Barnes rightly points out that an existential Françoise would have accepted the consequences of her actions and resolved to become the sort of person she would rather be since there could always be another Xavière (*The Literature of Possibility: A Study in Humanistic Existentialism* 136).
73. Beauvoir *The Second Sex* 261.
74. Beauvoir *The Second Sex* 706–708.
75. Beauvoir *Letters to Sartre* 183.
76. Beauvoir *Letters to Sartre* 459–460.
77. Beauvoir *The Prime of Life* 26, *Force of Circumstance* 134, and "Pyrrhus and Cineas" 98.

78. Beauvoir *Who Shall Die?* 48.
79. Beauvoir *The Blood of Others* 234–235.
80. For example, Jeremy Bentham and John Stuart Mill argue for utilitarianism based on the promotion of maximizing total happiness for those whose interests are at stake. See Bentham *An Introduction to the Principles of Morals and Legislation* 310 and Mill "Utilitarianism" 282, 288.
81. Beauvoir *The Mandarins* 670.
82. Beauvoir *Letters to Sartre* 31, 81, 286, 348, 350, 354.
83. Beauvoir *The Second Sex* 443.
84. Beauvoir *Force of Circumstance* 133.
85. Beauvoir *Force of Circumstance* 133.
86. Fullbrook and Fullbrook *Sex and Philosophy: Rethinking de Beauvoir and Sartre* xiii.
87. Beauvoir *A Transatlantic Love Affair: Letters to Nelson Algren* 208.
88. Rowley *Tête-à-Tête: Simone de Beauvoir and Jean-Paul Sartre* 106.
89. Sartre *War Diaries: Notebooks from a Phoney War 1939–1940* 274.
90. Lilar *Aspects of Love in Western Society* 207.
91. Beauvoir *The Prime of Life* 25–26.
92. Beauvoir *The Mandarins* 457.
93. Beauvoir *Force of Circumstance* 134.
94. Beauvoir *Letters to Sartre* 389.
95. Beauvoir *Force of Circumstance* 136.
96. Brison *Beauvoir and Feminism: Interview and Reflections* 201.
97. Contat, Rybalka, and Sartre *The Writings of Jean-Paul Sartre* 163–164.
98. Beauvoir *The Woman Destroyed* 45.
99. Beauvoir *Who Shall Die?* 29.
100. Beauvoir *Who Shall Die?* 48.
101. Beauvoir *A Transatlantic Love Affair: Letters to Nelson Algren* 69.
102. Beauvoir *A Transatlantic Love Affair: Letters to Nelson Algren* 94.
103. Beauvoir *A Transatlantic Love Affair: Letters to Nelson Algren* 51–52.
104. Beauvoir *A Transatlantic Love Affair: Letters to Nelson Algren* 67, 197.
105. Beauvoir *A Transatlantic Love Affair: Letters to Nelson Algren* 202.
106. Beauvoir *Force of Circumstance* 137.
107. Beauvoir *The Mandarins* 589. Beauvoir said that *The Mandarins* resembled her affair with Nelson Algren, and some of her personal qualities were reflected in both the Anne and the Henri characters (*Force of Circumstance* 280).
108. Beauvoir *She Came to Stay* 207, 279.
109. Beauvoir *She Came to Stay* 230.
110. Jean Leighton argues that Beauvoir's definition of devotion is overly narrow and mistakenly assumes that devotion equates to self-annihilation (*Simone de Beauvoir on Woman* 192–193).
111. Beauvoir *The Second Sex* 664.
112. Beauvoir *The Second Sex* 755.
113. Brison *Beauvoir and Feminism: Interview and Reflections* 191.
114. Judith Okely, Jean Leighton, and Toril Moi all criticize Beauvoir for glorifying masculine values and underestimating feminine values (Okely *Simone de Beauvoir: A Re-reading* 98, Leighton *Simone de Beauvoir on Woman* 39, and Moi *Simone de Beauvoir: The Making of an Intellectual Woman* 211).

115. Beauvoir *The Second Sex* 721.
116. For example, see Andrea Veltman "The Sisyphean Torture of Housework: Simone de Beauvoir and Inequitable Divisions of Domestic Work in Marriage" 126.
117. Beauvoir *She Came to Stay* 158–159.
118. Beauvoir *She Came to Stay* 159.
119. Beauvoir *She Came to Stay* 163.
120. Beauvoir *She Came to Stay* 123–124.
121. Beauvoir "An Eye for an Eye" 258–259.
122. Beauvoir *Who Shall Die?* 64.

References

Ackermann, Robert John. *Nietzsche: A Frenzied Look*. Amherst: The University of Massachusetts Press, 1990.
Adorno, T.W. "On Kierkegaard's Doctrine of Love." *Studies in Philosophy and Social Science* 8 (1940): 413–429.
Aron, Arthur and Elaine N. Aron. *Love and the Expansion of Self*. Washington: Hemisphere Publishing Corporation, 1986.
Badinter, Elisabeth. *Dead End Feminism*. 2003. Trans. Borossa, Julia. Cambridge: Polity Press, 2006.
Barnes, Hazel E. *The Literature of Possibility: A Study in Humanistic Existentialism*. London: Tavistock Publications, 1961.
Beauvoir, Simone de. *All Said and Done*. Trans. O'Brian, Patrick. New York: G. P. Putnam's Sons, 1974.
——. *The Blood of Others*. 1945. Trans. Moyse, Yvonne and Roger Senhouse. Victoria, Australia: Penguin Books, 1964.
——. *The Ethics of Ambiguity*. Trans. Frechtman, Bernard. Secaucus, NJ: Citadel Press, 1948.
——. "An Eye for an Eye." Trans. Arp, Kristana. *Philosophical Writings*. 1946. Eds Simons, Margaret A., et al. Urbana and Chicago: University of Illinois Press, 2004.
——. *Force of Circumstance*. Trans. Howard, Richard. Middlesex, England: Penguin Books, 1968.
——. *Les Belles Images*. 1966. Trans. O'Brian, Patrick. London: Fontana Paperbacks, 1985.
——. *Letters to Sartre*. Trans. Hoare, Quintin. New York: Arcade Publishing, 1992.
——. *The Mandarins*. 1954. Trans. Friedman, Leonard M. London and Glasgow: Fontana Books, 1960.
——. "Must We Burn Sade?" Trans. Michelson, Annette. *The Marquis de Sade*. New York: Grove Press, 1953.
——. *Old Age*. Trans. O'Brian, Patrick. London: Deutsch, Weidenfeld and Nicolson, 1972.
——. *The Prime of Life*. Trans. Green, Peter. Cleveland and New York: The World Publishing Company, 1962.
——. "Pyrrhus and Cineas." Trans. Timmermann, Marybeth. *Philosophical Writings*. 1944. Eds Simons, Margaret A., et al. Urbana and Chicago: University of Illinois Press, 2004.
——. *The Second Sex*. 1949. Trans. Borde, Constance and Sheila Malovany-Chevallier. New York: Alfred A. Knopf, 2010.
——. *She Came to Stay*. 1943. Trans. Moyse, Yvonne and Roger Senhouse. London: Fontana, 1975.
——. *A Transatlantic Love Affair: Letters to Nelson Algren*. New York: The New Press, 1998.
——. "What is Existentialism?" Trans. Timmermann, Marybeth. *Philosophical Writings*. Eds Simons, Margaret A., et al. Urbana and Chicago: University of Illinois Press, 2004.

———. *When Things of the Spirit Come First*. 1979. Trans. O'Brian, Patrick. New York: Pantheon Books, 1982.

———. *Who Shall Die?* 1945. Trans. Francis, Claude and Fernande Gontier. Florissant, Missouri: River Press, 1983.

———. *The Woman Destroyed*. 1967. Trans. O'Brian, Patrick. London: Fontana, 1984.

Ben-Ze'ev, Aaron and Ruhama Goussinsky. *In the Name of Love: Romantic Ideology and Its Victims*. Oxford and New York: Oxford University Press, 2008.

Bentham, Jeremy. "An Introduction to the Principles of Morals and Legislation." 1789. *The Making of Modern Law*. Oxford, New York: Clarendon Press, 1907.

Bergmann, Martin S. *The Anatomy of Loving: The Story of Man's Quest to Know What Love Is*. New York: Columbia University Press, 1987.

Berscheid, Ellen and Elaine Hatfield Walster. *Interpersonal Attraction*. Reading, MA: Addison-Wesley, 1978.

Boesen, E. "Boesen's Account of his Hospital Conversations with Kierkegaard: 14 & 16 October 1855." Trans. Kirmmse, Bruce H. and Virginia R. Laursen. *Encounters with Kierkegaard*. Ed. Kirmmse, B.H. Princeton, NJ: Princeton University Press, 1996.

Brison, Susan J. "Beauvoir and Feminism: Interview and Reflections." *The Cambridge Companion to Simone de Beauvoir*. Ed. Card, Claudia. Cambridge and New York: Cambridge University Press, 2003. 189–207.

Brobjer, Thomas H. "Philologica: A Possible Solution to the Stirner-Nietzsche Question." *The Journal of Nietzsche Studies* 25 (2003): 109–114.

Camus, Albert. *L'Homme révolté*. Paris: Gallimard, 1951.

———. *Lyrical and Critical Essays*. Trans. Kennedy, Ellen Conroy. Ed. Thody, Philip. New York: Vintage Books, 1970.

Carroll, John. *Break-Out from the Crystal Palace*. London: Routledge & Kegan Paul, 1974.

Clark, John P. *Max Stirner's Egoism*. London: Freedom Press, 1976.

Contat, Michel, Michel Rybalka, and Jean-Paul Sartre. *The Writings of Jean-Paul Sartre*. Trans. McCleary, Richard C. Vol. 1. Evanston: Northwestern University Press, 1974.

Cooper, David. *Existentialism: A Reconstruction*. 2 ed. Oxford: Blackwell, 1999.

Cox, Gary. *The Existentialist's Guide to Death, the Universe and Nothingness*. London and New York: Continuum, 2012.

———. *The Sartre Dictionary*. London and New York: Continuum, 2008.

Croxall, T.H. "Kierkegaard and Mozart." *Music and Letters* 26.3 (1945): 151–158.

Daigle, Christine, ed. *Existentialist Thinkers and Ethics*. Montreal, Ithaca: McGill-Queen's University Press, 2006.

———. "Nietzsche: Virtue Ethics…Virtue Politics?" *The Journal of Nietzsche Studies* 32 (2006): 1–21.

Daigle, Christine and Jacob Golomb, eds. *Beauvoir and Sartre: The Riddle of Influence*. Bloomington, IN and Indianapolis, IN: Indiana University Press, 2008.

Davis, Colin. "Existentialism and Literature." *The Continuum Companion to Existentialism*. Eds Joseph, Felicity, Jack Reynolds, and Ashley Woodward. London and New York: Continuum, 2011. 138–154.

Derrida, Jacques. *Spurs: Nietzsche's Styles*. Trans. Harlow, Barbara. Chicago and London: The University of Chicago Press, 1979.

Dewey, Bradley R. "Seven Seducers: A Typology of Interpretations of the Aesthetic Stage in Kierkegaard's 'The Seducer's Diary'." *Either/Or I*. Ed. Perkins, Robert L.

International Kierkegaard Commentary. Macon, GA: Mercer University Press, 1995.
Diethe, Carol. "Nietzsche and the Woman Question." *History of European Ideas* 11 (1989): 865–875.
Dillon, Martin C. *Beyond Romance*. Albany, NY: State University of New York Press, 2001.
Duran, Jane. "The Kierkegaardian Feminist." *Feminist Interpretations of Søren Kierkegaard*. Eds Leon, Celine and Sylvia Walsh. University Park, PA: Pennsylvania State University Press, 1997.
Evans, C. Stephen. *Kierkegaard's Ethic of Love – Divine Commands and Moral Obligations*. Oxford: Oxford University Press, 2004.
Evans, Debbie. "Sartre and Beauvoir on Hegel's Master-Slave Dialectic and the Question of the 'Look'." *Beauvoir and Sartre: The Riddle of Influence*. Eds Daigle, Christine and Jacob Golomb. Bloomington, IN: Indiana University Press, 2009. 90–115.
Ferreira, M. Jamie. "Equality, Impartiality, and Moral Blindness in Kierkegaard's *Works of Love*." *Journal of Religious Ethics* 25.1 (1997): 21.
Flynn, Thomas. *Existentialism*. Oxford and New York: Oxford University Press, 2006.
Frankfurt, Harry G. *The Reasons of Love*. Princeton, NJ: Princeton University Press, 2004.
Fromm, Erich. *Escape from Freedom*. 1941. New York: Henry Holt, 1994.
Fullbrook, Edward. "She Came to Stay and Being and Nothingness." *Hypatia* 14.4 (1999): 50–69.
Fullbrook, Edward and Kate Fullbrook. *Sex and Philosophy: Rethinking de Beauvoir and Sartre*. London and New York: Continuum, 2008.
Fuss, Peter and Henry Shapiro, eds. *Nietzsche: A Self-Portrait from His Letters*. Cambridge, Massachusetts: Harvard University Press, 1971.
Gerassi, John. *Talking with Sartre: Conversations and Debates*. New Haven and London: Yale University Press, 2009.
Gilman, Sander L. and David J. Parent, eds. *Conversations with Nietzsche: A Life in the Words of His Contemporaries*. New York: Oxford University Press, 1991.
Glassford, John. "Did Friedrich Nietzsche (1844–1900) Plagiarise from Max Stirner (1806–56)?" *The Journal of Nietzsche Studies* 18 (1999): 73–79.
Greve, Wilfried. *Kierkegaards maieutische Ethik*. Frankfurt am Main: Suhrkamp, 1990.
Hartmann, Eduard von. *Philosophy of the Unconscious*. New ed. Vol. III. London: Kegan Paul, Trench, Trubner & Co., 1931.
Hatfield, Elaine and G. William Walster. *A New Look at Love*. Reading, MA: Addison-Wesley, 1981.
Hegel, G.W.F. "A Fragment on Love." *The Philosophy of (Erotic) Love*. Eds Solomon, Robert C. and Kathleen M. Higgins. Lawrence, Kansas: University Press of Kansas, 1991.
———. *Phenomenology of Spirit*. 1807. Trans. Miller, A.V. Oxford: Clarendon Press, 1977.
Hendrick, Susan S. and Clyde Hendrick. "Romantic Love." *Close Relationships*. Eds Hendrick, Clyde and Susan S. Hendrick. Thousand Oaks, London, New Delhi: Sage Publications, 2000. 201–215.
Higgins, Kathleen Marie. "The Whip Recalled." *Journal of Nietzsche Studies*.12 (1996): 1–18.

―――. "Gender in *The Gay Science*." *Philosophy and Literature* 19.2 (1995): 227–247.
Hodgkinson, Christopher. *The Philosophy of Leadership*. Oxford: Basil Blackwell, 1983.
Hollingdale, R.J. *Nietzsche: The Man and His Philosophy*. Revised ed. Cambridge: Cambridge University Press, 1999.
Honderich, Ted, ed. *The Oxford Companion to Philosophy*. Oxford: Oxford University Press, 1995.
Johnson, Robert A. *The Psychology of Romantic Love*. London, Melbourne and Henley: Routledge and Kegan Paul, 1984.
Joseph, Felicity, Jack Reynolds, and Ashley Woodward, eds. *The Continuum Companion to Existentialism*. London and New York: Continuum, 2011.
Joullié, Jean-Etienne. *Will to Power, Nietzsche's Last Idol*. Basingstoke and New York: Palgrave Macmillan, 2013.
Kant, Immanuel. *The Critique of Judgement*. 1790. Indianapolis, IN: Hackett Publishing Company, 1987.
Kierkegaard, Søren. *The Concept of Anxiety*. 1844. Trans. Thomte, Reidar and Albert B. Anderson. Princeton, NJ: Princeton University Press, 1980.
―――. *Concluding Unscientific Postscript*. 1846. Trans. Swenson, David F. and Walter Lowrie. Princeton, NJ: Princeton University Press, 1968.
―――. *The Crowd is Untruth*. Trans. Bellinger, Charles K.: Amazon Kindle Edition, 1847.
―――. *Either/Or*. 1843. Trans. Hannay, Alastair. London: Penguin, 1992.
―――. *Fear and Trembling*. 1843. Trans. Walsh, Sylvia. Cambridge and New York: Cambridge University Press, 2006.
―――. *Kierkegaard's Journals and Notebooks*. Ed. Kirmmse, Bruce H. Vol. 1. Princeton, NJ and Oxford: Princeton University Press, 2007.
―――. *The Point of View*. 1848. Trans. Hong, Howard V. and Edna H. Hong. Princeton, NJ: Princeton University Press, 1998.
―――. *Purify Your Hearts! A "Discourse for a Special Occasion" the first of three "Edifying Discourses in a Different Vein," published in 1847 at Copenhagen*. 1847. Trans. Aldworth, A.S. and W.S. Ferrie. London: The C. W. Daniel Company, 1937.
―――. *Søren Kierkegaard's Journals and Papers (Volume 3)*. Trans. Hong, Howard V., Edna H. Hong, and Gregor Malantschuk. Bloomington, IN and London: Indiana University Press, 1975.
―――. *Søren Kierkegaard's Journals and Papers (Volume 5)*. Trans. Hong, Howard V. and Edna H. Hong. Bloomington, IN: Indiana University Press, 1978.
―――. *Søren Kierkegaard's Journals and Papers (Volume 6)*. Trans. Hong, Howard V., Edna H. Hong, and Gregor Malantschuk. Bloomington, IN and London: Indiana University Press, 1978.
―――. *Works of Love*. 1847. Trans. Hong, Howard and Edna Hong. New York: Harper & Row, 1962.
Koestenbaum, Peter. *Existential Sexuality: Choosing to Love*. Englewood Cliffs, NJ: Prentice-Hall, 1974.
Kofman, Sarah. "Baubo: Theological Perversion and Fetishism." Trans. Strong, Tracy B. *Feminist Interpretations of Friedrich Nietzsche*. Eds Oliver, Kelly and Marilyn Pearsall. University Park, PA: Pennsylvania State University Press, 1998. 21–49.
Köhler, Joachim. *Zarathustra's Secret*. Trans. Taylor, Ronald. New Haven and London: Yale University Press, 2002.

Lamblin, Bianca. *A Disgraceful Affair*. Trans. Plovnick, Julie. Boston: Northeastern University Press, 1996.
Leighton, Jean. *Simone de Beauvoir on Woman*. Rutherford, NJ and London: Fairleigh Dickinson University Press and Associated University Presses, 1975.
Levinas, Emmanuel. *Proper Names*. 1976. Trans. Smith, Michael B. London: The Athlone Press, 1996.
Lilar, Suzanne. *Aspects of Love in Western Society*. 1963. Trans. Griffin, Jonathan. London: Thames and Hudson, 1965.
Lindholm, Charles. "Romantic Love and Anthropology." *Etnofoor* 19.1 (2006): 5–21.
Löwith, Karl. *From Hegel to Nietzsche*. Trans. Green, David E. 1 ed. New York: Holt, Rinehart and Winston, 1964.
Lungstrum, Janet. "Nietzsche Writing Woman/Woman Writing Nietzsche: The Sexual Dialectic of Palingenesis." *Nietzsche and the Feminine*. Ed. Burgard, Peter J. Charlottesville, VA and London: University Press of Virginia, 1994. 135–157.
MacIntyre, Alasdair. *After Virtue*. 2 ed. London: Duckworth, 1985.
Mackay, John Henry. *Max Stirner: His Life and His Work*. Trans. Kennedy, Hubert. From the 3rd German ed. Concord, CA: Peremptory Publications, 2005.
Macquarrie, John. *Existentialism*. London: Penguin Books, 1972.
Marx, Karl and Frederick Engels. *The German Ideology*. Ed. Ryazanskaya, S. London: Lawrence & Wishart, 1965.
McKinnon, Alastair. "Kierkegaard and the 'Leap of Faith'." *Kierkegaardiana* 16 (1993): 107–125.
Mikulincer, Mario, Victor Florian and Gilad Hirschberger. "The Terror of Death and the Quest for Love: An Existential Perspective on Close Relationships." *Handbook of Experimental Existential Psychology*. Eds Greenberg, Jeff, Sander L. Koole, and Tom Pyszczynski. New York and London: The Guilford Press, 2004.
Mill, John Stuart. "Utilitarianism." *John Stuart Mill and Jeremy Bentham: Utilitarianism and Other Essays*. 1861. Ed. Ryan, Alan. London: Penguin Books, 2004.
Moi, Toril. *Simone de Beauvoir: The Making of an Intellectual Woman*. Oxford and Cambridge: Blackwell, 1994.
Monk, Ray. "Philosophical Biography: The Very Idea." *Wittgenstein: Biography and Philosophy*. Ed. Klagge, James C. Cambridge: Cambridge University Press, 2001. 3–15.
Nietzsche, Friedrich. "The Anti-Christ." Trans. Norman, Judith. *The Anti-Christ, Ecce Homo, Twilight of the Idols, and Other Writings*. Eds Ridley, Aaron and Judith Norman. Cambridge: Cambridge University Press, 2005.
———. *Beyond Good and Evil*. 1886. Trans. Hollingdale, R.J. London: Penguin Books, 1990.
———. "The Case of Wagner: A Musician's Problem." Trans. Norman, Judith. *The Anti-Christ, Ecce Homo, Twilight of the Idols and Other Writings*. 1888. Eds Ridley, Aaron and Judith Norman. Cambridge: Cambridge University Press, 2005. 231–262.
———. *Daybreak*. 1881. Trans. Hollingdale, R.J. Cambridge: Cambridge University Press, 1982.
———. "Ecce Homo." Trans. Norman, Judith. *The Anti-Christ, Ecce Homo, Twilight of the Idols, and Other Writings*. Eds Ridley, Aaron and Judith Norman. Cambridge: Cambridge University Press, 2005. 69–151.

———. *The Gay Science*. 1882–1887. Trans. Nauckhoff, Josefine and Adrian Del Caro. Ed. Williams, Bernard. Cambridge and New York: Cambridge University Press, 2001.

———. *Human, All Too Human*. 1878–1880. Trans. Hollingdale, R.J. Cambridge: Cambridge University Press, 1996.

———. "On The Genealogy of Morals." Trans. Kaufmann, Walter and R.J. Hollingdale. *On The Genealogy of Morals and Ecce Homo*. Ed. Kaufmann, Walter. New York: Vintage Books, 1989.

———. "Schopenhauer as Educator." Trans. Hollingdale, R.J. *Untimely Meditations*. 1874. Ed. Breazeale, Daniel. Cambridge: Cambridge University Press, 1997. 125–194.

———. *Thus Spoke Zarathustra*. 1883–1885. Trans. Hollingdale, R.J. London: Penguin Books, 1969.

———. "Twilight of the Idols." Trans. Hollingdale, R.J. *Twilight of the Idols and The Anti-Christ*. 1889. London: Penguin, 1990.

———. "The Wanderer and His Shadow." Trans. Hollingdale, R.J. *Human, All Too Human*. Cambridge: Cambridge University Press, 1996.

———. *The Will to Power*. Trans. Kaufmann, Walter and R.J. Hollingdale. Ed. Kaufmann, Walter. New York: Vintage Books, 1968.

Nozick, Robert. "Love's Bond." *The Philosophy of (Erotic) Love*. Eds Solomon, Robert C. and Kathleen M. Higgins. Lawrence, Kansas: University Press of Kansas, 1991. 417–432.

Ogilvy, James. "Mastery and Sexuality: Hegel's Dialectic in Sartre and Post-Freudian Psychology." *Human Studies*.3 (1980): 201–219.

Okely, Judith. *Simone de Beauvoir: A Re-reading*. London: Virago, 1986.

Oliver, Kelly. "Nietzsche's Abjection." *Nietzsche and the Feminine*. Ed. Burgard, Peter J. Charlottesville, VA and London: University Press of Virginia, 1994. 53–67.

Oppel, Frances Nesbitt. *Nietzsche on Gender: Beyond Man and Woman*. Charlottesville, VA and London: University of Virginia Press, 2005.

Padgett, Alan G. and Steve Wilkens. *Christianity and Western Thought: A History of Philosophers, Ideas and Movements*. Vol. 3: Journey to Postmodernity in the 20th Century. Downers Grove, IL: InterVarsity Press, 2009.

Paterson, R.W.K. *The Nihilistic Egoist: Max Stirner*. New York: For University of Hull by Oxford University Press, 1971.

Penn, Roger. "Arranged Marriages in Western Europe: Media Representations and Social Reality." *Journal of Comparative Family Studies* 42.5 (2011): 637–650.

Priest, Stephen, ed. *Jean-Paul Sartre: Basic Writings*. London and New York: Routledge, 2001.

Read, Herbert. *Anarchy and Order*. London: Faber & Faber, 1954.

Reginster, Bernard. *The Affirmation of Life: Nietzsche on Overcoming Nihilism*. Cambridge and London: Harvard University Press, 2006.

Reynolds, Jack. *Understanding Existentialism*. Chesham, Bucks: Acumen, 2006.

Reynolds, Jack and Ashley Woodward. "Existentialism and Poststructuralism: Some Unfashionable Observations." *The Continuum Companion to Existentialism*. Eds Joseph, Felicity, Jack Reynolds, and Ashley Woodward. London and New York: Continuum, 2011.

Rowley, Hazel. *Tête-à-Tête: Simone de Beauvoir and Jean-Paul Sartre*. New York: HarperCollins, 2005.

Sadler Jr, William A. *Existence and Love: A New Approach in Existential Phenomenology*. New York: Charles Scribner's Sons, 1969.

Safranski, Rüdiger. *Nietzsche: A Philosophical Biography*. Trans. Frisch, Shelley. New York: W. W. Norton, 2002.
Salomé, Lou. *Nietzsche*. Trans. Mandel, Siegfried. Urbana, IL and Chicago: University of Illinois Press, 2001.
Santoni, Robert E. *Bad Faith, Good Faith, and Authenticity in Sartre's Early Philosophy*. Philadelphia: Temple University Press, 1995.
Sartre, Jean-Paul. *Being and Nothingness*. 1943. Trans. Barnes, Hazel E. New York: Washington Square Press, 1992.
——. *Between Existentialism and Marxism*. Trans. Matthews, John. London: Gallimard, 1974.
——. *The Chips are Down*. 1947. Trans. Varése, Louise. London: Rider and Company, 1951.
——. *The Emotions: Outline of a Theory*. 1939. Trans. Frechtman, Bernard. New York: Philosophical Library, 1948.
——. *Existentialism is a Humanism*. 1946. Trans. Macomber, Carol. New Haven, CT: Yale University Press, 2007.
——. "The Flies." Trans. Gilbert, Stuart. *Altona, Men Without Shadows, The Flies*. 1943. Harmondsworth: Penguin, 1962.
——. "Huis Clos." Trans. Gilbert, Stuart. *Huis Clos and Other Plays*. 1944. London: Penguin Books, 2000.
——. "Interview with Jean-Paul Sartre." *The Philosophy of Jean-Paul Sartre*. Ed. Schilpp, Paul Arthur. Carbondale, IL: Southern Illinois University, 1981.
——. "Lucifer and the Lord." Trans. Black, Kitty. *Huis Clos and Other Plays*. 1951. London: Penguin Books, 2000.
——. *Nausea*. 1938. Trans. Alexander, Lloyd. New York: New Directions, 1964.
——. *Notebooks for an Ethics*. 1983. Trans. Pellauer, David. Chicago and London: University of Chicago Press, 1992.
——. *The Problem of Method*. 1960. Trans. Barnes, Hazel E. London: Meuthen & Co., 1963.
——. *Quiet Moments in a War: The Letters of Jean-Paul Sartre to Simone de Beauvoir 1940–1963*. 1983. Trans. Fahnestock, Lee and Norman MacAfee. Ed. de Beauvoir, Simone. New York: Scribner, 1993.
——. "The Room." Trans. Alexander, Lloyd. *The Wall (Intimacy) and Other Stories*. 1939. New York: New Directions, 1969.
——. *Sartre in the Seventies: Interviews and Essays*. Trans. Auster, Paul and Lydia Davis. London: Deutsch, 1978.
——. *War Diaries: Notebooks from a Phoney War 1939–1940*. Trans. Hoare, Quintin. London and New York: Verso, 1984.
——. *Witness to My Life: The Letters of Jean-Paul Sartre to Simone de Beauvoir 1926–1939*. Trans. Fahnestock, Lee and Norman MacAfee. New York: Scribner, 1992.
Schwarzer, Alice. *After The Second Sex: Conversations with Simone de Beauvoir*. Trans. Horwarth, Marianne. New York: Pantheon Books, 1984.
Secomb, Linnell. *Philosophy and Love: From Plato to Popular Culture*. Bloomington, IN: Indiana University Press, 2007.
Segal, Steven. "The Yearning for Philosophy Today: Its Transformational and Therapeutic Value." *The Capa Quarterly* (February 2012): 8–11.
Shalin, Dmitri N. "The Romantic Antecedents of Meadian Social Psychology." *Symbolic Interaction* 7.1 (1984): 43–65.

Simmel, Georg. *Schopenhauer and Nietzsche.* Trans. Loiskandl, Helmut, Deena Weinstein, and Michael Weinstein. Urbana, IL and Chicago: University of Illanois Press, 1991.

Simons, Margaret A., Jessica Benjamin, and Simone de Beauvoir. "Simone de Beauvoir: An Interview." *Feminist Studies* 5.2 (1979): 330–345.

Singer, Irving. *The Nature of Love: The Modern World.* 2 ed. Chicago and London: The University of Chicago Press, 1987.

——. *The Pursuit of Love.* Baltimore and London: John Hopkins University Press, 1994.

Small, Robin. *Nietzsche and Rée: A Star Friendship.* Oxford and New York: Oxford University Press, 2005.

Solomon, Robert C. "The Virtue of (Erotic) Love." *The Philosophy of (Erotic) Love.* Eds Solomon, Robert C. and Kathleen M. Higgins. Lawrence, Kansas: University Press of Kansas, 1991. 492–518.

——. *Living with Nietzsche.* New York: Oxford University Press, 2003.

——. *Love: Emotion, Myth, and Metaphor.* Buffalo: Prometheus Books, 1990.

Solomon, Robert C. and Kathleen M. Higgins, eds. *The Philosophy of (Erotic) Love.* Lawrence, KS: University Press of Kansas, 1991.

——. *What Nietzsche Really Said.* New York: Shocken Books, 2000.

Spillane, Robert. *An Eye for An I: Living Philosophy.* Melbourne: Michelle Anderson Publishing, 2007.

Stepelevich, Lawrence. "Max Stirner as Hegelian." *Journal of the History of Ideas* 46.4 (1985): 597–614.

Sternberg, Robert J. *Love is a Story.* New York and Oxford: Oxford University Press, 1998.

——. "A Triangular Theory of Love." *Psychological Review* 93.2 (1986): 119–135.

Stirner, Max. *The Ego and His Own.* 1845. Trans. Byington, Steven T. Ed. Martin, James J. Mineola, NY: Dover Publications, Inc., 2005.

——. *Kleinere Schriften und seine Entgegnungen auf die Kritik seines Werkes "Der Einzige und sein Eigenthum" aus den Jahren 1842–1848.* Ed. Mackay, John Henry. 2 ed. Berlin: Bernhard Zack's Verlag, 1914.

Szabados, Béla. "Autobiography and Philosophy: Variations on a Theme of Wittgenstein." *Metaphilosophy* 26.1&2 (1995): 63–80.

Utterback, Sylvia Walsh. "Don Juan and the Representation of Spiritual Sensuousness." *Journal of the American Academy of Religion* 47.4 (1979): 627–644.

Veltman, Andrea. "The Sisyphean Torture of Housework: Simone de Beauvoir and Inequitable Divisions of Domestic Work in Marriage." *Hypatia* 19.3 (2004): 121–143.

Warnock, Mary. *The Philosophy of Sartre.* London: Hutchinson University Library, 1965.

Welsh, John. *Max Stirner's Dialectical Egoism: A New Interpretation.* Lanham, MD: Lexington Books, 2010.

Widner, Marc. "Love in *Don Giovanni.*" *Nature and Pursuit of Love.* Ed. Goicoechia, D. New York: Prometheus, 1995. 287–294.

Index

aesthetic loving/sphere, 48–57, 64–7, *see also* Kierkegaard, Søren
agape, 41, 74, 77–8
Algren, Nelson, 138, 146, 150–4
angst, *see* anxiety
anguish, *see* anxiety
anxiety, 11, 13, 14, 17, 29, 44, 50, 56, 57, 59–64, 68, 102, 106, 114–15, 140, 157–8, 165, 168–9, 174
Aristophanes, 4–5, 79, 111
Aron, Arthur, and Elaine Aron, 7
Aron, Raymond, 10
art (love as), 52–3, 75
authenticity, 12, 14–15, 17, 18, 25, 43, 59, 76, 81, 96, 115, 118–19, 124
authentic loving, 9, 12, 115–16, 141–7, 151, 155–9, 169, 176, *see also* Beauvoir, Simone de

bad faith, 11, 15, 17, 108, 112, 115, 117, 118–19, 124, 126, 130–41, 143, 149, 151, 160, 172, 175–6
Badinter, Elisabeth, 3–4
beauty, 40, 52–3, 66, 76, 80, 94, 133, 162
Beauvoir, Simone de, 6, 9, 10, 13, 15, 17, 18, 99, 115, 116–17, 120, 122, 123–4, 125–59, 161–77
  on anxiety of love, 157–9
  on destiny, 139–41
  on devotion, 135–6, 153–5
  on diversifying interests, 137–9
  on economic independence, 156–7
  on feminine values, 155–6
  on fidelity, 151–3
  on idolizing and subordinating, 132–3
  on justifying oneself, 136–7, 148–9
  on loving authentically, 141–7
  on loving inauthentically, 130–41
  on merging, 133–4
  on possessing and dominating, 135, 148

and her relationship with Jean-Paul Sartre, see Jean-Paul Sartre on secondary lovers, 150–1
  on transcending, 145–6
  on transparency, 149–50
being-for-itself, 101
being-for-others, 55, 100, 103–5, 120
being-in-itself, 101
being-with (others), 12, 103, 105, 127–30
Bentham, Jeremy, 22
Ben-Ze'ev, Aaron, and Ruhama Goussinsky, 5
Bergson, Henri, 100
Bienenfeld, Bianca, 108, 151
Brison, Susan J., 151, 192
Buber, Martin, 18
Byron, Lord George Gordon, 91

Camus, Albert, 10, 18, 26, 29, 35
care, *see* concern
caress, 109–10
Carroll, John, 18
childbearing/childcare, 4, 7, 67, 76, 85, 90–2, 96, 97, 127, 132, 139, 142–3, 146, 156
choice, 10–11, 13, 14–15, 23–5, 28, 32–3, 43, 52–3, 57–8, 61–5, 86, 101, 104, 111–14, 118–19, 129, 131, 173–6, *see also* leap
Christianity, 46, 60, 74, 77–9, 83–4
commitment, 6–7, 8, 13, 36–7, 43, 48, 57, 60, 61, 65, 86, 115, 118–19, 147, 151–2, *see also* leap
communication
  immediate, 144
  indirect, 19–20, 47
  in love, 90–1, 122
community, 4, 11, 12, 23–4, 46, 128
companionship, *see* friendship
concern (for the other's welfare), 5, 8, 31–3, 66–7, 82, 96, 98, 120, 123, 162, 168–9

204

connections to others, 7, 57–8, 93, 104, 122, 123, 128, 129, 144, 146, 163, 167
contingent love, 117, 123, 150–1, *compare* primary love
Cooper, David, 12, 17, 18
Cordelia (Wahl), 51–7, 67–8
Cox, Gary, 8
creative nothing/nothingness, 18, 22, 28–9, 100, 166
creativity, 28, 53, 66, 92, 98, 127, 156–7

Dähnhardt, Marie, 21, 34, 40
Davis, Colin, 20
death, 3, 10, 11, 41, 57, 58–9, 92, 100, 101, 104, 107, 118, 131, 152, 165
desire, *see* sexual desire
despair, *see* anxiety
destiny, 126, 127, 139–41, 172
determinism, 11, 107, 112, 124, 126, 139
devotion, 23, 32, 78, 81, 135–6, 149, 153–5, 164, 194n
dialectic, *see* master–slave dialectic
Dillon, Martin, 5
distance (from others), 36, 92–94, 121, 171
diversifying, 137–40, 158
dominating, 81, 82, 96, 130, 135, 140, 144, 148, 159, 161, 171
Don Giovanni, 48–51, 57–8, 64–8, 146
Don Juan, 5, 49–50
Dostoyevsky, Fyodor, 111, 128, 170
dread, *see* anxiety

economic independence, 3–4, 125, 141–2, 156–7
education, 55, 84–5, 89, 91, 94, 96, 142
egoism, 26, 38, 78, 81, 127
egoistic loving, *see* Stirner, Max
emotions, 26, 29, 112–13, 144–5
enemies, 78, 95, 121, 123, 170–1
Engels, Friedrich, 21, 43
ens causa sui, 102
Eros/erotic love, 8, 48–50, 59–60, 67, 79, 84, 161, *see also* loving; sex/sexual desire

essential love, 117, 123, 151, *compare* contingent love
ethical sphere, 57–9, 67–9
existentialism (definition of), 2, 9–13

facticity, 11, 27, 127, 131, *see also* immanence
family, 3, 4, 11, 76, 90–2, 103, 112, 120, 121, 142, 145, 146, 149, 154, 155
fascination, 53, 82, 108–9
fear, 56, 61, 102, *compare* anxiety
femininity, 55, 76, 77, 96, 133, 155–6
fidelity, 149–50, 152, 154
freedom, 3, 10–11, 12, 14–15, 17, 22, 24, 26–7, 31, 43–4, 48, 52, 55, 58, 70, 76, 89–90, 98, 107–10, 115–17, 119, 124, 125–26, 128–31, 137, 141–3, 148, 149–57, 159, 161–2, 169–76
friendship, 6, 8, 13, 17, 34–5, 38, 55, 71, 87–8, 90, 94–8, 105, 116–17, 121, 123, 137–8, 144–5, 148, 150, 159, 168, 170

gaze (or look) of the other, 80, 100, 103–4, 108–9, 110, 120–2, 133, 146, 156, 169, 171

harmony (in relationships), 13, 109, 134, 162, 163, 165, 170
hedonism, 39, 48, 66, 71, 74, 80, 84, 96, 147, 162
Hegel, G.W.F., 9–10, 22, 36, 45, 100, 104–5, 106, 163
Heidegger, Martin, 10, 12, 18, 100
Hendrick, Susan, and Clyde Hendrick, 6
Higgins, Kathleen, 3
Husserl, Edmund, 10, 100, 102

idolizing, 74, 132–3, 140, 141, 161
immanence, 127, 131, 132, 142, 152, 156, *compare* transcendence
inauthentic loving, 130–41, 145, 153, 158, *see also* bad faith, *compare* authentic loving
intersubjectivity, 24, 144

intimacy, 6–7, 8, 103, 105, 110, 121, 136, 138, 152
intoxication, 45, 53–4, 80, 98, 130, 144–5, 149, 169

Jaspers, Karl, 10, 18
jealousy, 60, 78, 81, 117, 150, 164
Johannes the Seducer, 16, 45, 48, 51–9, 62, 63, 64–8, 106, 108, 146
Jollivet, Simone, 108
Joseph, Felicity, Jack Reynolds, and Ashley Woodward, 20
justifying (existence), 107, 123, 128, 132, 135, 136–7, 138, 141, 145, 148–9, 161–2, 165

Kant, Immanuel, 52, 100, 129
Kierkegaard, Søren, 8, 9, 13, 15, 16, 18, 19–20, 45–70, 72, 86, 87, 89, 101, 102, 106, 108, 113, 114, 118, 161–77
 on leaping, 61–4, 68
 on loving aesthetically, 48–57, 64–7
 on loving ethically, 57–9, 67–9
 on loving reflectively (Johannes the Seducer), 51–6
 on loving unreflectively (Mozart's Don Giovanni), 49–51
 on religious love, 59–60, 67–9
Koestenbaum, Peter, 7, 11, 12
Köhler, Joachim, 72–3

lack, 101–2, 136
language, 105, 108
leap, 12–13, 24, 43, 45, 57, 61–4, 67–8
Le Bon, Sylvie, 120
Levinas, Emmanuel, 18, 46
Lindholm, Charles, 7
look, *see* gaze (of the other)
loving/love
 aesthetic, 48–57
 companionate, 6, 8, 19, 162, 168, *see also* friendship
 consummate, 6
 courtly, 3
 empty, 6
 ethical, 57–9
 and evolutionary theory, 7
 fatuitous, 6

infatuated, 6, 23, 26
 as merging, 4–6, 7, 8, 9, 14, 24, 41, 85, 92–3, 98, 108, 110, 122–4, 133–5, 144, 163–5, 167, *see also* unity
 passionate, 3, 4, 6, 7, *see also* passions
 reflective, 51–6
 religious, 59–60
 romantic (definition of), 2–9
 sadomasochistic, 109–10, 114, 115–16, 164
 self, 25–31, 60, 120
 as self-expansion, 7
 sensual, 16, 23, 26, 38, 48, 50, 58, 65–7, 70, 83–4, 86, 103, 121, 144–5, 166, 167
 sexual, *see* sex/sexual desire
 as similar stories, 6
 unreflective, 49–51
lust, 51, 79, 97–8, 133

Mackay, John Henry, 34
Macquarrie, John, 12
Marcel, Gabriel, 10, 18
Marx, Karl/Marxism, 13, 21, 43, 99, 126, 149
marriage, 3, 4, 5, 6, 7, 8, 11, 16–17, 19, 34, 40, 45, 57–9, 62–4, 67–8, 71, 72, 74–5, 85–91, 94, 95, 97, 98, 118, 127, 139, 142, 149, 163, 164, 172–3
masculinity, 77, 85, 139, 140, 156, 172
masochism, 17, 109, 110, 114, 115–16, 164, *compare* sadism
master–slave dialectic, 10, 100, 104, 124, 130, 135, 141, 161, 163
Merleau-Ponty, Maurice, 10, 18
Mikulincer, Mario, Victor Florian, and Gilad Hirschberger, 11
Mill, John Stuart, 22
Monk, Ray, 15
monogamy, 5, 87–90, 92, 117, 140
Mozart, Wolfgang Amadeus, 48–51

narcissism, 37, 79, 93, 119–20, 182n
Nietzsche, Friedrich, 6, 8, 9, 13, 16, 18, 28, 71–98, 101, 102, 105, 107, 121, 125, 126, 128, 133, 148, 156, 159, 161–77

Nietzsche, Friedrich – *continued*
  on Christian morality, 77–8
  on friendship, 94–5
  on idealizing women, 75–6
  on keeping distance, 92–4
  on leveraging strengths, 77
  on marriage, 85–91
  on monogamy, 87–90
  and his personal relationships, 72–3
  on procreating, 90–2
  on promises, 86–7
  on risks and challenges, 82–3
  on self-mastery, 78–82
  on sex, bodies, and passions, 83–4
  on sex education, 84–5
nihilism, 13, 28–9, 35, 71, 72, 74, 98, 127
nothingness, 101, *see also* creative nothing, lack
Nozick, Robert, 5

Olsen, Regine, 58, 62
overcoming (oneself), 11, 28, 36, 71, 83, 89, 94–5, 102, 116, 127, 156, 174
ownness, 25, 33, 41–3, *see also* self–ownership

passions, 1, 6–8, 11, 14, 15, 16, 26, 31, 33, 38–9, 41, 45–7, 50, 51, 53–4, 59–62, 67, 68, 78, 80–1, 83–4, 97, 113, 115, 126, 129, 130, 133, 139, 142, 144, 147–9, 162–3, 169–70, 173–5
phenomenology, 10, 15, 18, 100
Plato, 2, 4, 16, *see also* Aristophanes
possession/possessiveness, 8, 26–7, 31, 35–6, 39, 41, 42, 58, 81–2, 98, 101, 106–7, 116, 124, 135, 144, 163–5, 170, *see also* jealousy, property, self–mastery, self–ownership
power, 3, 10, 16, 21, 22, 26–7, 31, 35–6, 41–4, 53–4, 55, 56, 74–7, 80, 82, 94–5, 97–8, 116, 128–9, 133, 135, 140–1, 148, 155–6, 157, 164–7, 168, 169–71, 173–4 *see also* will to power

powerful loving, *see* Nietzsche, Friedrich
pregnancy, 92, *see also* childbearing
primary lovers, 117, 123, 151, *compare* contingent lovers
procreation, *see* childbearing
promises, 23–4, 37, 39, 86–7, 128, 165–6
property, 21–3, 25–7, 32–3, 36, 39, 41–2, 182n, *see also* possession
Proust, Marcel, 106

radical conversion, 114
raison d'etre, 9, 14, 17, 111, 132, 136, 148–9, 154
reciprocity, 5, 14, 35–6, 41, 58, 60, 67, 69–70, 104–5, 108, 110, 113–14, 141, 162, 167
religious sphere, 59–60, 67–9
responsibility, 11, 12, 13, 23, 46, 47, 48, 56, 112, 118, 119, 125, 129, 131–2, 136, 137, 143, 145, 146, 151, 152, 158, 163, 164, 172, 175
Romanticism, 3, 4, 5, 7, 9, 37, 39
romantic loving (definition of), 2–9, *see also* love

sacrifices (in love), 15, 23–4, 32–3, 40–2, 51, 64, 71, 77–8, 81–2, 96, 98, 132, 175–6
Sade, Marquis de, 100, 144
sadism, 109–10, 114, 115, 120, 164
Sadler, William, 12
sadomasochism, 17, 110, 116, 143, 161, *see also* masochism, sadism
sadomasochistic loving, *see* Sartre, Jean-Paul
Salomé, Lou, 73, 88, 89
Sartre, Jean-Paul, 8–9, 10, 11, 13, 15, 17, 18, 20, 99–123, 161–77
  on anxiety, 102, 114–15
  on authentic loving, 115–16, 119
  on choosing to love, 111–14
  on masochism, 109
  and the master–slave dialectic, 100, 104–6, 106, 124
  and narcissism, 119–20
  on possession, 106–7
  on prioritizing (lovers), 117–19

Sartre, Jean-Paul – *continued*
  and his relationships with women, 116, 120, 150–51
  and his relationship with Simone de Beauvoir, 99, 116–17, 122, 123, 149–50, 153–54
  on sadism, 109–10
  on seduction, 107–9
  and transparency, 116–17
Schmidt, Johann Kaspar, *see* Stirner, Max
Schopenhauer, Arthur, 7, 74
Secomb, Linnell, 6
secondary love, *see* contingent love
seduction, 49–56, 75–6, 107–9, 133, *see also* Johannes the Seducer, Don Giovanni
Segal, Steven, 13
self-expansion, 7
self-love, 25–31, 60, 120
self-mastery, 12, 26, 58, 74, 78–82, 87, 93, 97–8, 161, 169–70, 174–5
self-ownership, 25–31, 43
selfishness, 8, 23–4, 26, 30–1, 34, 35, 49, 60, 78, 81, 136, 144, 147, 168, *see also* egoism
sex/sexual desire, 5, 6, 7, 8, 49, 50, 66, 67, 96, 97, 98, 109, 116, 122, 162–4, 174
sex education, 84–5
Shakespeare, William, 2, 3, 4
shame, 83–5, 103–4
Singer, Irving, 5, 39
Smith, Adam, 22
Socrates, 89, 94
Solomon, Robert, 3, 4, 5, 11
soul mates, 9, 111, 172, 174
Spillane, Robert, 9
star friendship, 87–8, 95, 96, 148, 170, *see also* friendship
Stendhal, 79
Sternberg, Robert, 6–7
Stirner, Max, 8, 9, 13, 16, 18, 21–44, 161–77
  on creative nothings, 28–9
  on embracing power, 26–8
  on loving unions, 35–7

  and his personal relationships, 34
  on self-acceptance, 29–30
  on self-interest, 30–1
  on self-ownership, 25–9, *see also* ownness
submitting/subordinating, 5, 22, 23, 25, 26, 35, 36, 39, 42, 55–6, 65, 67, 77, 81, 82, 96, 100, 115, 125, 130, 132–3, 139, 140, 141, 143, 145, 155, 159, 161, 162, 171, 172, 175
Symposium, 4, 16, *see also* Aristophanes
Szabados, Béla, 15

touch, *see* caress
transcendence/transcending, 7, 11, 12, 26, 28, 31, 43, 71, 92, 110, 126, 127, 131, 133, 139, 141, 142, 143, 145–6, 149, 151, 154–7, 159, 165, 171
transparency, 116–17, 149–50, 176
Tristan and Isolde, 3, 8, 130
trust, 79, 108, 117, 141, 150, 167, 175
truth, 15, 24, 40, 46–7, 76, 105, 112, 117, 122, 150, *see also* transparency

Übermensch, 13, 16, 71, 74, 89–98, 101, 102, 126, 161, 170, 176, 177
Union of Egoists, 36
unique one, 21–43, 170, 174
unity/unions (loving), 3–7, 14, 16, 35–7, 58–9, 93, 106, 123, 127, 133–5, 145, 147, 160, 163, *see also* merging

Wagner, Cosima, 73
Wagner, Richard, 3, 73
war (love as), 55–6, 82, 164, 171
we, 5, 7, 14, 41, 105, 123, 133, 151, 159, 162, 163
whip (*in Thus Spoke Zarathustra*), 93–4
William, Judge, 16, 48, 54, 58–9, 63–5, 67
will to power, 18, 82, 95, 97, 98, 102, 128
will to slavery, 82

CPSIA information can be obtained
at www.ICGtesting.com
Printed in the USA
LVOW03*0032020216
473271LV00016B/216/P